VPNs and NAT for Cisco Networks

A CCIE v5 guide to tunnels, DMVPN, VPNs, and NAT

By Stuart Fordham

Copyright

Notice of Rights

Copyright © 2015 Stuart Fordham / 802101 Ltd.

All rights reserved. This book or any portion thereof may not be reproduced or used in any manner whatsoever without the express written permission of the publisher except for the use of brief quotations in a book review.

Front cover image copyright of echo3005 / Shutterstock, Inc.

Notice of Liability

Although the author and publisher have made every effort to ensure that the information in this book was correct at press time, the author and publisher do not assume and hereby disclaim any liability to any party for any loss, damage, or disruption caused by errors or omissions, whether such errors or omissions result from negligence, accident, or any other cause.

Trademarks

CCNA, CCNP, CCDP, CCIE and Cisco are registered trademarks of Cisco Systems, Inc.

To Trish

Promised you a dedication!

To the best sis ever!

Table of Contents

1. About 6
   - 1.1 About the Author 6
   - 1.2 About this series of books 6
   - 1.3 Following this book 8
   - 1.4 About the reader 9
   - 1.5 Cisco IOS basics 9

2. Topology 11

Part 1: Tunnels, DMVPN and VPNs 12
   - 3. Tunnels 13
     - 3.1 Basic GRE tunnels 14
     - 3.2 Recursive routing 23
     - 3.3 Dynamic GRE 27
     - 3.4 IP in IP tunnels 32
     - 3.5 Securing GRE with IPSec 38
       - AH and ESP 39
     - 3.6 IPv6 transition mechanisms 52
       - IPv6 in IPv4 tunnels (6over4) 52
       - Automatic 6to4 tunnels 54
       - 6RD 61
       - ISATAP 67
   - 4. DMVPN 73
     - 4.1 NHRP 74
     - 4.2 DMVPN phases 74
       - Phase 1: 74
       - Phase 2: 74
       - Phase 3: 75
     - 4.3 Switching from Phase 1 to Phase 2 78
     - 4.4 Switching from Phase 2 to Phase 3 103
     - 4.5 DMVPN and RIP 109
     - 4.6 DMVPN and BGP 109
     - 4.7 DMVPN and OSPF 114
     - 4.8 Securing DMVPN 120
       - NHRP Authentication 120
       - Tunnel protection using IPSec 123
       - Transport vs. Tunnel mode 124
     - 4.9 Tweaking DMVPN 131
       - Packet fragmentation 131
       - Interoperability with routing protocols 132

- NHRP tweaks 133
- 4.10 DMVPN and QoS 135
- 4.11 DMVPN and IPv6 138
- 4.12 DMVPN and NAT 143
- 4.13 DMVPN and VRFs 146
- 5. GETVPN 158
- 6. Site-to-Site VPNs 160

Part 2: NAT 167

- 7. Network Address Translation 168
  - 7.1 Static NAT 171
    - Static NAT with route-maps 175
    - Static NAT with IP aliasing 177
    - Policy-based NAT 180
    - Static NAT with Load distribution 186
    - NAT order of Operation 190
    - Static Extendable NAT 194
    - NAT ALG 195
  - 7.2 Dynamic NAT 196
  - 7.3 PAT (Port Address Translation) 199
  - 7.4 Reversible NAT 203
  - 7.4 NAT and IPv6 209
    - NAT-PT 209
    - NAT64 216
    - NPTv6 217
    - NAT Virtual Interface (NVI) 217
- 8. Troubleshooting 223
  - Troubleshooting tunnels 223
  - Troubleshooting DMVPN 224
  - Troubleshooting VPNs 225
  - Troubleshooting IPv6 225
  - Troubleshooting NAT 225
  - Confirming end-to-end connectivity 226
  - Troubleshooting mini lab 228
- 9. This book and the CCIE 254
- 10. Further reading 256
- 11. Cloudshark capture links 257

1. About

1.1 About the Author

I have been working in IT for over 10 years - starting off in desktop support, moving up the chain to third line and more recently and specifically finding my "home" within networking. I have worked for a number of companies, including local health authorities, Hedge Funds, and software houses. My current role is Network Manager for a global SaaS company.

I studied Psychology at university; however, at the end of the degree, I really didn't fancy spending years and years studying in order to progress up the ladder. So, I moved into IT, and have spent years and years studying in order to progress up the ladder. I have a number of qualifications including; CCDP, CCNP, CCNA, JNCIP, CEH, RHCSA, MCITP, MCSE, MCSA: Security, Network+, Security+, A+ and I think that's about it. I tend to collect certifications; some I have purposely let lapse in order to concentrate more on the Cisco side of things. Others are still current. I released my first book, BGP for Cisco Networks, in March 2014. I enjoyed the process of creating it so much that I continued with Volume II; MPLS for Cisco Networks, right away.

I am married with twin sons, and I live in Bedfordshire in the UK.

I can be contacted at stu@802101.com. I am always happy to hear feedback and suggestions.

My website address is http://www.802101.com.

1.2 About this series of books

It seems that as the number of certifications being passed grows, so does the recommended reading list of books that need to be purchased. For the CCNA it was two books, for the CCNP it's three books. The technical jump from CCNP to CCIE is vast. With that, so is the required reading list. The publicized reading list from Cisco is a whopping 21 books[1]. Even with judicious purchasing of second hand books (via the likes of eBay or Amazon marketplace), you would still end up paying in the region of $15 (if very lucky) or more. So buying the entire book list even at this minimum price, would total about $300 (about £200). I have bought a large number of the books on the reading list, but a number of them will go untouched. Large portions of others will go unread (at least until I need to

---

[1] http://www.802101.com/2013/05/ccie-book-list.html

cover bits I have missed). With twenty-odd books, time is a significant factor. If you figure, at best, you would be able to finish one book a month, that's still nearly two years just to complete the reading list. Granted, not all books are created equal in length, and some people have more time than others to go through the reading. Even so, there is still a lot of reading to be done. Let's face it; no one really wants to spend two years reading for one exam.

That said, finding a book that is affordable, contains all the relevant information, but at the same time can be precise and short enough (but without lacking the detail) to finish within a week or so can be a bit of a mission.

After more than 10 years of being in this industry, I have read a large number of computer books on a variety of subjects, from the very best to the very worst. There are a number of things that, in my mind, make for a good networking book.

Networks are by their very nature constantly evolving, by that token, any book that teaches anything about networks should also follow this evolutionary path. It should build and scale as the book progresses in the same way that someone faced with a network. They will first start from the ground up, such as basic connectivity. Their skills and knowledge grow as the network grows and additions to the network are added. This including more complex routing, access rules and redundancy. The types of books that don't present an evolutionary network to the reader are also, in my experience, one of two types. Type A is full of tables of commands, with little actual examples of the commands and their results. Type B is slightly better and offers the commands within the context of a network, showing the results and effects of the commands. Generally, type B uses singular examples, each being self-contained. Example X bears no relevance to example Y. Therefore, the reader cannot actually see the evolution of the network, and how the intricacies of pathways are built and changed as the network grows.

With this in mind I decided to write one myself. The hope is that the end result would serve two purposes. The first, being to solidify my own knowledge towards the CCIE certification. The second being to start a series of Cisco-centric networking books that will:

- Be affordable
- Be easy to read within a couple of weeks
- Be of use at any level of networking competency
- Follow a topology to show how a network is built and evolves
- Allow the reader to follow using either physical or virtual (i.e. GNS3) equipment

This is the third book in this series. Technically, it should be called Tunnels, VPNs and NAT for Cisco Networks, but this would mean the spine layout would differ from the other volumes. Due to trying to keep the costs as low as possible, I have had to opt for black and white printing for the paperback version. Please see the links in the topology chapter to download the full color images.

1.3 Following this book

I have used GNS3 for the majority of the topology, primarily as this is the virtual environment that many people studying Cisco exams are familiar with (after packet tracer for CCNA of course) buth also, it is free and easy to use.

The initial router configurations and topologies used can be downloaded from:

http://l.802101.com/802books

Please refer to chapter 2 for the main topology that will be used through the majority of this book.

There are a couple of scenarios where I have had to move away from the main topology and set up smaller examples. Although this goes against the evolutionary style, I hope to accomplish with this book, I hope you'll understand the reasoning behind not pushing it all into one topology.

During the book, you will encounter a number of different exercises. Not all of these actually require all the routers to be switched on. Therefore, I will include a smaller picture (without the IP address details) indicating which routers are in use, the routers will look like this:

Router (on)   Router (off)

In order to ensure a stable topology that will run on the majority of computers, we can turn off some of the routers that are not in use. Obviously, if you can run all the routers then go for it, but the mini-topology diagrams are meant to show the minimum routers required.

The idea that the exercises within the book could be performed with a degree of router selection was as a result of some feedback I received on my first book, from Tyler on Facebook:

"It's very well written book, and has helped a lot. I would highly recommend it to be honest. I can turn on a few routers at a time, and easily do labs for a variety of reasons, without turning all of them on " – Tyler P, on Facebook

I didn't need to include the first two sentences to illustrate the gist. It's nice to get positive feedback, so I thought I would include it. Back to the point in hand, memory wasn't so much of an issue with the first volume as that used an older, less memory intensive router and image, but it is more of a consideration with this volume. So you can all thank Tyler if you meet him for saving your computer memory! It did mean a bit more work to make all the associated images, but I hope it'll make for a better over-all experience.

1.4 About the reader

The hope with this book, is that anyone looking to get a good grounding in VPN and NAT technologies can find this book useful without a large amount of prerequisite knowledge about Cisco commands or networking in general. That said, this is primarily designed for readers with at least a basic knowledge of Cisco routers and their basic commands. Similarly, as the examples given in this book are all based around the use of GNS3, I hope that you are familiar with this as well. The series is designed for those pursuing the CCIE certification and as the CCIE has no prerequisites, I have tried hard to start with the basics and then to advance as the book progresses. Hopefully, you as the reader, will have had previous exposure to Cisco networking and know your way around the IOS CLI.

1.5 Cisco IOS basics

There is a lot of command truncation in this book. Although this book is aimed at CCIE level readers, I do hope that anyone at any level can pick it up and get going. So a few quick words about the commands used.

Most of the show commands will be truncated to "sh" and will use further truncation such as "neigh" being the short version of neighbor. I also use the output modifier a lot. This is the bar, or "pipe" character "|". I follow this by an "i" for include, an "e" for exclude, and "beg" for begin [at]. If you have never even looked at the Cisco IOS before, there are plenty of guides around to get you going. If you know a bit about the Cisco IOS and are looking for a good resource, hopefully this is the right place for you.

When entering configuration mode, IOS always adds "Enter configuration commands, one per line. End with CNTL/Z" I have removed these lines from all output. Occasionally, due to space requirements, I will truncate GigabitEthernet to Gi and in console output as wel:

Tunnel to "Tun". This is purely for formatting reasons, and only where necessary. Generally, I will remove interface up notifications as well.

2. Topology

Our topology is based around a central router: Hub-1. Connecting to Hub-1, on the right-hand side, there will be three "spoke" routers, which we will use to create our tunnels and VPN connections. The "services" router on the left, will be used for part 2 when we look at NAT.

Our physical topology looks like this:

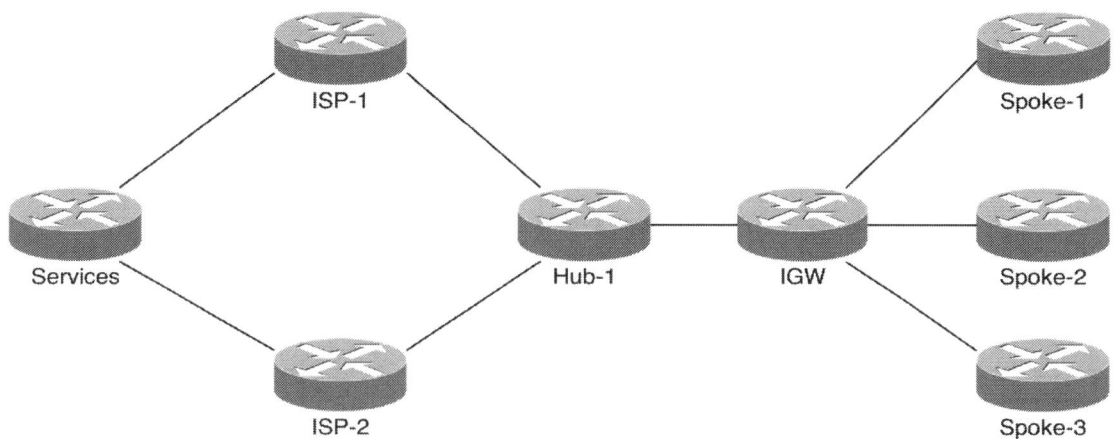

IGW will play a very limited role. The Spoke routers will only see it as their "next hop" destination, so it will be the ISP for the spokes.

Our tunnel network will use the IP subnet of 192.168.1.0/24. The physical connections between the routers, Hub-1 and IGW, will be 10.10.1.0/24. For IGW to the spoke routers it will be 10.10.2.0/24, 10.10.3.0/24 and 10.10.4.0.24. The IGW router will take the .2 addresses for these subnets (i.e. 10.10.1.2/24, 10.10.2.2/24 and so on). Each router will have loopback 0 configured, which will be advertised, through an IGP into the network created by the tunnels and later, by the VPNs. The loopback interfaces will be 1.1.1.1/32 for Hub-1, 2.2.2.2/32 for Spoke-1, 3.3.3.3/32 for Spoke-2 and 4.4.4.4/32 for Spoke-3. The Services router will also have loopback interfaces configured but we will discuss those later.

Please note that the IOS version is pretty important, especially when we come to Phase 3 DMVPN, and NAT. I am using IOS 15.2(4)M4 (the filename to look for is c7200-adventerprisek9-mz.152-4.M4.bin).

Let's get started!

Part 1: Tunnels, DMVPN and VPNs

3. Tunnels

Tunnels, in a physical, man-made, perspective have been around for thousands of years. Some have been created for defensive purposes, such as the 4000 year-old Hezekiah's tunnel in Jerusalem. Some have been created for irrigation, such as the Qanat of Persia, and some have been created for transportation, such as the Via Flaminia, which dates back roughly 2100 years and is still used today. In essence, a tunnel provides a quicker way to get from point A to point B and going through this tunnel, you are oblivious to the world outside of the tunnel.

We use tunnels in routing for the same reasons. We can move traffic from point A to B, as if it were one hop away - despite the fact that it may move through a number of intermediate routers, either under our control, or, under that of a service provider.

Generic Routing Encapsulation (GRE) is the most widely used tunnelling mode and is the tunnelling focus of the CCIE v5 exam. GRE has been around since around 2000, when Cisco, Juniper, Procket Networks and Enron Communications standardized it in RFC 2784. Procket Networks' intellectual property rights and key personnel were bought up by Cisco a few years later. Enron famously crashed and burned in 2001 but Cisco and Juniper continue to do pretty well for themselves.

GRE sought to replace a number of other encapsulation methods, including RFC 1226 (Internet Protocol Encapsulation of AX.25 Frames) and RFC 1234 (Tunnelling IPX Traffic through IP Networks). With encapsulation, a packet, known as the payload, is encapsulated (placed) within another packet, in this case it is a GRE packet. This GRE packet can then be encapsulated within another protocol and passed along to its destination. We will look at the resulting packet, once we have set up our first tunnel, which we will do next.

3.1 Basic GRE tunnels

Our first tunnel will be the most basic form of GRE. Spoke-A will connect to Hub-1 though the IGW router (which is our "internet").

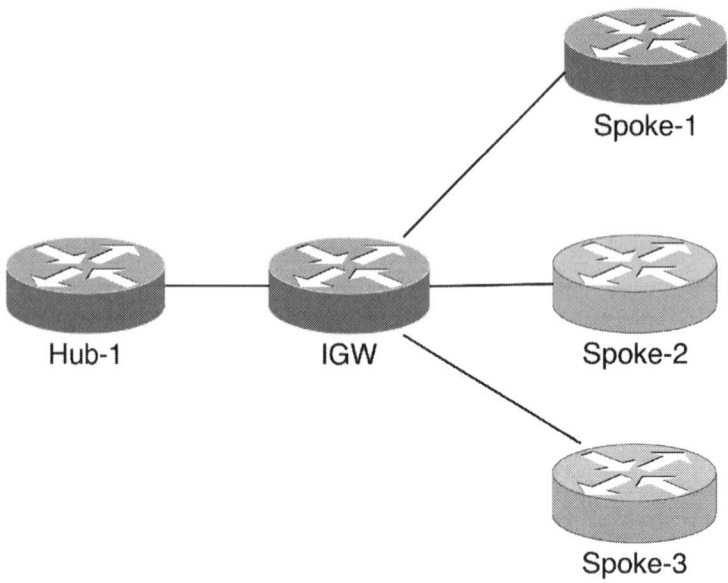

We will start off with some basic connectivity between our routers. Our spoke routers will just have a default route, which we will set statically. Hub-1 and IGW will not have a default route but these will be within the same OSPF area.

```
IGW(config)#int gi 1/0
IGW(config-if)#description Connection to Hub-1
IGW(config-if)#ip add 10.10.1.2 255.255.255.0
IGW(config-if)#no shut
IGW(config-if)#int gi 2/0
IGW(config-if)#description Connection to Spoke-1
IGW(config-if)#ip add 10.10.2.2 255.255.255.0
IGW(config-if)#no shut
IGW(config-if)#router ospf 1
IGW(config-router)#router-id 10.10.10.10
IGW(config-router)#network 10.10.1.0 0.0.0.255 area 0
IGW(config-router)#redistribute static subnets
IGW(config-router)#redistribute connected subnets
IGW(config-router)#

Hub-1(config)#int gi 1/0
Hub-1(config-if)#ip add 10.10.1.1 255.255.255.0
```

```
Hub-1(config-if)#desc Connection to IGW
Hub-1(config-if)#no shut
Hub-1(config-if)#do ping 10.10.1.2
Type escape sequence to abort.
Sending 5, 100-byte ICMP Echos to 10.10.1.2
.!!!!
Success rate is 80 percent (4/5)
Hub-1(config-if)#int lo0
Hub-1(config-if)#ip add 1.1.1.1 255.255.255.255
Hub-1(config-if)#router ospf 1
Hub-1(config-router)#router-id 1.1.1.1
Hub-1(config-router)#network 10.10.1.0 0.0.0.255 area 0
Hub-1(config-router)#
%OSPF-5-ADJCHG: Process 1, Nbr 10.10.10.10 on GigabitEthernet1/0 from
LOADING to FULL, Loading Done
Hub-1(config-router)#

Spoke-1(config)#int lo0
Spoke-1(config-if)#ip add 2.2.2.2 255.255.255.255
Spoke-1(config-if)#int gi 1/0
Spoke-1(config-if)#ip add 10.10.2.1 255.255.255.0
Spoke-1(config-if)#desc Connection to IGW
Spoke-1(config-if)#no shut
Spoke-1(config-if)#do ping 10.10.2.2
Type escape sequence to abort.
Sending 5, 100-byte ICMP Echos to 10.10.2.2
.!!!!
Success rate is 80 percent (4/5)
Spoke-1(config-if)#ip route 0.0.0.0 0.0.0.0 10.10.2.2
Spoke-1(config)#
```

Now that we have some basic connectivity, we can confirm our reachability from our spoke to our hub:

```
Hub-1(config-router)#do sh ip route | beg Gate
Gateway of last resort is not set

      1.0.0.0/32 is subnetted, 1 subnets
C        1.1.1.1 is directly connected, Loopback0
      10.0.0.0/8 is variably subnetted, 3 subnets, 2 masks
C        10.10.1.0/24 is directly connected, Gi1/0
L        10.10.1.1/32 is directly connected, Gi1/0
O E2     10.10.2.0/24 [110/20] via 10.10.1.2, 00:05:26, Gi1/0
Hub-1(config-router)#

Spoke-1(config)#do ping 10.10.1.1
Type escape sequence to abort.
```

```
Sending 5, 100-byte ICMP Echos to 10.10.1.1:
!!!!!
Success rate is 100 percent (5/5)
Spoke-1(config)#
```

With this in place, we can start to create our first GRE tunnel, which will be a point-to-point link (as GRE tunnels are). It requires three components; a source, a destination and an encapsulation method. In creating a tunnel, GRE is the default encapsulation type, so this doesn't need to be specified, but this will be evident later on when we confirm that our tunnel is working:

```
Hub-1(config-router)#int tunnel 0
Hub-1(config-if)#
%LINEPROTO-5-UPDOWN: Line protocol on Interface Tunnel0, changed state
to down
Hub-1(config-if)#
Hub-1(config-if)#ip address 192.168.1.1 255.255.255.0
Hub-1(config-if)#tunnel source GigabitEthernet 1/0
Hub-1(config-if)#tunnel destination 10.10.2.1
Hub-1(config-if)#
%LINEPROTO-5-UPDOWN: Line protocol on Interface Tunnel0, changed state
to up
Hub-1(config-if)#

Spoke-1(config)#int tunnel 0
%LINEPROTO-5-UPDOWN: Line protocol on Interface Tunnel0, changed state
to down
Spoke-1(config-if)#ip address 192.168.1.2 255.255.255.0
Spoke-1(config-if)#tunnel source GigabitEthernet 1/0
Spoke-1(config-if)#tunnel destination 10.10.1.1
Spoke-1(config-if)#
%LINEPROTO-5-UPDOWN: Line protocol on Interface Tunnel0, changed state
to up
Spoke-1(config-if)#
```

Our tunnel is up now on both routers:

```
Spoke-1(config-if)#do sh int tunnel 0
Tunnel0 is up, line protocol is up
  Hardware is Tunnel
  Internet address is 192.168.1.2/24
  MTU 17916 bytes, BW 100 Kbit/sec, DLY 50000 usec,
     reliability 255/255, txload 1/255, rxload 1/255
  Encapsulation TUNNEL, loopback not set
  Keepalive not set
  Tunnel source 10.10.2.1 (Gi1/0), destination 10.10.1.1
```

```
      Tunnel Subblocks:
        src-track:
          Tunnel0 source tracking subblock associated with
GigabitEthernet1/0
          Set of tunnels with source GigabitEthernet1/0, 1 member
(includes iterators), on interface <OK>
  Tunnel protocol/transport GRE/IP
    Key disabled, sequencing disabled
    Checksumming of packets disabled
  Tunnel TTL 255, Fast tunneling enabled
  Tunnel transport MTU 1476 bytes
  Tunnel transmit bandwidth 8000 (kbps)
  Tunnel receive bandwidth 8000 (kbps)
  Last input never, output never, output hang never
  Last clearing of "show interface" counters 00:01:29
  Input queue: 0/75/0/0 (size/max/drops/flushes); Total output drops:0
  Queueing strategy: fifo
  Output queue: 0/0 (size/max)
  5 minute input rate 0 bits/sec, 0 packets/sec
  5 minute output rate 0 bits/sec, 0 packets/sec
     0 packets input, 0 bytes, 0 no buffer
     Received 0 broadcasts (0 IP multicasts)
     0 runts, 0 giants, 0 throttles
     0 input errors, 0 CRC, 0 frame, 0 overrun, 0 ignored, 0 abort
     0 packets output, 0 bytes, 0 underruns
     0 output errors, 0 collisions, 0 interface resets
     0 unknown protocol drops
     0 output buffer failures, 0 output buffers swapped out
Spoke-1(config-if)#
```

To get a more succinct output, we can limit the output down to include just the protocol:

```
Hub-1(config-if)#do sh int tunnel 0 | i protocol
Tunnel0 is up, line protocol is up
  Tunnel protocol/transport GRE/IP
     0 unknown protocol drops
Hub-1(config-if)#
```

So far, we don't have any traffic running across the tunnel, so let's do that now by joining the two networks using EIGRP:

```
Spoke-1(config-if)#router eigrp 1
Spoke-1(config-router)#network 192.168.1.0 0.0.0.255
Spoke-1(config-router)#network 2.2.2.2 0.0.0.0
Spoke-1(config-router)#
```

```
Hub-1(config-if)#router eigrp 1
Hub-1(config-router)#network 1.1.1.1 0.0.0.0
Hub-1(config-router)#network 192.168.1.0 0.0.0.255
%DUAL-5-NBRCHANGE: EIGRP-IPv4 1: Neighbor 192.168.1.2 (Tunnel0) is up:
new adjacency
Hub-1(config-router)#
```

Let's check our routing tables:

```
Hub-1(config-router)#do sh ip route | beg Gate
Gateway of last resort is not set

      1.0.0.0/32 is subnetted, 1 subnets
C        1.1.1.1 is directly connected, Loopback0
      2.0.0.0/32 is subnetted, 1 subnets
D        2.2.2.2 [90/27008000] via 192.168.1.2, 00:03:00, Tun0
      10.0.0.0/8 is variably subnetted, 3 subnets, 2 masks
C        10.10.1.0/24 is directly connected, Gi1/0
L        10.10.1.1/32 is directly connected, Gi1/0
O E2     10.10.2.0/24 [110/20] via 10.10.1.2, 00:16:59, Gi1/0
      192.168.1.0/24 is variably subnetted, 2 subnets, 2 masks
C        192.168.1.0/24 is directly connected, Tunnel0
L        192.168.1.1/32 is directly connected, Tunnel0
Hub-1(config-router)#

Spoke-1(config-router)#do sh ip route | beg Gate
Gateway of last resort is 10.10.2.2 to network 0.0.0.0

S*    0.0.0.0/0 [1/0] via 10.10.2.2
      1.0.0.0/32 is subnetted, 1 subnets
D        1.1.1.1 [90/27008000] via 192.168.1.1, 00:03:54, Tun0
      2.0.0.0/32 is subnetted, 1 subnets
C        2.2.2.2 is directly connected, Loopback0
      10.0.0.0/8 is variably subnetted, 2 subnets, 2 masks
C        10.10.2.0/24 is directly connected, Gi1/0
L        10.10.2.1/32 is directly connected, Gi1/0
      192.168.1.0/24 is variably subnetted, 2 subnets, 2 masks
C        192.168.1.0/24 is directly connected, Tunnel0
L        192.168.1.2/32 is directly connected, Tunnel0
Spoke-1(config-router)#
```

Perfect, we can start to advertise more networks over our tunnel now, but before we do that, let's have a look at the packets we are transmitting.

When we use GRE, we have an outer header appended to the original packet, along with a GRE header.

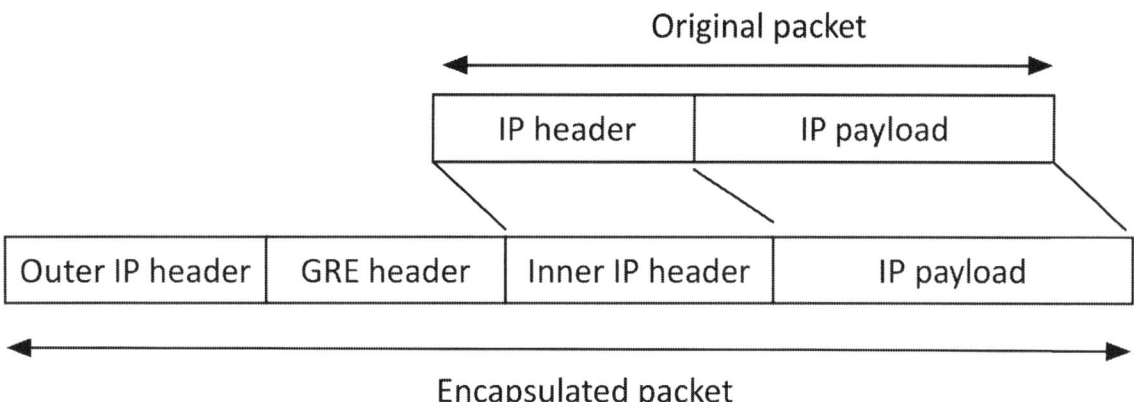

Using Wireshark, we can capture the ping traffic as it leaves Spoke-1 towards Hub-1:

```
Spoke-1(config-router)#do ping 1.1.1.1 rep 25
Type escape sequence to abort.
Sending 25, 100-byte ICMP Echos to 1.1.1.1:
!!!!!!!!!!!!!!!!!!!!!!!!!
Success rate is 100 percent (25/25)
Spoke-1(config-router)#end
```

The first thing we notice is that we now have an entry in the packet for the Generic Routing Encapsulation (IP) header.

```
59 22.8630000 192.168.1.2           1.1.1.1              ICMP     138 Echo (ping) requ
⊞ Frame 59: 138 bytes on wire (1104 bits), 138 bytes captured (1104 bits) on interface 0
⊞ Ethernet II, Src: ca:03:4a:24:00:1c (ca:03:4a:24:00:1c), Dst: ca:02:44:e4:00:38 (ca:02:
⊞ Internet Protocol Version 4, Src: 10.10.2.1 (10.10.2.1), Dst: 10.10.1.1 (10.10.1.1)
⊞ Generic Routing Encapsulation (IP)
⊞ Internet Protocol Version 4, Src: 192.168.1.2 (192.168.1.2), Dst: 1.1.1.1 (1.1.1.1)
⊞ Internet Control Message Protocol
```

Capture: 1

Before we drill down into this, though, we need to go one level higher, into the outer header. In here, we can see that the protocol is set to GRE (which is type 47). We also have the source and destination IP addresses of our tunnel's entry and exit points.

```
⊞ Frame 59: 138 bytes on wire (1104 bits), 138 byte
⊞ Ethernet II, Src: ca:03:4a:24:00:1c (ca:03:4a:24:
⊟ Internet Protocol Version 4, Src: 10.10.2.1 (10.1
    Version: 4
    Header length: 20 bytes
    ⊞ Differentiated Services Field: 0x00 (DSCP 0x00:
    Total Length: 124
    Identification: 0x0067 (103)
    ⊞ Flags: 0x00
    Fragment offset: 0
    Time to live: 255
  ➔ Protocol: GRE (47)
    ⊞ Header checksum: 0xa3d6 [correct]
  ➔ Source: 10.10.2.1 (10.10.2.1)
  ➔ Destination: 10.10.1.1 (10.10.1.1)
    [Source GeoIP: Unknown]
    [Destination GeoIP: Unknown]
⊞ Generic Routing Encapsulation (IP)
⊞ Internet Protocol Version 4, Src: 192.168.1.2 (19
⊞ Internet Control Message Protocol
```

Next, we can drill down into the GRE header.

```
⊞ Frame 59: 138 bytes on wire (1104 bits), 138 bytes captured (1104 bits) on interface
⊞ Ethernet II, Src: ca:03:4a:24:00:1c (ca:03:4a:24:00:1c), Dst: ca:02:44:e4:00:38 (ca:0
⊞ Internet Protocol Version 4, Src: 10.10.2.1 (10.10.2.1), Dst: 10.10.1.1 (10.10.1.1)
⊟ Generic Routing Encapsulation (IP)
  ⊟ Flags and Version: 0x0000
       0... .... .... .... = Checksum Bit: No
       .0.. .... .... .... = Routing Bit: No
       ..0. .... .... .... = Key Bit: No
       ...0 .... .... .... = Sequence Number Bit: No
       .... 0... .... .... = Strict Source Route Bit: No
       .... .000 .... .... = Recursion control: 0
       .... .... 0000 0... = Flags (Reserved): 0
       .... .... .... .000 = Version: GRE (0)
    Protocol Type: IP (0x0800)
⊞ Internet Protocol Version 4, Src: 192.168.1.2 (192.168.1.2), Dst: 1.1.1.1 (1.1.1.1)
⊞ Internet Control Message Protocol
```

The GRE header is full of zeros and this is for good reasons. From the RFC, the first bit is the checksum present bit. Bits 1 through to 12 are reserved, in the RFC document this is referred to as Reserved0. If any of the bits from 1 to 5 are non-zero, then the receiver must discard them. Bits 6 to 12 must also be set at zero, these are reserved for future use. These must be ignored. Bits 13 to 15 are the version number, which again must be set at 0. Finally, we get to the Protocol Type. This is the EtherType of the payload packet, as defined under RFC 1700. In our case, our payload is IP, or, more specifically, IPv4, which is 0x0800. A good list of EtherTypes is available on Wikipedia: http://en.wikipedia.org/wiki/EtherType.

Lastly, in the packet, we have the "true" data we sent. Its source is 192.168.1.2 and its destination is 1.1.1.1, both of which are within the tunnel we created. This is the (original) IPv4 payload.

Now, that we have a working tunnel, with its own IGP running through it, we can advertise more of our networks. Let's add another network and see what happens:

```
Hub-1(config-router)#network 10.10.1.0 0.0.0.255
Hub-1(config-router)#
```

Our tunnel goes down:

```
Spoke-1#
%ADJ-5-PARENT: Midchain parent maintenance for IP midchain out of
Tunnel0 - looped chain attempting to stack
Spoke-1#
%TUN-5-RECURDOWN: Tunnel0 temporarily disabled due to recursive
routing
%LINEPROTO-5-UPDOWN: Line protocol on Interface Tunnel0, changed state
to down
%DUAL-5-NBRCHANGE: EIGRP-IPv4 1: Neighbor 192.168.1.1 (Tunnel0) is
down: interface down
Spoke-1#
```

This, in turn, makes our routing table rather sparse now:

```
Spoke-1#sh ip route | beg Gate
Gateway of last resort is 10.10.2.2 to network 0.0.0.0

S*      0.0.0.0/0 [1/0] via 10.10.22
        2.0.0.0/32 is subnetted, 1 subnets
C          2.2.2.2 is directly connected, Loopback0
        10.0.0.0/8 is variably subnetted, 2 subnets, 2 masks
C          10.10.2.0/24 is directly connected, Gi1/0
L          10.10.2.1/32 is directly connected, Gi1/0
Spoke-1#
```

After a few moments the tunnel comes back up again

```
%LINEPROTO-5-UPDOWN: Line protocol on Interface Tunnel0, changed state
to up
```

```
Spoke-1#
%DUAL-5-NBRCHANGE: EIGRP-IPv4 1: Neighbor 192.168.1.1 (Tunnel0) is up:
new adjacency
%ADJ-5-PARENT: Midchain parent maintenance for IP midchain out of
Tunnel0 - looped chain attempting to stack
Spoke-1#
```

If we are quick enough, we can see that we are learning about the 10.10.1.0/24 network through our tunnel's EIGRP adjacency to Hub-1:

```
Spoke-1#sh ip route | beg Gate
Gateway of last resort is 10.10.2.2 to network 0.0.0.0

S*    0.0.0.0/0 [1/0] via 10.10.2.2
      1.0.0.0/32 is subnetted, 1 subnets
D        1.1.1.1 [90/27008000] via 192.168.1.1, 00:00:08, Tun0
      2.0.0.0/32 is subnetted, 1 subnets
C        2.2.2.2 is directly connected, Loopback0
      10.0.0.0/8 is variably subnetted, 3 subnets, 2 masks
D        10.10.1.0/24 [90/26880256] via 192.168.1.1, 00:00:08,Tun0
C        10.10.2.0/24 is directly connected, Gi1/0
L        10.10.2.1/32 is directly connected, Gi1/0
      192.168.1.0/24 is variably subnetted, 2 subnets, 2 masks
C        192.168.1.0/24 is directly connected, Tunnel0
L        192.168.1.2/32 is directly connected, Tunnel0
Spoke-1#
```

Again our tunnel goes down.

```
Spoke-1#
%TUN-5-RECURDOWN: Tunnel0 temporarily disabled due to recursive
routing
%LINEPROTO-5-UPDOWN: Line protocol on Interface Tunnel0, changed state
to down
DUAL-5-NBRCHANGE: EIGRP-IPv4 1: Neighbor 192.168.1.1 (Tunnel0) is
down: interface down
Spoke-1#
```

For the moment, let's fix this the easy way:

```
Hub-1(config-router)#no network 10.10.1.0 0.0.0.255
```

Looking at the console messages, it is very easy to see why the tunnel goes down. The keywords to note in the warning messages are "recursive routing".

3.2 Recursive routing

Route recursion is where we learn about a routes' destination through a method that requires the destination to already be known. To put it in context, we are trying to reach the tunnel destination through the tunnel itself. In a motorway tunnel sense, this is plausible enough when we are driving through it, but when the tunnel was first made, the engineers could not just pick a point and start drilling, otherwise the tunnel could exit over a cliff edge and that would certainly not make for a good driving experience. The engineers had to already know where the tunnel needed to end up, before they started drilling.

Issues with recursion come down, in part, to administrative distance (AD). Spoke-1 has a default route, with a metric of 1, to the IGW router. Once Hub-1 starts to advertise the 10.10.1.0/24 route to Spoke-1, this is installed in Spoke-1's routing table with an AD of 90 (Internal EIGRP). Although an AD of 1, for the static route, is preferred to the AD of 90, because the router will choose the closest matching route, the EIGRP route is chosen.

We can fix the recursion in a number of ways. We could have a static route to the 10.10.1.0/24 network, pointing to the IGW router. This would be the closest matching prefix and the AD would be more favourable. If, however, we are forced to remain with EIGRP running over the tunnel and we are not allowed a static route, then, according to the list of administrative distances, we would have to choose eBGP, as its AD of 20 is lower than EIGRP's 90.

Routing Protocol	Administrative Distance
Connected interface	0
Static route	1
EIGRP Summary route	5
External BGP	20
Internal EIGRP	90
IGRP	100
OSPF	110
IS-IS	115
RIP	120
EGP	140
ODR	160
External EIGRP	170
Internal BGP	200

We would have to run eBGP between IGW and Spoke-1, as after a static route, this would be the next best-preferred AD before Internal EIGRP. We do have another option though. Assuming that we *have* to advertise the 10.10.1.0/24 network from Hub-1, our other option would be a "distribute list".

We start with a simple access list, denying the 10.10.1.0/24 network and permitting all our other traffic. Under our EIGRP autonomous system we can then re-advertise the same network, we then use a distribute list to call our access list (1) and send the traffic out using our tunnel interface. It is important here, that we use the correct interface. If we used the GigabitEthernet 1/0 interface, we would still encounter the recursion, therefore it must be applied to the tunnel interface. The commands are below:

```
Hub-1(config-router)#exit
Hub-1(config)#access-list 1 deny 10.10.1.0 0.0.0.255
Hub-1(config)#access-list 1 permit any
Hub-1(config)#router eigrp 1
Hub-1(config-router)#network 10.10.1.0 0.0.0.255
Hub-1(config-router)#distribute-list 1 out tunnel 0
Hub-1(config-router)#end
```

Once again, our tunnel is up and healthy:

```
Spoke-1#
%DUAL-5-NBRCHANGE: EIGRP-IPv4 1: Neighbor 192.168.1.1 (Tunnel0) is up: new adjacency
Spoke-1#sh ip route | beg Gate
Gateway of last resort is 10.10.2.2 to network 0.0.0.0

S*      0.0.0.0/0 [1/0] via 10.10.2.2
        1.0.0.0/32 is subnetted, 1 subnets
D          1.1.1.1 [90/27008000] via 192.168.1.1, 00:00:03, Tun0
        2.0.0.0/32 is subnetted, 1 subnets
C          2.2.2.2 is directly connected, Loopback0
        10.0.0.0/8 is variably subnetted, 2 subnets, 2 masks
C          10.10.2.0/24 is directly connected, Gi1/0
L          10.10.2.1/32 is directly connected, Gi1/0
        192.168.1.0/24 is variably subnetted, 2 subnets, 2 masks
C          192.168.1.0/24 is directly connected, Tunnel0
L          192.168.1.2/32 is directly connected, Tunnel0
Spoke-1#sh int tunnel 0 | i (packets input|packets output)
     1011 packets input, 85918 bytes, 0 no buffer
     998 packets output, 97917 bytes, 0 underruns
Spoke-1#
```

Spoke-1, now (because of the distribute list), does not have an entry for the 10.10.1.0/24 network, despite the fact that we are advertising it. Instead it must use the default route to get to it.

Now, it is time to bring Spoke-2 into the network.

We start with the basic connectivity:

```
IGW(config-router)#int gi 3/0
IGW(config-if)#ip add 10.10.3.2 255.255.255.0
IGW(config-if)#desc Connection to Spoke-2
IGW(config-if)#no shut
IGW(config-if)#

Spoke-2(config)#int lo0
Spoke-2(config-if)#ip add 3.3.3.3 255.255.255.255
Spoke-2(config-if)#int gi 1/0
Spoke-2(config-if)#ip add 10.10.3.1 255.255.255.0
Spoke-2(config-if)#no shut
Spoke-2(config-if)#desc Connection to IGW
Spoke-2(config-if)#ip route 0.0.0.0 0.0.0.0 10.10.3.2
Spoke-2(config)#
```

We can confirm that Hub-1 can see Spoke-2:

```
Hub-1#sh ip route 10.10.3.0
Routing entry for 10.10.3.0/24
  Known via "ospf 1", distance 110, metric 20, type extern 2, forward metric 1
  Last update from 10.10.1.2 on GigabitEthernet1/0, 00:02:37 ago
  Routing Descriptor Blocks:
  * 10.10.1.2, from 10.10.10.10, 00:02:37 ago, via Gi1/0
      Route metric is 20, traffic share count is 1
Hub-1#
```

We also confirm that Spoke-2 can actually reach Hub-1:

```
Spoke-2(config)#do ping 10.10.1.1
Type escape sequence to abort.
Sending 5, 100-byte ICMP Echos to 10.10.1.1:
!!!!!
Success rate is 100 percent (5/5)
Spoke-2(config)#
```

What are our options now that we need introduce Spoke-2 to Hub-1?

We could create another tunnel on Hub-1 and Hub-1's tunnel 1 could talk to Spoke-2's tunnel 0 (the tunnel numbers do not need to match). We could set this up in the same way that we set up Spoke-1. But that wouldn't be much fun really, now would it?! If we had a larger number of spokes, Hub-1 would need a tunnel per-spoke. So for 100 spokes, we would have 100 tunnels, if we wanted these spokes to have connectivity to each other, then each would need an additional 99 tunnels. This is far from ideal. Instead, we can do something a little more interesting here. Spoke-2 can be set up the same as Spoke-1, but we don't need to create a second tunnel on Hub-1. Instead we can have one tunnel, and multiple end points, which is known as Dynamic GRE, or mGRE.

3.3 Dynamic GRE

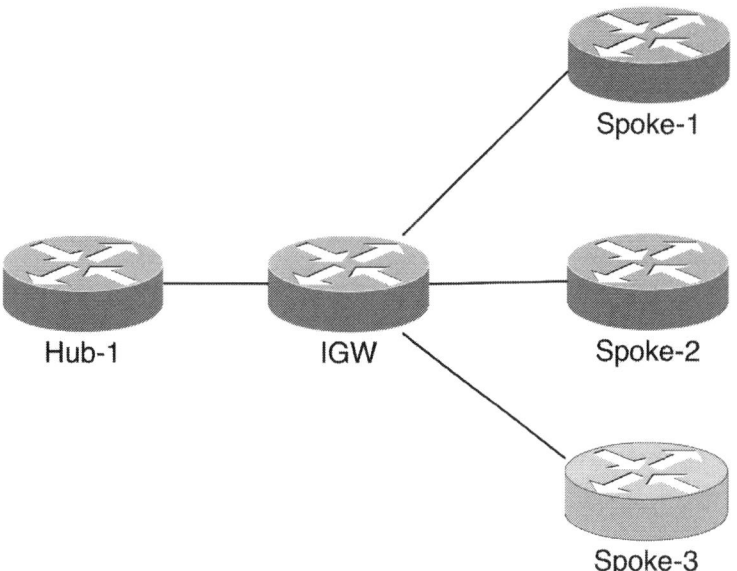

Let's get Spoke-2 set up first:

```
Spoke-2(config)#int tunnel 0
%LINEPROTO-5-UPDOWN: Line protocol on Interface Tunnel0, changed state
to down
Spoke-2(config-if)#ip address 192.168.1.3 255.255.255.0
Spoke-2(config-if)#tunnel source Gi 1/0
Spoke-2(config-if)#tunnel destination 10.10.1.1
Spoke-2(config-if)#
%LINEPROTO-5-UPDOWN: Line protocol on Interface Tunnel0, changed state
to up
Spoke-2(config-if)#
```

Now, we need to do some reconfiguration on Hub-1.

Firstly, we need to change our tunnel mode. As the default mode is point-to-point, this would mean that we need to stay with the concept of one tunnel per peer and does not offer the flexibility that we need.

What then, are our suitable options?

```
Hub-1(config)#int tun 0
Hub-1(config-if)#tun mode ?
  aurp    AURP TunnelTalk AppleTalk encapsulation
```

```
    cayman    Cayman TunnelTalk AppleTalk encapsulation
    dvmrp     DVMRP multicast tunnel
    eon       EON compatible CLNS tunnel
    gre       generic route encapsulation protocol
    ipip      IP over IP encapsulation
    ipsec     IPSec tunnel encapsulation
    iptalk    Apple IPTalk encapsulation
    ipv6      Generic packet tunneling in IPv6
    ipv6ip    IPv6 over IP encapsulation
    mpls      MPLS encapsulations
    nos       IP over IP encapsulation (KA9Q/NOS compatible)
    rbscp     RBSCP in IP tunnel
Hub-1(config-if)#tunnel mode
```

At this stage we want to stay with GRE, and under GRE we have an option for multipoint:

```
Hub-1(config-if)#tunnel mode gre ?
    ip           over IP
    ipv6         over IPv6
    multipoint   over IPv4 (multipoint)
Hub-1(config-if)#tunnel mode gre
```

Let's try that:

```
Hub-1(config-if)#tunnel mode gre multipoint
 Tunnel set mode failed. p2mp tunnels cannot have a tunnel
destination.
Hub-1(config-if)#
```

It would appear that we can't have a destination already defined, when switching to mGRE, so let's remove our destinations:

```
Hub-1(config-if)#no tunnel destination
Hub-1(config-if)#tunnel mode gre multipoint
Hub-1(config-if)#
%LINEPROTO-5-UPDOWN: Line protocol on Interface Tunnel0, changed state
to up
Hub-1(config-if)#
%DUAL-5-NBRCHANGE: EIGRP-IPv4 1: Neighbor 192.168.1.2 (Tunnel0) is up:
new adjacency
Hub-1(config-if)#
%DUAL-5-NBRCHANGE: EIGRP-IPv4 1: Neighbor 192.168.1.2 (Tunnel0) is
down: Interface PEER-TERMINATION received
Hub-1(config-if)#
%DUAL-5-NBRCHANGE: EIGRP-IPv4 1: Neighbor 192.168.1.2 (Tunnel0) is up:
new adjacency
```

```
Hub-1(config-if)#
%DUAL-5-NBRCHANGE: EIGRP-IPv4 1: Neighbor 192.168.1.2 (Tunnel0) is
down: retry limit exceeded
```

Our tunnel will start to flap now. Nevertheless, let's go ahead and add EIGRP to Spoke-2 anyway:

```
Spoke-2(config-if)#router eigrp 1
Spoke-2(config-router)#network 3.3.3.3 0.0.0.0
Spoke-2(config-router)#network 192.168.1.0 0.0.0.255
Spoke-2(config-router)#
```

Hub-1 can now form an adjacency with Spoke-3, but, again, it will flap:

```
Hub-1#(config-if)
%DUAL-5-NBRCHANGE: EIGRP-IPv4 1: Neighbor 192.168.1.3 (Tunnel0) is up:
new adjacency
Hub-1#(config-if)
%DUAL-5-NBRCHANGE: EIGRP-IPv4 1: Neighbor 192.168.1.3 (Tunnel0) is
down: retry limit exceeded
Hub-1#(config-if)
%DUAL-5-NBRCHANGE: EIGRP-IPv4 1: Neighbor 192.168.1.3 (Tunnel0) is up:
new adjacency
Hub-1#(config-if)
```

Obviously it is not as simple, as just changing or adding the configurations we have done so far. What then, are we missing?

With the default point-to-point configuration, that we have seen thus far, it is easy for the router to figure out whom it should be talking to. The connection request comes into the source interface from the destination IP address and the tunnel is made.

With multipoint, we will have multiple connections, but how do we distinguish one spoke from another? In a normal Ethernet LAN network we have a MAC addresses linked to IP addresses through ARP (Address Resolution Protocol), so similarly we need something like for our dynamic tunnel network.

Next Hop Resolution Protocol (NHRP) is needed here. Defined under RFC 2332, NHRP can be used by a router to "determine the internetworking layer address and NBMA subnetwork addresses of the "NBMA next hop" towards a destination station". It works very much like ARP does. ARP maintains an IP address to a physical address (MAC address) mapping, and likewise NHRP maintains an internal address to its NBMA address (its "external" address).

So, how does it achieve this? Well, let's look at our available options:

```
Hub-1(config-if)#ip nhrp ?
  attribute       NHRP attribute set
  authentication  Authentication string
  cache           NHRP Cache related commands.
  connect         NHRP resolution request connect
  group           NHRP group name
  holdtime        Advertised holdtime
  interest        Specify an access list
  map             Map dest IP addresses to NBMA addresses
  max-send        Rate limit NHRP traffic
  network-id      NBMA network identifier
  nhs             Specify a next hop server
  record          Allow NHRP record option
  redirect        Enable NHRP redirect traffic indication
  registration    Settings for registration packets.
  reject          NHRP resolution reject request
  responder       Responder interface
  server-only     Disable NHRP requests
  shortcut        Enable shortcut switching
  trigger-svc     Create NHRP cut-through based on traffic load
  use             Specify usage count for sending requests
```

The map option looks ideal for this:

```
Hub-1(config-if)#ip nhrp map ?
  A.B.C.D    IP address of destination
  group      NHRP group mapping
  multicast  Use this NBMA mapping for broadcasts/multicasts
```

We know our destination, this is the tunnel's IP address, so, what do we map to?

```
Hub-1(config-if)#ip nhrp map 192.168.1.2 ?
  A.B.C.D    IP NBMA address
  A.B.C.D    IP mask of destination
  X:X:X:X::X IPv6 NBMA address
```

The outside interface address of our spoke routers!

```
Hub-1(config-if)#ip nhrp map 192.168.1.2 10.10.2.1
Hub-1(config-if)#ip nhrp map 192.168.1.3 10.10.3.1
```

We have not finished yet. We still need to add our NHRP network ID, which we will set to 1, and also, as we are using EIGRP which relies on multicast, we should enable this as well:

```
Hub-1(config-if)#ip nhrp network-id 1
Hub-1(config-if)#ip nhrp map multicast 10.10.2.1
Hub-1(config-if)#ip nhrp map multicast 10.10.3.1
Hub-1(config-if)#
```

We will go into more detail about the NHRP network-id later on, but for now, all we need to know is that the network-id is required to enable NHRP on a tunnel interface. With this in place, we can see our EIGRP adjacencies form:

```
Spoke-1#
%DUAL-5-NBRCHANGE: EIGRP-IPv4 1: Neighbor 192.168.1.1 (Tunnel0) is up:
new adjacency
Spoke-1#

Spoke-2(config-router)#
%DUAL-5-NBRCHANGE: EIGRP-IPv4 1: Neighbor 192.168.1.1 (Tunnel0) is up:
new adjacency
Spoke-2(config-router)#
```

Both of our spoke routers receive the 1.1.1.1/32 prefix from Hub-1:

```
Spoke-1#sh ip route eigrp | beg Gate
Gateway of last resort is 10.10.2.2 to network 0.0.0.0
      1.0.0.0/32 is subnetted, 1 subnets
D        1.1.1.1 [90/27008000] via 192.168.1.1, 00:01:37, Tun0
Spoke-1#

Spoke-2(config-router)#do sh ip route eigrp | b Gate
Gateway of last resort is 10.10.3.2 to network 0.0.0.0

      1.0.0.0/32 is subnetted, 1 subnets
D        1.1.1.1 [90/27008000] via 192.168.1.1, 00:02:22, Tunnel0
Spoke-2(config-router)#
```

Note that we still do not receive the 10.10.1.0/24 network, as this is denied through our EIGRP distribute list, which is assigned to our tunnel.

We are off to a pretty good start, so let's bring Spoke-3 into the mix as well. Spoke-3 is going to be a little different. Due to some restrictions, placed by the ISP, we cannot use GRE encapsulation between Spoke-3 and Hub-1. Out of the box, GRE does not offer any form of security; encapsulation is not the same as encryption. Due to this, many ISPs filter GRE traffic. So instead of a GRE tunnel, we are going to create an IP tunnel, which is a common way to circumvent this restriction.

3.4 IP in IP tunnels

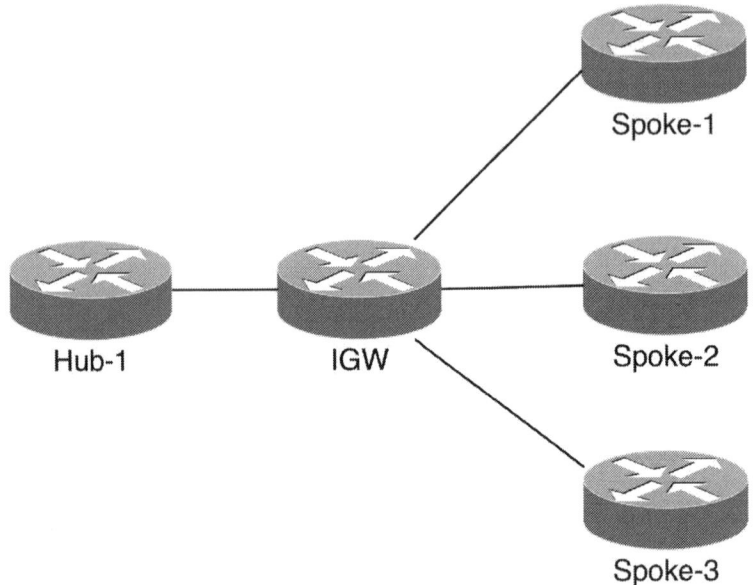

With IP in IP tunnels, an IP packet is encapsulated within another IP packet. An outer header is added, which contains the source and the destination IP addresses.

The basic packet structure looks like this, it is very similar to our GRE packet, but without the GRE portion:

Outer IP header	Inner IP header	IP payload

The basic connectivity configuration is below:

```
IGW(config-if)#int gi 4/0
IGW(config-if)#desc Connection to Spoke-3
IGW(config-if)#ip add 10.10.4.2 255.255.255.0
IGW(config-if)#no shut
IGW(config-if)#

Spoke-3(config)#int lo0
```

```
Spoke-3(config-if)#ip add 4.4.4.4 255.255.255.255
Spoke-3(config-if)#int gi 1/0
Spoke-3(config-if)#desc Connection to IGW
Spoke-3(config-if)#ip add 10.10.4.1 255.255.255.0
Spoke-3(config-if)#no shut
Spoke-3(config-if)#router eigrp 1
Spoke-3(config-router)#network 4.4.4.4 0.0.0.0
Spoke-3(config-router)#network 192.168.1.0 0.0.0.255
Spoke-3(config-router)#ip route 0.0.0.0 0.0.0.0 10.10.4.2
```

We can start to create our tunnel in the same manner that we did with Spokes 1 and 2:

```
Spoke-3(config-router)#int tunnel 0
Spoke-3(config-if)#ip address 192.168.1.4 255.255.255.0
Spoke-3(config-if)#tunnel source gi 1/0
Spoke-3(config-if)#tunnel destination 10.10.1.1
Spoke-3(config-if)#
```

We know we are not allowed to run a GRE tunnel on Spoke-3, so what options do we have instead?

```
Spoke-3(config-if)#tunnel mode ?
  aurp    AURP TunnelTalk AppleTalk encapsulation
  cayman  Cayman TunnelTalk AppleTalk encapsulation
  dvmrp   DVMRP multicast tunnel
  eon     EON compatible CLNS tunnel
  gre     generic route encapsulation protocol
  ipip    IP over IP encapsulation
  ipsec   IPSec tunnel encapsulation
  iptalk  Apple IPTalk encapsulation
  ipv6    Generic packet tunneling in IPv6
  ipv6ip  IPv6 over IP encapsulation
  mpls    MPLS encapsulations
  nos     IP over IP encapsulation (KA9Q/NOS compatible)
  rbscp   RBSCP in IP tunnel

Spoke-3(config-if)#tunnel mode
```

Immediately, we can see some that would be less likely options, such as AppleTalk and MPLS, but we do have IP over IP.

```
Spoke-3(config-if)#tunnel mode ipip
```

Now, unfortunately for us, we cannot mix and match our tunnels on Hub-1, so we will have to create a new tunnel. You will see EIGRP adjacencies form, but they will be torn down again. We will create a new tunnel, borrowing the IP address from our first tunnel (through the *ip unnumbered* command), and we will set the tunnel mode to match that of Spoke-3:

```
Hub-1(config-if)#int tunnel 1
Hub-1(config-if)#ip unnumbered tunnel 0
Hub-1(config-if)#tunnel source gi 1/0
Hub-1(config-if)#tunnel dest 10.10.4.1
Hub-1(config-if)#tunnel mode ipip
Hub-1(config-if)#
%DUAL-5-NBRCHANGE: EIGRP-IPv4 1: Neighbor 192.168.1.4 (Tunnel1) is up: new adjacency
Hub-1(config-if)#
```

Our tunnel comes up, and goes back down again:

```
Hub-1(config-if)#
%DUAL-5-NBRCHANGE: EIGRP-IPv4 1: Neighbor 192.168.1.4 (Tunnel1) is up: new adjacency
Hub-1(config-if)#
%DUAL-5-NBRCHANGE: EIGRP-IPv4 1: Neighbor 192.168.1.4 (Tunnel1) is down: holding time expired
Hub-1(config-if)#
%DUAL-5-NBRCHANGE: EIGRP-IPv4 1: Neighbor 192.168.1.4 (Tunnel1) is up: new adjacency
Hub-1(config-if)#
%DUAL-5-NBRCHANGE: EIGRP-IPv4 1: Neighbor 192.168.1.4 (Tunnel1) is down: holding time expired
Hub-1(config-if)#
%DUAL-5-NBRCHANGE: EIGRP-IPv4 1: Neighbor 192.168.1.4 (Tunnel1) is up: new adjacency
Hub-1(config-if)#
```

If we check Spoke-3 we can see the reason why again:

```
Spoke-3(config-if)#
%TUN-5-RECURDOWN: Tunnel0 temporarily disabled due to recursive routing
%LINEPROTO-5-UPDOWN: Line protocol on Interface Tunnel0, changed state to down
%DUAL-5-NBRCHANGE: EIGRP-IPv4 1: Neighbor 192.168.1.1 (Tunnel0) is down: interface down
Spoke-3(config-if)#
```

We can fix this by using the same distribute list as we did earlier. If we look at the EIGRP configuration, we can confirm that we are using it for both our tunnels:

```
Hub-1(config-if)#router eigrp 1
Hub-1(config-router)#distribute-list 1 out tunnel 1
Hub-1(config-router)#do sh run | sec eigrp
router eigrp 1
 distribute-list 1 out Tunnel0
 distribute-list 1 out Tunnel1
 network 1.1.1.1 0.0.0.0
 network 10.10.1.0 0.0.0.255
 network 192.168.1.0
Hub-1(config-router)#
```

Spoke-3, now, has a very healthy routing table:

```
Spoke-3(config-if)#do sh ip route eigrp | beg Gate
Gateway of last resort is 10.10.4.2 to network 0.0.0.0

   1.0.0.0/32 is subnetted, 1 subnets
D    1.1.1.1 [90/27008000] via 192.168.1.1, 00:00:17, Tunnel0
   2.0.0.0/32 is subnetted, 1 subnets
D    2.2.2.2 [90/28288000] via 192.168.1.1, 00:00:17, Tunnel0
   3.0.0.0/32 is subnetted, 1 subnets
D    3.3.3.3 [90/28288000] via 192.168.1.1, 00:00:17, Tunnel0
Spoke-3(config-if)#
```

It can see and reach Hub-1, Spoke-1, and Spoke-2.

```
Spoke-3(config-if)#do ping 1.1.1.1 so lo0
Type escape sequence to abort.
Sending 5, 100-byte ICMP Echos to 1.1.1.1:
Packet sent with a source address of 4.4.4.4
!!!!!
Success rate is 100 percent (5/5)
Spoke-3(config-if)#do ping 2.2.2.2 so lo0
Type escape sequence to abort.
Sending 5, 100-byte ICMP Echos to 2.2.2.2:
Packet sent with a source address of 4.4.4.4
!!!!!
Success rate is 100 percent (5/5)
Spoke-3(config-if)#do ping 3.3.3.3 so lo0
Type escape sequence to abort.
Sending 5, 100-byte ICMP Echos to 3.3.3.3:
Packet sent with a source address of 4.4.4.4
!!!!!
Success rate is 100 percent (5/5)
Spoke-3(config-if)#
```

Spoke-3 has access to all of the routers within our tunnel network. Which is good for Spoke-3. Why is it good for Spoke-3? Well, because the other spoke routers are not so lucky:

```
Spoke-1#sh ip route eigrp | beg Gate
Gateway of last resort is 10.10.2.2 to network 0.0.0.0

      1.0.0.0/32 is subnetted, 1 subnets
D       1.1.1.1 [90/27008000] via 192.168.1.1, 00:20:45, Tunnel0
      4.0.0.0/32 is subnetted, 1 subnets
D       4.4.4.4 [90/28288000] via 192.168.1.1, 00:01:58, Tunnel0
Spoke-1#

Spoke-2(config-router)#do sh ip route eigrp | beg Gate
Gateway of last resort is 10.10.3.2 to network 0.0.0.0

      1.0.0.0/32 is subnetted, 1 subnets
D       1.1.1.1 [90/27008000] via 192.168.1.1, 00:21:03, Tunnel0
      4.0.0.0/32 is subnetted, 1 subnets
D       4.4.4.4 [90/28288000] via 192.168.1.1, 00:02:16, Tunnel0
Spoke-2(config-router)#
```

How is it that Spoke-1 has no visibility of Spoke-2 and vice-versa? This is due to the nature of our design, which is a traditional Hub-and-Spoke topology. Spoke-3 is, effectively, in its own little domain, it has the visibility that Spoke-1 and Spoke-2 do not have between each other. We will change this behaviour later on. For those of you thinking "Hang on, what about split-horizon?", don't worry, we will get to that in a little while.

If we have a look at a Wireshark capture (a ping from Spoke-3's loopback interface to Hub-1's loopback interface), we can see that the basic format is the same as the GRE version. Both have an outer header appended and this outer header shares the same structure as the GRE version's outer header:

```
   20 22.023975000    4.4.4.4                    1.1.1.1                    ICMP
▷ Frame 20: 134 bytes on wire (1072 bits), 134 bytes captured (1072 bits) on interface
▷ Ethernet II, Src: ca:05:b2:5c:00:1c (ca:05:b2:5c:00:1c), Dst: ca:02:98:18:00:70 (ca:
▷ Internet Protocol Version 4, Src: 10.10.4.1 (10.10.4.1), Dst: 10.10.1.1 (10.10.1.1)
▷ Internet Protocol Version 4, Src: 4.4.4.4 (4.4.4.4), Dst: 1.1.1.1 (1.1.1.1)
▷ Internet Control Message Protocol
```

Capture: 2

```
▷ Frame 20: 134 bytes on wire (1072 bits), 134 bytes captured (1072 bits) on
▷ Ethernet II, Src: ca:05:b2:5c:00:1c (ca:05:b2:5c:00:1c), Dst: ca:02:98:18:0
▽ Internet Protocol Version 4, Src: 10.10.4.1 (10.10.4.1), Dst: 10.10.1.1 (10
     Version: 4
     Header length: 20 bytes
   ▷ Differentiated Services Field: 0x00 (DSCP 0x00: Default; ECN: 0x00: Not-E
     Total Length: 120
     Identification: 0x0021 (33)
   ▷ Flags: 0x00
     Fragment offset: 0
     Time to live: 255
  → Protocol: IPIP (4)
   ▷ Header checksum: 0xa24b [correct]
     Source: 10.10.4.1 (10.10.4.1)
     Destination: 10.10.1.1 (10.10.1.1)
     [Source GeoIP: Unknown]
     [Destination GeoIP: Unknown]
▷ Internet Protocol Version 4, Src: 4.4.4.4 (4.4.4.4), Dst: 1.1.1.1 (1.1.1.1)
▷ Internet Control Message Protocol
```

The difference here though, is that the protocol is set to IP (4). Therefore, if the ISP does not permit GRE tunnels, this is a good way to create a tunnel through their network, and keeping them happy.

We have had some good news about Spoke-3; their ISP has said that they can switch to using GRE, but only if it is secured with IPSec!

3.5 Securing GRE with IPSec

Our first steps are to make sure that everyone is on the same page; by switching Spoke-3 to using GRE and having it under the same tunnel on Hub-1, as Spoke-1 and Spoke-2:

```
Spoke-3(config-if)#int tunnel 0
Spoke-3(config-if)#tunnel mode gre ip
Spoke-3(config-if)#do sh int tunnel 0 | i Tunnel protocol
  Tunnel protocol/transport GRE/IP
Spoke-3(config-if)#

Hub-1(config-if)#no int tunnel 1
Hub-1(config)#int tunnel 0
Hub-1(config-if)#ip nhrp map multicast 10.10.4.1
Hub-1(config-if)#ip nhrp map 192.168.1.4 10.10.4.1
Hub-1(config-if)#exit

Spoke-3(config-if)#
%DUAL-5-NBRCHANGE: EIGRP-IPv4 1: Neighbor 192.168.1.1 (Tunnel0) is up:
new adjacency
Spoke-3(config-if)#do sh ip route eigrp | beg Gate
Gateway of last resort is 10.10.4.2 to network 0.0.0.0

      1.0.0.0/32 is subnetted, 1 subnets
D        1.1.1.1 [90/27008000] via 192.168.1.1, 00:00:38, Tun0
Spoke-3(config-if)#exit
```

Now that Spoke-3 has the same limited view of the world as Spoke-1 and Spoke-2, we can set up the IPSec encryption.

There are a number of steps to creating an IPSec tunnel; these boil down to what we are going to say, who we are going to say it to and how we are going to say it.

The "what" will be the traffic we want to encrypt, in the form of an access list. The "who" will be the other router, specified in a crypto map, and the "how" will be through the use of a password, and a transform set - which defines the encryption. Finally, this is then added to our interfaces.

Let's start with Hub-1.

We will have an access list that will permit GRE traffic between our physical interface and our peers' physical interface:

```
Hub-1(config)#access-list 104 permit gre host 10.10.1.1 host 10.10.4.1
```

Next, we set up our ISAKMP policy. ISAKMP stands for Internet Security Association and Key Management Protocol, it was defined under RFC 2408 and is a procedure for authenticating a communicating peer. It controls how to create and manage the Security Associations (SAs), controls the key generation techniques and looks after threat mitigation. ISAKMP allows the tunnel to be created and the IPSec SA to be negotiated. This is also known as IKE Phase 1. The SA contains all the parameters that the two routers need to set up phase 2. It is an agreement to use the same encryption method, the same algorithm to verify message integrity (MD5 or SHA) and how the two will authenticate (PKI, or shared secret key).

Our ISAKMP policy will use a pre-shared password of "802101.com" between our peer (10.10.4.1) and us. In this way, we can have different passwords for each peer.

```
Hub-1(config)#crypto isakmp policy 1
Hub-1(config-isakmp)#authentication pre-share
Hub-1(config-isakmp)#crypto isakmp key 802101.com address 10.10.4.1
```

With this part set up, we can create the transform set for phase 2. Phase 2 (the IPSec part) controls whether we will use the Authentication Header protocol (AH), or Encapsulating Security Payload protocol (ESP), or both. It then determines which encryption method will be used for ESP and (if we are using it), which authentication method for AH.

The choice of AH or ESP will determine how our end packet looks and will have greater ramifications later on.

AH and ESP

AH protects the packet from tampering, replay attacks and spoofing. It digitally signs the entire packet, inserting an AH header between the layer 3 IP header and the layer 4 TCP or UDP header.

IP Header	AH Header	TCP/UDP Header	Data

A checksum is computed based on the entire packet (above) and is stored in the AH header.

Digging down a bit deeper, the AH header looks like this:

Next Header (8 bits)	Payload Length (8 bits)	Reserved (16 bits)
Security Parameter Index (SPI) (32 bits)		
Sequence Number Field (32 bits)		
Authentication Data (ICV) (32 bits)		

The next header identifies the type of the next payload after the AH, the payload length specifies the length of AH. "Reserved" means just what it says, this is reserved for future use and must always be set at 0. SPI combines the destination IP address and the AH to uniquely identify the SA that is being used. The sequence number is an increasing counter, to identify the sequence and the authentication data contains the Integrity Check value, which, strictly speaking, is a multiple of 32 bits and is used for padding, so that the field aligns with either the IPv4, or IPv6 boundary.

Our options for AH are to use a keyed-hash message authentication code (HMAC), with either MD5, or SHA. AH uses IP protocol ID 51.

AH does not actually prevent people from seeing the data; they cannot tamper with it, but they can still see it. ESP, on the other hand, encrypts the entire payload of the packet.

ESP, which uses IP protocol ID 50, can provide authentication, replay-proofing, and integrity checking. It adds more to the packet than AH does (ESP header, ESP trailer, and ESP authentication), an ESP packet will look like this:

IP Header	ESP Header	TCP or UDP Header	Data	ESP Trailer	ESP Auth

ESP uses the same fields that were present in the AH header, though they are separated out.

The ESP header contains the 32-bit Security Parameter Index (SPI) and sequence number.

The ESP trailer contains the padding, which varies depending on what algorithm we use, along with the 8-bit pad length and the 8-bit next header.

The ESP Auth contains the ICV.

ESP is used more frequently than AH, as it works with NAT traversal, which we will see is important later on.

Our transform set controls how the information is encrypted. We will give the transform set a name and specify that we want to use, from the wide variety of options, esp-3des and esp-md5-hmac. For our transform set to work we require two components, a valid encryption method, such as esp-3des, and a valid authentication method, such as esp-md5-hmac.

```
Hub-1(config)#crypto ipsec transform-set ?
  WORD  Transform set tag

Hub-1(config)#crypto ipsec transform-set HUB-TO-SPOKE ?
  ah-md5-hmac        AH-HMAC-MD5 transform
  ah-sha-hmac        AH-HMAC-SHA transform
  ah-sha256-hmac     AH-HMAC-SHA256 transform
  ah-sha384-hmac     AH-HMAC-SHA384 transform
  ah-sha512-hmac     AH-HMAC-SHA512 transform
  comp-lzs           IP Compression using the LZS algorithm
  esp-3des           ESP transform using 3DES cipher (168 bits)
  esp-aes            ESP transform using AES cipher
  esp-des            ESP transform using DES cipher (56 bits)
  esp-gcm            ESP transform using GCM cipher
  esp-gmac           ESP transform using GMAC cipher
  esp-md5-hmac       ESP transform using HMAC-MD5 auth
  esp-null           ESP transform w/o cipher
  esp-seal           ESP transform using SEAL cipher (160 bits)
  esp-sha-hmac       ESP transform using HMAC-SHA auth
  esp-sha256-hmac    ESP transform using HMAC-SHA256 auth
  esp-sha384-hmac    ESP transform using HMAC-SHA384 auth
  esp-sha512-hmac    ESP transform using HMAC-SHA512 auth

Hub-1(config)#crypto ipsec transform-set HUB-TO-SPOKE esp-3des esp-md5-hmac
Hub-1(cfg-crypto-trans)#exit
```

We have exited out of the transform set here, but we do have the option to set the mode (either tunnel or transport), which we will look at in greater detail in section 4.8, when we look at protecting DMVPN with IPSec.

Next, we create our crypto map, which will reference the peer, the transform set, and the interesting traffic.

```
Hub-1(config)#crypto map HubToSpokeVPN ?
```

```
    <1-65535>        Sequence to insert into crypto map entry
    client           Specify client configuration settings
    gdoi             Configure crypto map gdoi features
    isakmp           Specify isakmp configuration settings
    isakmp-profile   Specify isakmp profile to use
    local-address    Interface to use for local address for this crypto
map
    redundancy       High availability options for this map

Hub-1(config)#crypto map HubToSpokeVPN 10 ?
    gdoi           GDOI
    ipsec-isakmp   IPSEC w/ISAKMP
    ipsec-manual   IPSEC w/manual keying
    <cr>

Hub-1(config)#crypto map HubToSpokeVPN 10 ipsec-isakmp
% NOTE: This new crypto map will remain disabled until a peer
    and a valid access list have been configured.
Hub-1(config-crypto-map)#set peer 10.10.4.1
Hub-1(config-crypto-map)#set transform-set HUB-TO-SPOKE
Hub-1(config-crypto-map)#match address 104
```

The final stage is to apply this to our physical interface:

```
Hub-1(config-crypto-map)#int gi 1/0
Hub-1(config-if)#crypto map HubToSpokeVPN
Hub-1(config-if)#
%CRYPTO-6-ISAKMP_ON_OFF: ISAKMP is ON
Hub-1(config-if)#
```

Looking at the console messages, we can see that our other neighbors remain up, but only Spoke-3 loses its adjacency:

```
%CRYPTO-4-RECVD_PKT_NOT_IPSEC: Rec'd packet not an IPSEC packet. (ip)
vrf/dest_addr= /10.10.1.1, src_addr= 10.10.4.1, prot= 47
Hub-1(config-if)#
%DUAL-5-NBRCHANGE: EIGRP-IPv4 1: Neighbor 192.168.1.4 (Tunnel0) is
down: holding time expired
Hub-1(config-if)#
%CRYPTO-4-RECVD_PKT_NOT_IPSEC: Rec'd packet not an IPSEC packet. (ip)
vrf/dest_addr= /10.10.1.1, src_addr= 10.10.4.1, prot= 47
Hub-1(config-if)#end
```

Now, we can move on to Spoke-3 and implement the other side of our IPSec tunnel, making sure that our settings match:

```
Spoke-3(config)#access-list 104 permit gre host 10.10.4.1 host 10.10.1.1
Spoke-3(config)#crypto isakmp policy 1
Spoke-3(config-isakmp)#authentication pre-share
Spoke-3(config-isakmp)#crypto isakmp key 802101.com address 10.10.1.1
Spoke-3(config)#crypto ipsec transform-set HUB-TO-SPOKE esp-3des esp-md5-hmac
Spoke-3(cfg-crypto-trans)#exit
Spoke-3(config)#crypto map HubToSpokeVPN 10 ipsec-isakmp
% NOTE: This new crypto map will remain disabled until a peer
    and a valid access list have been configured.
Spoke-3(config-crypto-map)#set peer 10.10.1.1
Spoke-3(config-crypto-map)#set transform-set HUB-TO-SPOKE
Spoke-3(config-crypto-map)#match address 104
Spoke-3(config-crypto-map)#int gi 1/0
Spoke-3(config-if)#crypto map HubToSpokeVPN
Spoke-3(config-if)#
%CRYPTO-6-ISAKMP_ON_OFF: ISAKMP is ON
%DUAL-5-NBRCHANGE: EIGRP-IPv4 1: Neighbor 192.168.1.1 (Tunnel0) is up: new adjacency
Spoke-3(config-if)#do sh ip route eigrp | beg Gate
Gateway of last resort is 10.10.4.2 to network 0.0.0.0

      1.0.0.0/32 is subnetted, 1 subnets
D        1.1.1.1 [90/27008000] via 192.168.1.1, 00:00:20, Tun0
Spoke-3(config-if)#
```

Now, we have a fully secured IPSec tunnel, as part of our multipoint GRE configuration.

So how do our packets differ from non-IPSec encrypted packets?

```
10 11.786870000    10.10.4.1               10.10.1.1              ESP
▷ Frame 10: 190 bytes on wire (1520 bits), 190 bytes captured (1520 bits) on interface
▷ Ethernet II, Src: ca:05:b2:5c:00:1c (ca:05:b2:5c:00:1c), Dst: ca:02:98:18:00:70 (ca:0
▷ Internet Protocol Version 4, Src: 10.10.4.1 (10.10.4.1), Dst: 10.10.1.1 (10.10.1.1)
▷ Encapsulating Security Payload
```

Capture: 3

We have the same outer header, with the source and destination IP addresses of our ingress and egress points of the tunnel. The difference is in the IPv4 header; the protocol is set to ESP (50):

```
10          o    11.786870000              10.10.4.1

▷ Frame 10: 190 bytes on wire (1520 bits), 190 byte
▷ Ethernet II, Src: ca:05:b2:5c:00:1c (ca:05:b2:5c:
▽ Internet Protocol Version 4, Src: 10.10.4.1 (10.1
      Version: 4
      Header Length: 20 bytes
   ▷ Differentiated Services Field: 0x00 (DSCP 0x00
      Total Length: 176
      Identification: 0x016e (366)
   ▷ Flags: 0x00
      Fragment offset: 0
      Time to live: 255
      Protocol: Encap Security Payload (50)
   ▷ Header checksum: 0xa098 [validation disabled]
      Source: 10.10.4.1 (10.10.4.1)
      Destination: 10.10.1.1 (10.10.1.1)
▽ Encapsulating Security Payload
      ESP SPI: 0x4625bd6a (1176878442)
      ESP Sequence: 17
```

Then we have the ESP header. We do not have much visibility into this header, as we would expect. With the right mix of authentication and encryption protocols (which basically means it's less secure), then we could decrypt these using Wireshark. This is, however, beyond the scope of what we need to achieve here, but does make for an interesting delve into encryption. We can, however, see the SPI and the sequence number.

Returning to the command line, we can see some useful information about the status of our IPSec tunnels. These commands are all based around the command "sh crypto" and the keyword of either isakmp or ipsec – depending on if we want to look at the phase 1, or phase 2 details.

Without going into all of the options, for either isakmp or ipsec, there are a couple of commands that we should look at, for both confirmation and troubleshooting purposes.

```
Hub-1#sh crypto isakmp ?
  default  Show ISAKMP default
  key      Show ISAKMP preshared keys
  peers    Show ISAKMP peer structures
  policy   Show ISAKMP protection suite policy
  profile  Show ISAKMP profiles
  sa       Show ISAKMP Security Associations
```

```
Hub-1#
```

The first is to check the key we are using between our peers:

```
Hub-1#sh crypto isakmp key
Keyring         Hostname/Address        Preshared Key

default         10.10.4.1               802101.com
Hub-1#
```

Here, we can easily spot, assuming that we have access to both sides, differences in the preshared key. That said, if there were spaces at the end of the preshared key, these would not be evident. If this is the (suspected) case then reapplying the pre-shared key to both sides, ensuring that we do not enter any spaces, is usually the easiest option.

We can confirm who our peers should be, by using the command "sh crypto isakmp peers":

```
Hub-1#sh crypto isakmp peers
Peer: 10.10.4.1 Port: 500 Local: 10.10.1.1
 Phase1 id: 10.10.4.1
Hub-1#
```

The last command is to check the security associations:

```
Hub-1#sh crypto isakmp sa
IPv4 Crypto ISAKMP SA
dst             src             state           conn-id status
10.10.4.1       10.10.1.1       QM_IDLE            1002 ACTIVE
10.10.1.1       10.10.4.1       QM_IDLE            1001 ACTIVE

IPv6 Crypto ISAKMP SA

Hub-1#
```

QM_IDLE is good; this is what we want to see. If we see MM_KEY_EXCH, then either our pre-shared key is incorrect, or our peer IP addresses are incorrect.

Moving onto the IPSec side of things, again, there are a couple of "quick win" commands:

```
Hub-1#sh crypto ipsec ?
  policy                Show IPSEC client policies
  profile               Show ipsec profile information
```

```
    sa                      IPSEC SA table
    security-association    Show parameters for IPSec security
  associations
    spi-lookup              IPSEC SPI table
    transform-set           Crypto transform sets

Hub-1#sh crypto ipsec
```

Firstly, we can check the SPI table. The SPI is the Security Peer Information; a unique hash identifier created by each peer.

```
Hub-1#sh crypto ipsec spi-lookup
Active SPI table
     SPI Prot Local Address            M Type
4625BD6A ESP  10.10.1.1                * ?
B50954FB ESP  10.10.1.1                * ?

Hub-1#
```

Secondly, we can check our transform sets. Here, we can see the system default, and any additional ones that we have configured:

```
Hub-1#sh crypto ipsec transform-set
Transform set default: { esp-aes esp-sha-hmac  }
   will negotiate = { Transport,  },

Transform set HUB-TO-SPOKE: { esp-3des esp-md5-hmac  }
   will negotiate = { Tunnel,  },

Hub-1#
```

Finally, we get to the command with the longest output. If we look at the output from "sh crypto ipsec sa" then we can see all the information we need to (and more). This includes who we are talking to, how we are talking to them (in the shape of our transform sets and crypto maps), and how many packets we have encapsulated (encaps) or decapsulated (decaps). The pertinent lines have been bolded, also please note that the sibling_flags is actually 80000040 for SPI 0xB50954FB and 80004040 for SPI 0x4625BD6A, I have truncated these for readability:

```
Hub-1#sh crypto ipsec sa

interface: GigabitEthernet1/0
    Crypto map tag: HubToSpokeVPN, local addr 10.10.1.1

   protected vrf: (none)
```

```
local  ident (addr/mask/prot/port): (10.10.1.1/255.255.255.255/47/0)
remote ident (addr/mask/prot/port): (10.10.4.1/255.255.255.255/47/0)
current_peer 10.10.4.1 port 500
  PERMIT, flags={origin_is_acl,}
 #pkts encaps: 440, #pkts encrypt: 440, #pkts digest: 440
 #pkts decaps: 420, #pkts decrypt: 420, #pkts verify: 420
 #pkts compressed: 0, #pkts decompressed: 0
 #pkts not compressed: 0, #pkts compr. failed: 0
 #pkts not decompressed: 0, #pkts decompress failed: 0
 #send errors 0, #recv errors 0

  local crypto endpt.: 10.10.1.1, remote crypto endpt.: 10.10.4.1
  path mtu 1500, ip mtu 1500, ip mtu idb GigabitEthernet1/0
  current outbound spi: 0x6F4AE9E0(1867180512)
  PFS (Y/N): N, DH group: none

  inbound esp sas:
   spi: 0xB50954FB(3037287675)
     transform: esp-3des esp-md5-hmac ,
     in use settings ={Tunnel, }
     conn id: 1, flow_id: 1, sibling_flags 80040, crypto map: HubToSpokeVPN
     sa timing: remaining key lifetime (k/sec): (4158793/1619)
     IV size: 8 bytes
     replay detection support: Y
     Status: ACTIVE(ACTIVE)
   spi: 0x4625BD6A(1176878442)
     transform: esp-3des esp-md5-hmac ,
     in use settings ={Tunnel, }
     conn id: 3, flow_id: 3, sibling_flags 84040, crypto map: HubToSpokeVPN
     sa timing: remaining key lifetime (k/sec): (4287512/1625)
     IV size: 8 bytes
     replay detection support: Y
     Status: ACTIVE(ACTIVE)

  inbound ah sas:

  inbound pcp sas:

  outbound esp sas:
   spi: 0xAA004CD(178259149)
     transform: esp-3des esp-md5-hmac ,
     in use settings ={Tunnel, }
     conn id: 2, flow_id: 2, sibling_flags 80040, crypto map: HubToSpokeVPN
     sa timing: remaining key lifetime (k/sec): (4158793/1619)
     IV size: 8 bytes
     replay detection support: Y
     Status: ACTIVE(ACTIVE)
   spi: 0x6F4AE9E0(1867180512)
     transform: esp-3des esp-md5-hmac ,
     in use settings ={Tunnel, }
     conn id: 4, flow_id: 4, sibling_flags 84040, crypto map: HubToSpokeVPN
     sa timing: remaining key lifetime (k/sec): (4287509/1625)
     IV size: 8 bytes
```

```
            replay detection support: Y
         Status: ACTIVE(ACTIVE)

     outbound ah sas:

     outbound pcp sas:
Hub-1#
```

We do still have a few options to really highlight what we are looking for:

```
Hub-1#sh crypto ipsec sa ?
  address    IPSEC SA table in (dest) address order
  detail     show counter detail
  identity   IPSEC SADB identity tree
  interface  Show info for specific interface
  ipv6       Show IPv6 crypto IPsec SA info
  map        IPSEC SA table for a specific crypto map
  peer       Show peer sas
  vrf        VRF Routing/Forwarding instance
  |          Output modifiers
  <cr>

Hub-1#
```

We can get a more concise overview of our peers, using the "address" keyword:

```
Hub-1#sh crypto ipsec sa address
fvrf/address: (none)/10.10.1.1
   protocol: ESP
     spi: 0x3DC4E719(1036314393)
        transform: esp-3des esp-md5-hmac ,
        in use settings ={Tunnel, }
        conn id: 5, flow_id: 5, sibling_flags 84040, crypto map: HubToSpokeVPN
        sa timing: remaining key lifetime (k/sec): (4608000/2410)
        IV size: 8 bytes
        replay detection support: Y
        Status: ACTIVE(ACTIVE)

fvrf/address: (none)/10.10.4.1
   protocol: ESP
     spi: 0x817DA271(2172494449)
        transform: esp-3des esp-md5-hmac ,
        in use settings ={Tunnel, }
        conn id: 6, flow_id: 6, sibling_flags 84040, crypto map: HubToSpokeVPN
        sa timing: remaining key lifetime (k/sec): (4608000/2410)
        IV size: 8 bytes
        replay detection support: Y
        Status: ACTIVE(ACTIVE)
```

```
Hub-1#
```

We can also get some visibility into what we chose as our "interesting traffic":

```
Hub-1#sh crypto ipsec sa identity

interface: GigabitEthernet1/0
    Crypto map tag: HubToSpokeVPN, local addr 10.10.1.1

   protected vrf: (none)
   local  ident (addr/mask/prot/port): (0.0.0.0/0.0.0.0/0/0)
   remote ident (addr/mask/prot/port): (0.0.0.0/0.0.0.0/0/0)
   current_peer (none) port 500
     DENY, flags={ident_is_root,}
    #pkts encaps: 0, #pkts encrypt: 0, #pkts digest: 0
    #pkts decaps: 0, #pkts decrypt: 0, #pkts verify: 0
    #pkts compressed: 0, #pkts decompressed: 0
    #pkts not compressed: 0, #pkts compr. failed: 0
    #pkts not decompressed: 0, #pkts decompress failed: 0
    #send errors 0, #recv errors 31

   protected vrf: (none)
   local  ident (addr/mask/prot/port): (10.10.1.1/255.255.255.255/47/0)
   remote ident (addr/mask/prot/port): (10.10.4.1/255.255.255.255/47/0)
   current_peer 10.10.4.1 port 500
     PERMIT, flags={origin_is_acl,}
    #pkts encaps: 1021, #pkts encrypt: 1021, #pkts digest: 1021
    #pkts decaps: 908, #pkts decrypt: 908, #pkts verify: 908
    #pkts compressed: 0, #pkts decompressed: 0
    #pkts not compressed: 0, #pkts compr. failed: 0
    #pkts not decompressed: 0, #pkts decompress failed: 0
    #send errors 0, #recv errors 0
Hub-1#
```

Here, we can see that our interesting traffic was defined through an ACL, as shown in the PERMIT line above. It may not show us which particular ACL we used, but it does give us a good idea where to start looking.

We have some very good insight into what IPSec peers we have, but what about our other peers; those that are bound to us through NHRP? What tools do we have at our disposal for them?

Firstly, we can check our routing table and hub-to-spoke connectivity. Secondly, we can use NHRP to tell us what is going on with our tunnels. The command "sh nhrp ?" does not offer many options:

```
Hub-1#sh nhrp ?
```

```
debug-condition   Display NHRP conditional debugging

Hub-1#sh nhrp
```

Thankfully, "sh ip nhrp ?" does offer a few more, in fact too many to list here. Many of the options are concerned with NHRP functionality on an interface specific level. Of the 65 subcommands returned, only 24 do not have the word "interface" in the description and three of the remaining entries are still interfaces.

On it's own, "sh ip nhrp" can tell us who we are peered with.

```
Hub-1#sh ip nhrp
192.168.1.2/32 via 192.168.1.2
   Tunnel0 created 00:19:57, never expire
   Type: static, Flags: used
   NBMA address: 10.10.2.1
192.168.1.3/32 via 192.168.1.3
   Tunnel0 created 00:19:40, never expire
   Type: static, Flags: used
   NBMA address: 10.10.3.1
192.168.1.4/32 via 192.168.1.4
   Tunnel0 created 02:05:09, never expire
   Type: static, Flags: used
   NBMA address: 10.10.4.1
Hub-1#
```

Here, we can see our peer endpoints, how long the tunnel has been up, our type - which is static (for the moment at least) and the NBMA address.

We can look at these peers individually by specifying the IP address:

```
Hub-1#sh ip nhrp 192.168.1.2
192.168.1.2/32 via 192.168.1.2
   Tunnel0 created 00:28:05, never expire
   Type: static, Flags: used
   NBMA address: 10.10.2.1
Hub-1#
```

We can see a brief overview of our NHRP peers:

```
Hub-1#sh ip nhrp brief
   Target          Via           NBMA        Mode    Intfc  Claimed
   192.168.1.2/32  192.168.1.2   10.10.2.1   static  Tu0    <     >
   192.168.1.3/32  192.168.1.3   10.10.3.1   static  Tu0    <     >
```

```
    192.168.1.4/32   192.168.1.4   10.10.4.1 static    Tu0     <   >
Hub-1#
```

We can see the peers that are taking part in multicast:

```
Hub-1#sh ip nhrp multicast
   I/F      NBMA address
Tunnel0    10.10.3.1        Flags: static
Tunnel0    10.10.2.1        Flags: static
Tunnel0    10.10.4.1        Flags: static
Hub-1#
```

Lastly, we can have a very brief overview of our peers, those that are static, dynamic, or incomplete:

```
Hub-1#sh ip nhrp summary
IP NHRP cache 3 entries, 1104 bytes
   3 static  0 dynamic  0 incomplete
Hub-1#
```

So far, all our peers have been statically created. We can, though, have them dynamically created and this is where the lines between mGRE and DMVPN start to cross and blur. We will come to DMVPN shortly, but while our focus is still on tunnels, we will look at tunnels and IPv6.

3.6 IPv6 transition mechanisms

When we wish to tunnel IPv6 packets across an IPv4 "core", we have a few options as to how we can achieve this. These are collectively referred to as "transition mechanisms". There are a number of these "transitions mechanisms" we can use, such as "6over4", "6to4", "6RD", and "ISATAP".

IPv6 in IPv4 tunnels (6over4)

This is perhaps the simplest method. With 6over4, dual-stack nodes use an existing multicast-enabled IPv4 network, creating a virtual data link layer.

We start by enabling IPv6 routing on the router. We then create a second loopback interface, adding it to an EIGRP routing instance and then we create a second tunnel, again, adding this to the same routing instance. Lastly we create the routing instance.

```
Hub-1(config)#ipv6 unicast-routing
Hub-1(config)#int lo1
Hub-1(config-if)#ipv6 add 2001::1/128
Hub-1(config-if)#ipv6 eigrp 10
Hub-1(config-if)#exit
Hub-1(config)#int tunnel 1
Hub-1(config-if)#ipv6 enable
Hub-1(config-if)#ipv6 eigrp 10
Hub-1(config-if)#tunnel source gi 1/0
Hub-1(config-if)#tunnel dest 10.10.2.1
Hub-1(config-if)#tunnel mode ipv6ip
Hub-1(config-if)#ipv6 router eigrp 10
Hub-1(config-rtr)#


Spoke-1(config)#ipv6 unicast-routing
Spoke-1(config)#int lo1
Spoke-1(config-if)#ipv6 add 2001::2/128
Spoke-1(config-if)#ipv6 eigrp 10
Spoke-1(config-if)#ipv6 router eigrp 10
Spoke-1(config-rtr)#exit
Spoke-1(config)#int tunnel 1
Spoke-1(config-if)#no ip address
Spoke-1(config-if)#ipv6 enable
Spoke-1(config-if)#ipv6 eigrp 10
Spoke-1(config-if)#tunnel source gi 1/0
Spoke-1(config-if)#tunnel mode ipv6ip
Spoke-1(config-if)#tunnel destination 10.10.1.1
Spoke-1(config-if)#
```

```
%DUAL-5-NBRCHANGE: EIGRP-IPv6 10: Neighbor FE80::A0A:101 (Tunnel1) is
up: new adjacency
```

The requirements for an IPv6 tunnel are no different to an IPv4 tunnel. We need a source, an IPv4 destination and a tunnel mode, which, with ipv6ip, will default to 6over4.

The adjacencies come up and we have the expected entries in the IPv6 routing table. We also (more importantly) have reachability.

```
Hub-1(config-rtr)#do sh ipv6 route eigrp | beg 20
D   2001::2/128 [90/27008000]
     via FE80::A0A:201, Tunnel1
Hub-1(config-rtr)#

Spoke-1(config-if)#do sh ipv6 route eigrp | beg 20
D   2001::1/128 [90/27008000]
     via FE80::A0A:101, Tunnel1
Spoke-1(config-if)#

Spoke-1(config-if)#do ping 2001::1 so lo1
Type escape sequence to abort.
Sending 5, 100-byte ICMP Echos to 2001::1:
Packet sent with a source address of 2001::2
!!!!!
Success rate is 100 percent (5/5)
Spoke-1(config-if)#
```

If we sniff this traffic, using Wireshark, we can see the IPv6 packet being encapsulated within our IPv4 packet:

```
▷ Frame 12: 134 bytes on wire (1072 bits), 134 bytes captured (1072 bits) on interface 0
▷ Ethernet II, Src: ca:03:98:19:00:1c (ca:03:98:19:00:1c), Dst: ca:02:98:18:00:38 (ca:02:9
▷ Internet Protocol Version 4, Src: 10.10.2.1 (10.10.2.1), Dst: 10.10.1.1 (10.10.1.1)
▷ Internet Protocol Version 6, Src: 2001::2 (2001::2), Dst: 2001::1 (2001::1)
▷ Internet Control Message Protocol v6
```

Capture: 4

We have our IPv4 outer header, with the source and destination IP addresses of our physical interfaces. Beneath this is the IPv6 header and beneath that, is the IPv6 data.

A simplified diagram of the packet would look like this:

IPv4 header	IPv6 header	IPv6 data

The resulting packet is identical to one created by using 6to4 tunnels.

Automatic 6to4 tunnels

Like 6over4, 6to4 is a transition mechanism for migration from IPv4 to IPv6. Unlike 6over4, 6to4 must have a specially configured tunnel address, starting with 2002: - this is a requirement of 6to4 that the address must be within the 2002::/16 subnet. This address must also match up with the IPv4 source address used – which we will explain in a moment.

We are going to step away from our main topology for this example and use a simple, two-router network:

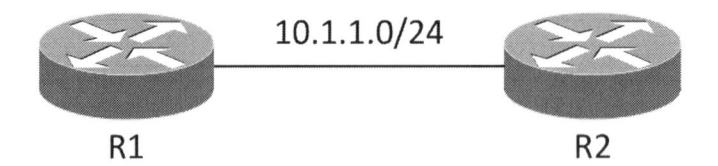

We start by enabling IPv6 unicast-routing and configuring our IPv4 addresses.

```
R1(config)#ipv6 unicast-routing
R1(config)#int gi 1/0
R1(config-if)#ip add 10.1.1.1 255.255.255.0
R1(config-if)#no shut
R1(config-if)#

R2(config)#ipv6 unicast-routing
R2(config)#int gi 1/0
R2(config-if)#ip add 10.1.1.2 255.255.255.0
R2(config-if)#no shut
R2(config-if)#
```

Setting the tunnel mode as "ipv6ip 6to4" and the source to be our physical interface creates the tunnel.

```
R1(config)#int tunnel 0
R1(config-if)#tunnel mode ipv6ip 6to4
```

```
R1(config-if)#tunnel source gi 1/0
R1(config-if)#exit
```

We know that our tunnel address must start with 2002, but how do we configure the rest of it to "match" our IPv4 address for the gigabit interface?

Thankfully, Cisco can help us out there (unless you really want to start playing around with hex conversion). Under configuration mode, using the "ipv6" command we can see that we have an option to create a "general-prefix". The general prefix can be used to generate the address we need to use. It takes the format of "ipv6 general-prefix <name> <conversion method> <interface>", where the name can be anything we want to use and the conversion method either being 6to4, or 6rd (IPv6 rapid deployment). The interface is the IPv4 interface that we want to use as the source.

```
R1(config)#ipv6 ?
  access-list        Configure access lists
  cef                Cisco Express Forwarding for IPv6
  dhcp               Configure IPv6 DHCP
  dhcp-client        Configure IPv6 DHCP client
  dhcp-relay         Configure IPv6 DHCP relay agent
  flowset            Set flow label random for originated packets
  general-prefix     Configure a general IPv6 prefix
  hop-limit          Configure hop count limit
  host               Configure static hostnames
  icmp               Configure ICMP parameters
  local              Specify local options
  mfib               Multicast Forwarding
  mld                Global mld commands
  mobile             Mobile IPv6
  multicast          Configure multicast related commands
  multicast-routing  Enable IPv6 multicast
  nd                 Configure IPv6 ND
  neighbor           Neighbor
  ospf               OSPF
  pim                Configure Protocol Independent Multicast
  prefix-list        Build a prefix list
  radius             RADIUS configuration commands


R1(config)#ipv6 general-prefix ?
  WORD  General prefix name

R1(config)#ipv6 general-prefix R1G1 ?
  6rd                 6rd
```

```
                      6to4              6to4
                      X:X:X:X::X/<0-128>  IPv6 prefix

  R1(config)#ipv6 general-prefix R1G1 6to4 ?
    ACR                Virtual ACR interface
    ATM-ACR            ATM interface with ACR
    Analysis-Module    cisco network analysis service module
    Async              Async interface
    Auto-Template      Auto-Template interface
    BVI                Bridge-Group Virtual Interface
    CDMA-Ix            CDMA Ix interface
    CEM-ACR            Circuit Emulation interface with ACR
    CTunnel            CTunnel interface
    Container          Container interface
    Dialer             Dialer interface
    EsconPhy           ESCON interface
    FastEthernet       FastEthernet IEEE 802.3
    Fcpa               Fiber Channel
    Filter             Filter interface
    Filtergroup        Filter Group interface
    GMPLS              MPLS interface
    GigabitEthernet    GigabitEthernet IEEE 802.3z
    IMA-ACR            IMA interface with ACR
    LISP               Locator/ID Separation Protocol Virtual Int
    LongReachEthernet  Long-Reach Ethernet interface
    Loopback           Loopback interface

  R1(config)#ipv6 general-prefix R1G1 6to4 Gi 1/0
```

We can find our newly created address, using the command "sh ipv6 general-prefix":

```
  R1(config)#do sh ipv6 general-prefix
  IPv6 Prefix R1G1, acquired via 6to4
    2002:A01:101::/48 Valid lifetime infinite, preferred lifetime
  infinite
  R1(config)#
```

We then apply this to our tunnel, appending ::1/64 to it:

```
  R1(config)#int tunnel 0
  R1(config-if)#ipv6 address ?
    WORD               General prefix name
    X:X:X:X::X         IPv6 link-local address
    X:X:X:X::X/<0-128> IPv6 prefix
    autoconfig         Obtain address using autoconfiguration
    negotiated         IPv6 Address negotiated via IKEv2 Modeconfig
```

```
R1(config-if)#ipv6 address R1G1 ?
  X:X:X:X::X/<0-128>  IPv6 prefix

R1(config-if)#ipv6 address R1G1 ::1/64
R1(config-if)#
```

We do the same on R2:

```
R2(config)#ipv6 general-prefix R2G1 6to4 Gi 1/0
R2(config)#do sh ipv6 general-prefix
IPv6 Prefix R2G1, acquired via 6to4
   2002:A01:102::/48 Valid lifetime infinite, preferred lifetime
infinite
R2(config)#int tunnel 0
R2(config-if)#tunnel mode ipv6ip 6to4
R2(config-if)#tunnel source gi 1/0
R2(config-if)#ipv6 add R2G1 ::1/64
R2(config-if)#end
R2#
```

In order for our tunnel ends to talk to each other, we need a static route for 2002::/16 pointing at our tunnel interface. While we are at it, let's give ourselves something to test with:

```
R1(config)#ipv6 route 2002::/16 tun 0
R1(config)#int lo0
R1(config-if)#ipv6 add 2001::1/128
R1(config-if)#ipv6 enable
R1(config-if)#exit
R1(config)#
```

Unlike 6over4, we cannot use EIGRP, or, for that matter OSPF through the tunnel. Both EIGRP and OSPF rely on link-local addresses to form adjacencies, and link-local addresses do not work with 6to4. We can, however, use BGP.

To form our BGP network we create the BGP AS and then create an IPv6 address family. Within this address family, we set our neighbour to be the IPv6 address we created using the general-prefix. We then activate our neighbour and advertise our loopback interface.

```
R1(config)#router bgp 100
R1(config-router)#no bgp default ipv4-unicast
R1(config-router)#address-family ipv6
R1(config-router-af)#neigh 2002:A01:102::1 remote-as 100
R1(config-router-af)#neigh 2002:A01:102::1 activate
```

```
R1(config-router-af)#
%BGP-5-NBR_RESET: Neighbor 2002:A01:102::1 passive reset (Peer closed
the session)
%BGP-5-ADJCHANGE: neighbor 2002:A01:102::1 Up
R1(config-router-af)#network 2001::1/128
R1(config-router-af)#end
```

We do the same for R2. First, by creating the static route, then creating our loopback interface and finally, creating our BGP AS.

```
R2(config)#ipv6 route 2002::/16 tun 0
R2(config)#int lo0
R2(config-if)#ipv6 add 2001::2/128
R2(config-if)#ipv6 enable
R2(config-if)#router bgp 100
R2(config-router)#no bgp default ipv4-unicast
R2(config-router)#address-family ipv6
R2(config-router-af)#neigh 2002:A01:101::1 remote-as 100
R2(config-router-af)#neigh 2002:A01:101::1 activate
R2(config-router-af)#
%BGP-5-ADJCHANGE: neighbor 2002:A01:101::1 Up
R2(config-router-af)#network 2001::2/128
R2(config-router-af)#end
```

We can confirm that our neighbour's loopback address is being advertised to us through BGP and that we have reachability:

```
R2#do sh ipv6 route | beg 20
B   2001::1/128 [200/0]
     via 2002:A01:101::1
LC  2001::2/128 [0/0]
     via Loopback0, receive
S   2002::/16 [1/0]
     via Tunnel0, directly connected
C   2002:A01:102::/64 [0/0]
     via Tunnel0, directly connected
L   2002:A01:102::1/128 [0/0]
     via Tunnel0, receive
L   FF00::/8 [0/0]
     via Null0, receive
R2#

R1#do sh ipv6 route | beg 20
LC  2001::1/128 [0/0]
     via Loopback0, receive
B   2001::2/128 [200/0]
```

```
           via 2002:A01:102::1
S    2002::/16 [1/0]
           via Tunnel0, directly connected
C    2002:A01:101::/64 [0/0]
           via Tunnel0, directly connected
L    2002:A01:101::1/128 [0/0]
           via Tunnel0, receive
L    FF00::/8 [0/0]
           via Null0, receive
R1#ping ipv6 2001::2
Type escape sequence to abort.
Sending 5, 100-byte ICMP Echos to 2001::2:
!!!!!
Success rate is 100 percent (5/5)
R1#ping ipv6 2001::2 so lo0
Type escape sequence to abort.
Sending 5, 100-byte ICMP Echos to 2001::2:
Packet sent with a source address of 2001::1
!!!!!
Success rate is 100 percent (5/5)
R1#
```

Looking at the ping packets, captured in Wireshark, there is no difference in the data carried by 6over4 to that carried by 6to4.

If we look at the IPv6 header, from our 6over4 tunnel, we notice that we have entries for "Teredo", which is an automated tunnelling mechanism. Teredo allows IPv6 hosts on an IPv4 network to communicate with each other, even though there is no IPv6 network joining them together.

```
 12 11.422356000    2001::2                    2001::1
▷ Frame 12: 134 bytes on wire (1072 bits), 134 bytes captured (1072 bits) on i
▷ Ethernet II, Src: ca:03:98:19:00:1c (ca:03:98:19:00:1c), Dst: ca:02:98:18:0(
▷ Internet Protocol Version 4, Src: 10.10.2.1 (10.10.2.1), Dst: 10.10.1.1 (10.
▽ Internet Protocol Version 6, Src: 2001::2 (2001::2), Dst: 2001::1 (2001::1)
    ▷ 0110 .... = Version: 6
    ▷ .... 0000 0000 .... .... .... .... .... = Traffic class: 0x00000000
          .... .... .... 0000 0000 0000 0000 0000 = Flowlabel: 0x00000000
      Payload length: 60
      Next header: ICMPv6 (58)
      Hop limit: 64
      Source: 2001::2 (2001::2)
      [Source Teredo Server IPv4: 0.0.0.0 (0.0.0.0)]
      [Source Teredo Port: 65535]
      [Source Teredo Client IPv4: 255.255.255.253 (255.255.255.253)]
      Destination: 2001::1 (2001::1)
      [Destination Teredo Server IPv4: 0.0.0.0 (0.0.0.0)]
      [Destination Teredo Port: 65535]
      [Destination Teredo Client IPv4: 255.255.255.254 (255.255.255.254)]
      [Source GeoIP: Unknown]
      [Destination GeoIP: Unknown]
▷ Internet Control Message Protocol v6
```

Teredo is referred to as a tunnelling mechanism, as it carries encapsulated IPv6 data within UDP/IPv4 packets. In this way, Teredo is better suited for NAT traversal. Next, we have the 6to4 packet:

```
 5 7.632000000    2001::1                    2001::2
▷ Frame 5: 134 bytes on wire (1072 bits), 134 bytes captured (1072 bits) on i
▷ Ethernet II, Src: ca:01:5d:8c:00:1c (ca:01:5d:8c:00:1c), Dst: ca:02:5c:14:0(
▷ Internet Protocol Version 4, Src: 10.1.1.1 (10.1.1.1), Dst: 10.1.1.2 (10.1.
▽ Internet Protocol Version 6, Src: 2001::1 (2001::1), Dst: 2001::2 (2001::2)
    ▷ 0110 .... = Version: 6
    ▷ .... 0000 0000 .... .... .... .... .... = Traffic class: 0x00000000
          .... .... .... 0000 0000 0000 0000 0000 = Flowlabel: 0x00000000
      Payload length: 60
      Next header: ICMPv6 (58)
      Hop limit: 64
      Source: 2001::1 (2001::1)
      [Source Teredo Server IPv4: 0.0.0.0 (0.0.0.0)]
      [Source Teredo Port: 65535]
      [Source Teredo Client IPv4: 255.255.255.254 (255.255.255.254)]
      Destination: 2001::2 (2001::2)
      [Destination Teredo Server IPv4: 0.0.0.0 (0.0.0.0)]
      [Destination Teredo Port: 65535]
      [Destination Teredo Client IPv4: 255.255.255.253 (255.255.255.253)]
      [Source GeoIP: Unknown]
      [Destination GeoIP: Unknown]
▷ Internet Control Message Protocol v6
```

Capture: 5

Let's now look at 6RD, which grew from 6to4.

6RD

IPv6 Rapid Deployment, or 6RD, is derived from 6to4 and was invented by Rémi Després and was ratified in RFC 5569. Whilst it stems from 6to4, it also looks to overcome some of the issues of its predecessor.

6to4 works by relaying IPv6 and IPv4 traffic between servers, which advertise common IPv4 and IPv6 prefixes to networks that they can relay to. There is however, no guarantee that all the IPv6 hosts have a working route to the relay. Therefore a 6to4 host does not have any guarantee of reachability.

6RD changes this by making each ISP use one of its own IPv6 prefixes, instead of the 2002::/16 prefix that 6to4 uses. The control of the relay is firmly in the hands of the ISP, and allows for QoS to be maintained across the network. This results in a truly scalable solution, as the ISP is not bound to using the 2002::/16 network required by 6to4.

6RD has two components, a Customer Edge Router (CE) and a Border Relay Router (BR). The CE is dual stack and sits in the customers network. The outgoing native IPv6 traffic is encapsulated in IPv4 and is then tunnelled to the BR (or to other CE routers), Traffic coming in from the BR, which is also dual-stack, will be de-capsulated and forwarded to the end user.

```
       .1              .2         .1              .20
CE-1       10.10.1.0/24    ISP       10.20.20/24       BR-1
```

Our basic connectivity is all IPv4 based:

```
CE-1(config-if)#int gi 1/0
CE-1(config-if)#ip add 10.10.1.1 255.255.255.0
CE-1(config-if)#no sh
CE-1(config-if)#ip route 0.0.0.0 0.0.0.0 10.10.1.2
CE-1(config)#

ISP(config)#int gi 1/0
ISP(config-if)#ip add 10.10.1.2 255.255.255.0
ISP(config-if)#no sh
ISP(config-if)#int gi 2/0
ISP(config-if)#ip add 10.20.20.1 255.255.255.0
ISP(config-if)#no sh
ISP(config-if)#
```

```
BR-1(config)#int gi 1/0
BR-1(config-if)#ip add 10.20.20.20 255.255.255.0
BR-1(config-if)#no sh
BR-1(config-if)#ip route 0.0.0.0 0.0.0.0 10.20.20.1
BR-1(config)#
```

For the IPv6 configuration, we will create a general-prefix, as we did with 6to4, and use this as the basis for our loopback 0 and tunnel 0 IPv6 addresses. We also make sure to enable IPv6 routing and IPv6 CEF for good measure:

```
CE-1(config-if)#ipv6 general-prefix 6RD-Prefixes 6rd Tunnel0
CE-1(config)#ipv6 unicast-routing
CE-1(config)#ipv6 cef
CE-1(config)#int lo0
CE-1(config-if)#ipv6 address 6RD-Prefixes ::10:0:0:0:1/64
CE-1(config-if)#ipv6 enable
CE-1(config-if)#

BR-1(config)#ipv6 general-prefix 6RD-Prefixes 6rd Tunnel0
BR-1(config)#ipv6 unicast-routing
BR-1(config)#ipv6 cef
BR-1(config)#int lo0
BR-1(config-if)#ipv6 enable
BR-1(config-if)#ipv6 address 6RD-Prefixes ::10:0:0:0:2/64
BR-1(config-if)#
```

Now, let us create the tunnel.

```
CE-1(config-if)#int tunnel 0
CE-1(config-if)#ipv6 address 6RD-Prefixes ::/128 anycast
CE-1(config-if)#ipv6 enable
CE-1(config-if)#tunnel source GigabitEthernet 1/0
CE-1(config-if)#tunnel mode ipv6ip 6rd
CE-1(config-if)#tunnel 6rd ipv4 prefix-len 8
CE-1(config-if)#tunnel 6rd prefix 2001:db80::/32
CE-1(config-if)#tunnel 6rd br 10.20.20.20
CE-1(config-if)#

BR-1(config-if)#int tun0
BR-1(config-if)#ipv6 address 6RD-Prefixes ::/128 anycast
BR-1(config-if)#ipv6 enable
BR-1(config-if)#tunnel source gi 1/0
BR-1(config-if)#tunnel mode ipv6ip 6rd
BR-1(config-if)#tunnel 6rd ipv4 prefix-len 8
BR-1(config-if)#tunnel 6rd prefix 2001:db80::/32
```

```
BR-1(config-if)#
```

Note, we are using a /128 address and the "anycast" keyword. This is not essential here. The anycast keyword just means that we could be using this address on multiple devices at the same time. As a result of this, the router will not perform duplicate address detection. We could have just as easily used the same method of IPv6 address generation as we did for our loopback interface.

All that is left now, is to add a couple of static routes:

```
CE-1(config-if)#ipv6 route ::/0 tunnel0 2001:DB80:1414:1400::
CE-1(config)#ipv6 route 2001:db80::/32 tun 0
CE-1(config)#

BR-1(config-if)#ipv6 route 2001:db80::/32 tun0
BR-1(config)#
```

CE-1 has a static route pointing to BR-1 – but how do we know what address to use? We can use the command "sh tunnel 6rd" to tell us and find it under "General Prefix":

```
BR-1(config-if)#do sh tunnel 6rd
Interface Tunnel0:
  Tunnel Source: 10.20.20.20
  6RD: Operational, V6 Prefix: 2001:DB80::/32
       V4 Prefix, Length: 8, Value: 10.0.0.0
       V4 Suffix, Length: 0, Value: 0.0.0.0
  General Prefix: 2001:DB80:1414:1400::/56
BR-1(config-if)#
```

The tunnel configuration has all our basics, the source interface, the mode, which is "ipv6ip 6rd", and it is IPv6 enabled. We then specify the IPv4 prefix-length, which we set to 8 bits. This is the number of bits that are common in all the IPv4 addresses of the CE and the BR. We are using 10.x.x.x/24 on both sides, so we set this to 8 – the equivalent of 10.0.0.0/8, which covers both sides. Both the CE and the BR have a 6rd prefix of 2001:DB80::/32.

Now we can test our reachability. First we must find an address to use:

```
BR-1(config)#do sh ipv6 int bri | e unas|down
GigabitEthernet1/0          [up/up]
Loopback0                   [up/up]
   FE80::C803:4FF:FEE3:8
   2001:DB80:1414:1410::2
Tunnel0                     [up/up]
```

```
    FE80::A14:1414
    2001:DB80:1414:1400::

BR-1(config)#
```

The loopback interface of BR-1 has an address of 2001:DB80:1414:1410::2, so let's try that:

```
CE-1(config)#do sh ipv6 route int tun0 | e -
S   ::/0 [1/0]
      via 2001:DB80:1414:1400::, Tunnel0
S   2001:DB80::/32 [1/0]
      via Tunnel0, directly connected
LC  2001:DB80:A01:100::/128 [0/0]
      via Tunnel0, receive

CE-1(config)#do ping 2001:DB80:1414:1410::2 rep 2
Type escape sequence to abort.
Sending 2, 100-byte ICMP Echos to 2001:DB80:1414:1410::2:
!!
Success rate is 100 percent (2/2)
CE-1(config)#do ping 2001:DB80:1414:1410::2 source lo0 rep 2
Type escape sequence to abort.
Sending 2, 100-byte ICMP Echos to 2001:DB80:1414:1410::2:
Packet sent with a source address of 2001:DB80:A01:110::1
!!
Success rate is 100 percent (2/2)
CE-1(config)#
```

Great! This shows that our default route is working well through the tunnel. Let's have a look in Wireshark at the traffic as it leaves ISP towards BR-1:

```
5 12.651846000   2001:db80:a01:110::1    2001:db80:1414:1410::2   ICMPv6   134 Echo (ping) req
▷ Frame 5: 134 bytes on wire (1072 bits), 134 bytes captured (1072 bits) on interface 0
▷ Ethernet II, Src: ca:02:04:e2:00:38 (ca:02:04:e2:00:38), Dst: ca:03:04:e3:00:1c (ca:03:04:e3:00:1c)
▷ Internet Protocol Version 4, Src: 10.10.1.1 (10.10.1.1), Dst: 10.20.20.20 (10.20.20.20)
▷ Internet Protocol Version 6, Src: 2001:db80:a01:110::1 (2001:db80:a01:110::1), Dst: 2001:db80:1414:1410::2 (2
▷ Internet Control Message Protocol v6
```

Capture: 6

We have, as we would expect, an IPv6 payload within an IPv4 packet.

```
 5 12.651846000   2001:db80:a01:110::1        2001:db80:1414:1410::2
```

▷ Frame 5: 134 bytes on wire (1072 bits), 134 bytes captured (1072 bits) o
▷ Ethernet II, Src: ca:02:04:e2:00:38 (ca:02:04:e2:00:38), Dst: ca:03:04:e
▽ Internet Protocol Version 4, Src: 10.10.1.1 (10.10.1.1), Dst: 10.20.20.2
    Version: 4
    Header length: 20 bytes
  ▷ Differentiated Services Field: 0x00 (DSCP 0x00: Default; ECN: 0x00: No
    Total Length: 120
    Identification: 0x0013 (19)
  ▷ Flags: 0x00
    Fragment offset: 0
    Time to live: 254
  → Protocol: IPv6 (41)
  ▷ Header checksum: 0x9317 [correct]
  → Source: 10.10.1.1 (10.10.1.1)
  → Destination: 10.20.20.20 (10.20.20.20)
    [Source GeoIP: Unknown]
    [Destination GeoIP: Unknown]

Within the IPv4 layer, the protocol is set to IPv6 (41) and the source and destination are the IPv4 addresses.

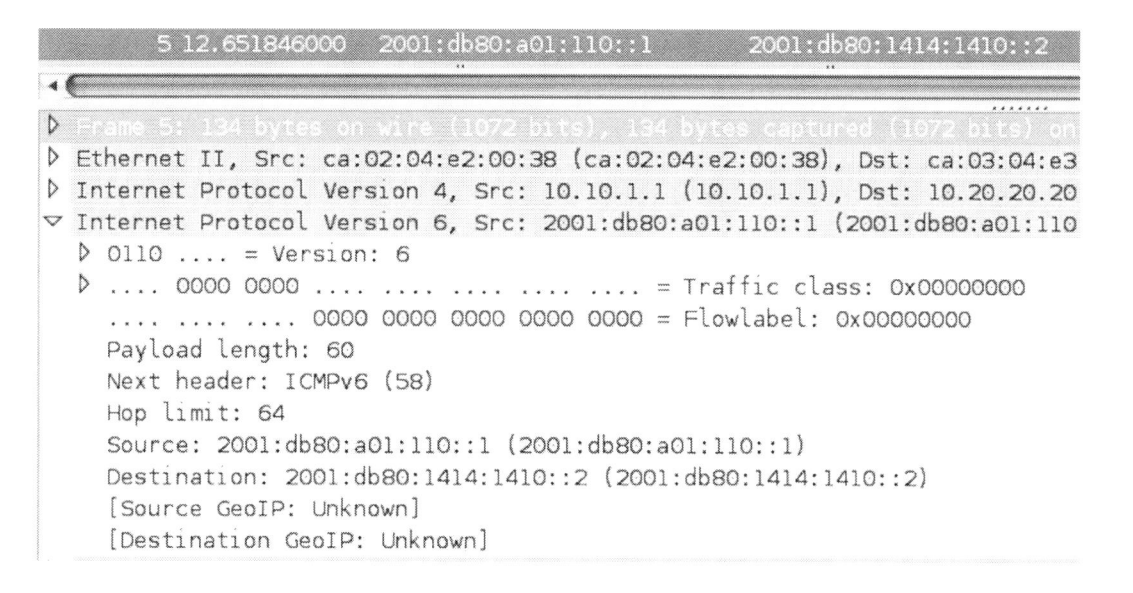

```
 5 12.651846000   2001:db80:a01:110::1        2001:db80:1414:1410::2
```

▷ Frame 5: 134 bytes on wire (1072 bits), 134 bytes captured (1072 bits) on
▷ Ethernet II, Src: ca:02:04:e2:00:38 (ca:02:04:e2:00:38), Dst: ca:03:04:e3
▷ Internet Protocol Version 4, Src: 10.10.1.1 (10.10.1.1), Dst: 10.20.20.20
▽ Internet Protocol Version 6, Src: 2001:db80:a01:110::1 (2001:db80:a01:110
  ▷ 0110 .... = Version: 6
  ▷ .... 0000 0000 .... = Traffic class: 0x00000000
    .... 0000 0000 0000 0000 0000 = Flowlabel: 0x00000000
    Payload length: 60
    Next header: ICMPv6 (58)
    Hop limit: 64
    Source: 2001:db80:a01:110::1 (2001:db80:a01:110::1)
    Destination: 2001:db80:1414:1410::2 (2001:db80:1414:1410::2)
    [Source GeoIP: Unknown]
    [Destination GeoIP: Unknown]

The IPv6 layer contains the IPv6 source and destination details.

So really, there is not a huge amount of difference in the end-packet, between 6to4 and 6RD. ISATAP, on the other hand, has a very different packet to both 6to4 and 6RD and we will look at this shortly. From scalability perspective, 6RD is definitely the better option when compared to 6to4. The ISPs are not bound to one particular subnet (2002::/16) and given this freedom, they can implement 6RD with a higher degree of ease.

Before we move on to ISATAP, we will look briefly at running a routing protocol over 6RD. Because of its similarities to 6to4, 6RD also shares some of the same limitations. Again, we see that we cannot run EIGRP or OSPF, because of the same reasons (lack of link-local addresses) but we can run BGP:

```
CE-1(config)#router bgp 100
CE-1(config-router)#no bgp default ipv4-unicast
CE-1(config-router)#address-family ipv6
CE-1(config-router-af)#neigh 2001:DB80:1414:1410::2 remote-as 100
CE-1(config-router-af)#neigh 2001:DB80:1414:1410::2 activate
CE-1(config-router-af)#

BR-1(config)#int lo1
BR-1(config-if)#ipv6 add 2001:abc:123::1/128
BR-1(config-if)#router bgp 100
BR-1(config-router)#no bgp default ipv4-unicast
BR-1(config-router)#address-family ipv6
BR-1(config-router-af)#neigh 2001:DB80:A01:110::1 remote-as 100
BR-1(config-router-af)#neigh 2001:DB80:A01:110::1 activate
BR-1(config-router-af)#
%BGP-5-ADJCHANGE: neighbor 2001:DB80:A01:110::1 Up
BR-1(config-router-af)#network 2001:abc:123::1/128
BR-1(config-router-af)#
```

The last step is to do some verification:

```
CE-1(config-router-af)#do sh ipv6 route bgp | e -
B   2001:ABC:123::1/128 [200/0]
     via 2001:DB80:1414:1410::2

CE-1(config-router-af)#do ping 2001:ABC:123::1
Type escape sequence to abort.
Sending 5, 100-byte ICMP Echos to 2001:ABC:123::1:
!!!!!
Success rate is 100 percent (5/5)
CE-1(config-router-af)# do trace 2001:ABC:123::1
Type escape sequence to abort.
Tracing the route to 2001:ABC:123::1

  1 2001:DB80:1414:1410::2 48 msec 52 msec 48 msec
```

```
CE-1(config-router-af)#
```

As you can see, the ping is going through our tunnel so BGP is a suitable protocol with 6RD as well. Let us now turn our attention to ISATAP.

ISATAP

Intra-Site Automatic Tunnel Addressing Protocol (ISATAP) is the final IPv6 transition mechanism that we will discuss. We haven't completely finished with IPv6, as we will return to it when we look at running it over DMVPN and again when we look at NAT later on, but this will conclude our dive into IPv6 and tunnels.

Unlike 6over4 and 6RD, ISATAP uses a virtual NBMA layer, so that there is no requirement on the underlying IPv4 network to support multicast.

ISATAP is predominantly used between a server and a client, yet we can emulate this using a couple of routers. We will use a three-router network here. The ISP router will be IPv4 only.

ISATAP-Server   ISP   ISATAP-Client

Our basic connectivity will use IPv4 addresses and an OSPF network to ensure end-to-end connectivity.

```
ISATAP-Server(config)#ipv6 unicast-routing
ISATAP-Server(config)#int gi 1/0
ISATAP-Server(config-if)#ip add 20.2.2.1 255.255.255.0
ISATAP-Server(config-if)#no shut
ISATAP-Server(config-if)#router ospf 1
ISATAP-Server(config-router)#netw 20.2.2.0 0.0.0.255 area 0
ISATAP-Server(config-router)#router-id 1.1.1.1
ISATAP-Server(config-router)#

ISP(config)#int gi 1/0
ISP(config-if)#ip add 20.2.2.2 255.255.255.0
ISP(config-if)#no shut
ISP(config-if)#router ospf 1
ISP(config-router)#network 20.2.2.0 0.0.0.255 area 0
ISP(config-router)#router-id 2.2.2.2
ISP(config-router)#int gi 2/0
```

```
ISP(config-if)#ip add 10.1.1.2 255.255.255.0
ISP(config-if)#no shut
ISP(config-if)#router ospf 1
ISP(config-router)#network 10.1.1.0 0.0.0.255 area 0
ISP(config-router)#

ISATAP-Client(config)#ipv6 unicast-routing
ISATAP-Client(config)#int gi 1/0
ISATAP-Client(config-if)#ip add 10.1.1.1 255.255.255.0
ISATAP-Client(config-if)#no shut
ISATAP-Client(config-if)#exit
ISATAP-Client(config)#router ospf 1
ISATAP-Client(config-router)#router-id 3.3.3.3
ISATAP-Client(config-router)#netw 10.1.1.0 0.0.0.255 area 0
ISATAP-Client(config-router)#
%OSPF-5-ADJCHG: Process 1, Nbr 2.2.2.2 on GigabitEthernet1/0 from
LOADING to FULL, Loading Done
ISATAP-Client(config-router)#
```

We can confirm that the ISATAP server can see the ISTAP client.

```
ISATAP-Server(config-router)#do sh ip route ospf | beg Gate
Gateway of last resort is not set

     10.0.0.0/24 is subnetted, 1 subnets
O       10.1.1.0 [110/2] via 20.2.2.2, 00:01:02, Gi1/0
ISATAP-Server(config-router)#exit
```

Our tunnel on the server will use a loopback interface as the source and the mode will be set to "ipv6ip isatap". We can use any address we wish to for our tunnel address, but note that there is no host id for the address. It is generated from the MAC address because we are using the EUI-64 method. The final line in our tunnel setup is to turn off suppression of nd and ra. These stand for "neighbour discovery" and for "router advertisement". The default behaviour is to suppress these messages. Note, again we do not specify a destination.

```
ISATAP-Server(config)#int lo0
ISATAP-Server(config-if)#ip add 1.1.1.1 255.255.255.255
ISATAP-Server(config-if)#int tunnel 0
ISATAP-Server(config-if)#tunnel mode ipv6ip isatap
ISATAP-Server(config-if)#tunnel source lo0
ISATAP-Server(config-if)#ipv6 add 2001:b00:802:101::/64 eui-64
ISATAP-Server(config-if)#no ipv6 nd ra suppress
ISATAP-Server(config-if)#exit
```

The configuration on the client is much simpler. Our IPv6 address can be automatically configured, our tunnel mode set to "standard" ipv6ip and our destination set to the IPv4 address of our server's loopback interface.

```
ISATAP-Client(config)#int tunnel 0
ISATAP-Client(config-if)#ipv6 address autoconfig
ISATAP-Client(config-if)#ipv6 enable
ISATAP-Client(config-if)#tunnel mode ipv6ip
ISATAP-Client(config-if)#tunnel source gi 1/0
ISATAP-Client(config-if)#tunnel destination 1.1.1.1
ISATAP-Client(config-if)#end
```

We must ensure that the client has reachability to the loopback interface, so we will advertise that through OSPF. As soon as we do this, our tunnel transitions to the up state on the client.

```
ISATAP-Server(config)#router ospf 1
ISATAP-Server(config-router)#netw 1.1.1.1 0.0.0.0 area 0
ISATAP-Server(config-router)#

ISATAP-Client#
%LINEPROTO-5-UPDOWN: Line protocol on Interface Tunnel0, changed state to up
ISATAP-Client#
```

We now have some IPv6 routes on the client. Our tunnel address has been automatically generated, in part by the server and in part, by our own source IP address being converted into hex. (A01:101).

```
ISATAP-Client#sh ipv6 route | beg 20
NDp  2001:B00:802:101::/64 [2/0]
       via Tunnel0, directly connected
L    2001:B00:802:101::A01:101/128 [0/0]
       via Tunnel0, receive
L    FF00::/8 [0/0]
       via Null0, receive
ISATAP-Client#
```

Our tunnel is up:

```
ISATAP-Client#sh ipv6 int tunnel 0
Tunnel0 is up, line protocol is up
  IPv6 is enabled, link-local address is FE80::A01:101
  No Virtual link-local address(es):
  Stateless address autoconfig enabled
  Global unicast address(es):
```

```
     2001:B00:802:101::A01:101, subnet is 2001:B00:802:101::/64
[EUI/CAL/PRE]
     valid lifetime 2591931 preferred lifetime 604731
  Joined group address(es):
    FF02::1
    FF02::2
    FF02::1:FF01:101
  MTU is 1480 bytes
  ICMP error messages limited to one every 100 milliseconds
  ICMP redirects are enabled
  ICMP unreachables are sent
  ND DAD is enabled, number of DAD attempts: 1
  ND reachable time is 30000 milliseconds (using 30000)
  ND RAs are suppressed (periodic)
  Hosts use stateless autoconfig for addresses.
ISATAP-Client#
```

We can also see the tunnel address here:

```
ISATAP-Client#sh ipv6 int bri
FastEthernet0/0         [administratively down/down]
    unassigned
FastEthernet0/1         [administratively down/down]
    unassigned
GigabitEthernet1/0      [up/up]
    unassigned
Tunnel0                 [up/up]
    FE80::A01:101
    2001:B00:802:101::A01:101
ISATAP-Client#
```

We can confirm reachability to both the clients tunnel link-local address, and to its assigned address.

```
ISATAP-Server#ping ipv6 FE80::A01:101
Output Interface: tun 0
Type escape sequence to abort.
Sending 5, 100-byte ICMP Echos to FE80::A01:101:
Packet sent with a source address of FE80::5EFE:101:101%Tunnel0
!!!!!
Success rate is 100 percent (5/5)
ISATAP-Server#

ISATAP-Server#ping 2001:B00:802:101::A01:101
Type escape sequence to abort.
Sending 5, 100-byte ICMP Echos to 2001:B00:802:101::A01:101:
!!!!!
```

```
Success rate is 100 percent (5/5)
ISATAP-Server#
```

Before we leave the world of IPv6 transition mechanisms, we should have a look at a cool feature of ISATAP.

Unlike our previous configurations, our ISATAP client does not need to have "ipv6 unicast-routing" enabled. We can remove this command completely and our tunnel will still work. Once we remove it we also get the added bonus of an IPv6 default route automatically installed into our routing table!

```
ISATAP-Client#conf t
ISATAP-Client(config)#no ipv6 unicast-routing
ISATAP-Client(config)#end
ISATAP-Client#sh ipv6 route | sec ex Codes:
IPv6 Routing Table - default - 4 entries
ND   ::/0 [2/0]
     via FE80::5EFE:101:101, Tunnel0
NDp  2001:B00:802:101::/64 [2/0]
     via Tunnel0, directly connected
L    2001:B00:802:101::A01:101/128 [0/0]
     via Tunnel0, receive
L    FF00::/8 [0/0]
     via Null0, receive

ISATAP-Client#

ISATAP-Server#ping 2001:B00:802:101::A01:101
Type escape sequence to abort.
Sending 5, 100-byte ICMP Echos to 2001:B00:802:101::A01:101:
!!!!!
Success rate is 100 percent (5/5)
ISATAP-Server#
```

If we look at the packet, captured in Wireshark, we can see how it differs from both the 6over4 and 6to4 packets:

```
  6 7.460000000    2001:b00:802:101:0:5efe:10 2001:b00:802:101::a01:101  ICMPv6
▷ Frame 6: 134 bytes on wire (1072 bits), 134 bytes captured (1072 bits) on interface
▷ Ethernet II, Src: ca:02:58:a8:00:38 (ca:02:58:a8:00:38), Dst: ca:03:5e:3c:00:1c (ca
▷ Internet Protocol Version 4, Src: 1.1.1.1 (1.1.1.1), Dst: 10.1.1.1 (10.1.1.1)
▽ Internet Protocol Version 6, Src: 2001:b00:802:101:0:5efe:101:101 (2001:b00:802:101
  ▷ 0110 .... = Version: 6
  ▷ .... 0000 0000 .... .... .... .... .... = Traffic class: 0x00000000
    .... .... .... 0000 0000 0000 0000 0000 = Flowlabel: 0x00000000
    Payload length: 60
    Next header: ICMPv6 (58)
    Hop limit: 64
    Source: 2001:b00:802:101:0:5efe:101:101 (2001:b00:802:101:0:5efe:101:101)
    [Source ISATAP IPv4: 1.1.1.1 (1.1.1.1)]
    Destination: 2001:b00:802:101::a01:101 (2001:b00:802:101::a01:101)
    [Source GeoIP: Unknown]
    [Destination GeoIP: Unknown]
▷ Internet Control Message Protocol v6
```

Capture: 7

As you can see, the source is set to ISATAP IPv4, and we have no mention of Teredo.

This pretty much concludes how far we can go within tunnelling. Already we have seen that the lines between a tunnel and a scalable VPN solution can start to blur very quickly.

With this in mind, let's return to our main topology.

4. DMVPN

In this chapter we will continue to build on our fledgling DMVPN network.

So far, we have covered GRE and mGRE. We have also looked, briefly, at NHRP and IPSec. We have also seen some issues with GRE; namely that we do not have any connectivity between the spokes. This brings us very nicely to talk about DMVPN. Dynamic Multipoint Virtual Private Networks (DMVPN) is a combination of mGRE, NHRP, IPSec (which is optional), CEF and a dynamic routing protocol.

We started out with a GRE tunnel, which required a source, a destination and a mode to be defined under the tunnel interface. This then changed (on our hub) to mGRE, which requires just a source and a mode.

Both GRE and mGRE are still point-to-point (in effect), which is fine, as point-to-point works well enough, but if we are running over an NBMA network, then issues can be seen in this particular environment.

What issues are we talking about, here? Well, the major issue is with the number of hops we need to take to reach our destination.

Imagine we have a network comprised of a number of routers that connect a number of offices:

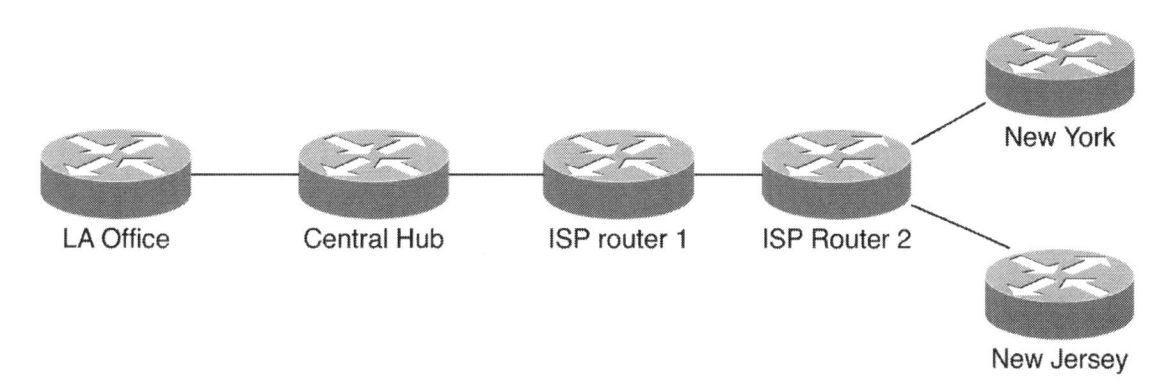

In the multipoint tunnel network above, traffic originating from New Jersey and destined for the New York office would have to travel up to the Central Hub and back down again in order to reach its destination, even though the number of hops it needs to actually take is far less.

We could always have created a tunnel directly between New York and New Jersey, but this would create an increase in complexity and reduce the scalability of the network design. Whilst adding another tunnel between the two would work well, if we carried on with this method we could easily end up with multiple tunnels, when only one is needed.

This is why DMVPN has become so popular. Due to the capabilities of NHRP we can allow for direct spoke-to-spoke traffic, but still maintain just one tunnel interface. We have already looked at NHRP from 10,000 feet, but now let's open it up and have a proper look.

4.1 NHRP

NHRP is defined under RFC 2332: "L2 address resolution protocol and caching series." It is used by the next-hop-client (NHC) to determine the NBMA IP address of the next-hop-server (NHS). In turn, they can then map the tunnel IP addresses to the NBMA ip address, either statically or dynamically. Once the network has been "built", the spokes can completely bypass the hub in order to get to each other (as we have just mentioned).

In order to better understand NHRP we should look at the different "phases" of DMVPN.

4.2 DMVPN phases

DMVPN can be deployed in one of three different phases. These phases control how traffic moves around the DMVPN network.

Phase 1:

Phase 1 is now considered to be obsolete. For DMVPN Phase 1 we would use mGRE on the hub router, and GRE on the spokes. Traffic will only be hub-to-spoke, never spoke-to-spoke. Phase 1 requires static or dynamic NHRP registration. This is the design we are currently using.

Phase 2:

With a phase 2 DMVPN network, the spokes also use mGRE; which allows for spoke-to-spoke communication. NHRP is required for spoke-to-hub registration and also for spoke-to-spoke resolution. The spoke-to-spoke tunnel creation is triggered by the spoke traffic, but route summarization and default routing are not permitted in this phase.

Phase 3:

The final phase is similar to phase 2, with the added bonus being that spoke-to-spoke traffic does not transit via the hub. The command "ip nhrp shortcut" is used on the spokes and "ip nhrp redirect" is used on the hub. Summarization and default routing are permitted and in spoke-to-spoke communication, the next hop ip address is changed from the hub's IP address to the spoke's IP address.

Now that we understand a little more about the DMVPN phases, let's see these in action as we continue to build our network.

In the interest of keeping things simple for the moment, we won't be mixing and matching IPv4 and IPv6 traffic, so let's quickly remove our IPv6 configurations:

```
Hub-1(config)#no int tun 1
Hub-1(config)#no ipv6 router eigrp 10
Hub-1(config)#no int lo1
Hub-1(config)#

Spoke-1(config)#no int tun 1
Spoke-1(config)#no ipv6 router eigrp 10
Spoke-1(config)#no int lo1
```

Now we can solely concentrate on our IPv4 DMVPN tunnel. Don't worry about missing out on IPv6 at the moment as we will tunnel this across it later on.

Let us remind ourselves about our current configuration. We are running in Phase 1 mode at the moment:

```
Hub-1(config)#do sh run int tun 0 | b int
interface Tunnel0
 ip address 192.168.1.1 255.255.255.0
 no ip redirects
 ip nhrp map 192.168.1.2 10.10.2.1
 ip nhrp map 192.168.1.3 10.10.3.1
 ip nhrp map multicast 10.10.2.1
 ip nhrp map multicast 10.10.3.1
 ip nhrp map multicast 10.10.4.1
 ip nhrp map 192.168.1.4 10.10.4.1
 ip nhrp network-id 1
 tunnel source GigabitEthernet1/0
 tunnel mode gre multipoint
end
```

```
Hub-1(config)#
```

We should also have a quick look at the routing tables on the spokes:

```
Spoke-1(config)#do sh ip route eigrp | b Gate
Gateway of last resort is 10.10.2.2 to network 0.0.0.0

    1.0.0.0/32 is subnetted, 1 subnets
D      1.1.1.1 [90/27008000] via 192.168.1.1, 00:15:30, Tun0
Spoke-1(config)#

Spoke-2#sh ip route eigrp | b Gate
Gateway of last resort is 10.10.3.2 to network 0.0.0.0

    1.0.0.0/32 is subnetted, 1 subnets
D      1.1.1.1 [90/27008000] via 192.168.1.1, 00:13:57, Tun0
Spoke-2#

Spoke-3#sh ip route eigrp | b Gate
Gateway of last resort is 10.10.4.2 to network 0.0.0.0

    1.0.0.0/32 is subnetted, 1 subnets
D      1.1.1.1 [90/27008000] via 192.168.1.1, 00:14:21, Tun0
Spoke-3#
```

Hopefully, you have already seen why Phase 1 is now considered obsolete. We have multiple point-to-point connections and at present, none of the spokes have visibility of each other. Depending on the network design this maybe ideal, such as a Point of Sales machine needing to communicate back to the head office to download price information, but having no need to contact other PoS machines. For our purposes, however, we should have spoke-to-spoke visibility, as this will help us in our understanding of NHRP.

We can achieve this visibility by disabling the split-horizon rule. The split-horizon rule dictates that a router will not advertise a route out of the interface that it learnt it on – which is why, when Spoke-3 had a separate tunnel, it had visibility of the other two spokes.

To disable the split-horizon rule we go into our tunnel and disable it for the routing process, we also disable the changing of the next-hop ip address:

```
Hub-1(config)#int tun 0
Hub-1(config-if)#no ip split-horizon eigrp 1
Hub-1(config-if)#no ip next-hop-self eigrp 1
```

This will cause a resync of our EIGRP peers:

```
Hub-1(config-if)#
%DUAL-5-NBRCHANGE: EIGRP-IPv4 1: Neighbor 192.168.1.4 (Tunnel0) is
resync: split horizon changed
%DUAL-5-NBRCHANGE: EIGRP-IPv4 1: Neighbor 192.168.1.3 (Tunnel0) is
resync: split horizon changed
%DUAL-5-NBRCHANGE: EIGRP-IPv4 1: Neighbor 192.168.1.2 (Tunnel0) is
resync: split horizon changed
Hub-1(config-if)#
```

Our spokes now have good visibility of each other:

```
Spoke-1(config)#do sh ip route eigrp | b Gate
Gateway of last resort is 10.10.2.2 to network 0.0.0.0

      1.0.0.0/32 is subnetted, 1 subnets
D        1.1.1.1 [90/27008000] via 192.168.1.1, 00:25:17, Tunnel0
      3.0.0.0/32 is subnetted, 1 subnets
D        3.3.3.3 [90/28288000] via 192.168.1.3, 00:01:42, Tunnel0
      4.0.0.0/32 is subnetted, 1 subnets
D        4.4.4.4 [90/28288000] via 192.168.1.4, 00:01:42, Tunnel0
Spoke-1(config)#

Spoke-2#sh ip route eigrp | b Gate
Gateway of last resort is 10.10.3.2 to network 0.0.0.0

      1.0.0.0/32 is subnetted, 1 subnets
D        1.1.1.1 [90/27008000] via 192.168.1.1, 00:23:59, Tunnel0
      2.0.0.0/32 is subnetted, 1 subnets
D        2.2.2.2 [90/28288000] via 192.168.1.2, 00:02:15, Tunnel0
      4.0.0.0/32 is subnetted, 1 subnets
D        4.4.4.4 [90/28288000] via 192.168.1.4, 00:02:15, Tunnel0
Spoke-2#

Spoke-3#sh ip route eigrp | b Gate
Gateway of last resort is 10.10.4.2 to network 0.0.0.0

      1.0.0.0/32 is subnetted, 1 subnets
D        1.1.1.1 [90/27008000] via 192.168.1.1, 00:24:18, Tunnel0
      2.0.0.0/32 is subnetted, 1 subnets
D        2.2.2.2 [90/28288000] via 192.168.1.2, 00:02:26, Tunnel0
      3.0.0.0/32 is subnetted, 1 subnets
D        3.3.3.3 [90/28288000] via 192.168.1.3, 00:02:26, Tunnel0
Spoke-3#
```

We can see that as well as having visibility, we also have reachability:

```
Spoke-1(config)#do ping 4.4.4.4
Type escape sequence to abort.
Sending 5, 100-byte ICMP Echos to 4.4.4.4:
!!!!!
Success rate is 100 percent (5/5)
Spoke-1#trace 4.4.4.4
Type escape sequence to abort.
Tracing the route to 4.4.4.4
VRF info: (vrf in name/id, vrf out name/id)
  1 192.168.1.1 48 msec 48 msec 36 msec
  2 192.168.1.4 60 msec 100 msec 88 msec
Spoke-1(config)#
```

Herein lies one of the "issues" with Phase 1; our spoke-to-spoke traffic will always transit via the hub. The other issue being that if we were to add more spokes to our network, we would have to also add more lines into our tunnel configuration. We would lose the dynamic nature of DMVPN and it leaves us with a greater room for error.

Let us therefore put the "dynamic" back into our Dynamic Multipoint VPN.

4.3 Switching from Phase 1 to Phase 2

We start by removing the static mappings:

```
Hub-1(config-if)#no ip nhrp map 192.168.1.2 10.10.2.1
Hub-1(config-if)#no ip nhrp map 192.168.1.3 10.10.3.1
Hub-1(config-if)#no ip nhrp map 192.168.1.4 10.10.4.1
Hub-1(config-if)#no ip nhrp map multicast 10.10.2.1
Hub-1(config-if)#no ip nhrp map multicast 10.10.3.1
Hub-1(config-if)#no ip nhrp map multicast 10.10.4.1
```

After a few moments our tunnels will be torn down and will come back up again.

```
Hub-1(config-if)#
%DUAL-5-NBRCHANGE: EIGRP-IPv4 1: Neighbor 192.168.1.3 (Tunnel0) is down: Interface PEER-TERMINATION received
%DUAL-5-NBRCHANGE: EIGRP-IPv4 1: Neighbor 192.168.1.2 (Tunnel0) is down: Interface PEER-TERMINATION received
%DUAL-5-NBRCHANGE: EIGRP-IPv4 1: Neighbor 192.168.1.4 (Tunnel0) is down: Interface PEER-TERMINATION received
Hub-1(config-if)#
%DUAL-5-NBRCHANGE: EIGRP-IPv4 1: Neighbor 192.168.1.2 (Tunnel0) is up: new adjacency
```

```
%DUAL-5-NBRCHANGE: EIGRP-IPv4 1: Neighbor 192.168.1.4 (Tunnel0) is up:
new adjacency
%DUAL-5-NBRCHANGE: EIGRP-IPv4 1: Neighbor 192.168.1.3 (Tunnel0) is up:
new adjacency
Hub-1(config-if)#
```

The tunnels will continue to flap up and down. In order to make them stable we need to change the nature of our tunnel on Hub-1:

```
Hub-1(config-if)#ip nhrp map multicast dynamic
```

We now have the ability for Hub-1 to dynamically register NHRP clients. We also, now, introduce a much stronger reliance on NHRP, in that we also need to implement it on our spokes. We will start with Spoke-1:

1. `Spoke-1(config)#int tun 0`
2. `Spoke-1(config-if)#ip nhrp map 192.168.1.1 10.10.1.1`
3. `Spoke-1(config-if)#ip nhrp map multicast 10.10.1.1`
4. `Spoke-1(config-if)#ip nhrp nhs 192.168.1.1`
5. `Spoke-1(config-if)#tunnel mode gre multipoint`
6. `The tunnel destination must be unconfigured before setting this mode`
7. `Spoke-1(config-if)#no tunnel destination 10.10.1.1`
8. `%LINEPROTO-5-UPDOWN: Line protocol on Interface Tunnel0, changed state to down`
9. `Spoke-1(config-if)#tunnel mode gre multipoint`
10. `Spoke-1(config-if)#`
11. `%LINEPROTO-5-UPDOWN: Line protocol on Interface Tunnel0, changed state to up`
12. `Spoke-1(config-if)#ip nhrp network-id 1`
13. `Spoke-1(config-if)#end`

With Spoke-1 we have mapped Hub-1's VPN address of 192.168.1.1 to its public address of 10.10.1.1 and also set our multicast traffic to map to this external address (lines 2 and 3). These steps are the same as the ones we used when creating our clients on Hub-1. We then introduce a new command on line 4: "ip nhrp nhs 192.168.1.1". This sets our NHRP Next-Hop server (NHS) to the VPN internal address of our hub. It is important that this is set to the internal VPN network address of the hub and not the external (public) address, otherwise IGP adjacencies will flap. Lines 5 through to 11 are also very familiar to us now; we change our tunnel mode to "gre multipoint", in doing so we need to remove the previously defined tunnel destination. On line 12 we have a new(ish) command, "ip nhrp network-id 1". This is required and enables NHRP on an interface, but does not have to match from hub to spoke or from spoke to spoke – at least not in the network that we have. The NHRP network ID is used to define the domain for an NHRP and to differentiate between domains, where two or more exist on the same router. The network ID is only locally significant, which is why you will not see it passed within NHRP packets (requests or replies). We are using the same network ID here for ease of understanding. If we were running dual-hub (which Is beyond the scope of the CCIE R&S at the time of writing) then this would be more of a concern.

The documentation on this can be a little confusing – even Cisco seems to contradict themselves, in one document they state that: "*In general, all NHRP stations within one logical NBMA network must be configured with the same network identifier.*"[2] Another document, which does explain it much more succinctly, aligns this requirement more closely to the OSPF process ID[3].

We can follow the same steps for our other spokes (I have removed the tunnel down / tunnel up messages for clarity):

```
Spoke-2(config)#int tun 0
Spoke-2(config-if)#no tunnel destination 10.10.1.1
Spoke-2(config-if)#ip nhrp map 192.168.1.1 10.10.1.1
Spoke-2(config-if)#ip nhrp map multicast 10.10.1.1
Spoke-2(config-if)#ip nhrp nhs 192.168.1.1
Spoke-2(config-if)#tunnel mode gre multipoint
Spoke-2(config-if)#ip nhrp network-id 1
Spoke-2(config-if)#end

Spoke-3(config)#int tun 0
Spoke-3(config-if)#no tunnel destination 10.10.1.1
Spoke-3(config-if)#ip nhrp map 192.168.1.1 10.10.1.1
Spoke-3(config-if)#ip nhrp map multicast 10.10.1.1
Spoke-3(config-if)#ip nhrp nhs 192.168.1.1
Spoke-3(config-if)#tunnel mode gre multipoint
Spoke-3(config-if)#ip nhrp network-id 1
Spoke-3(config-if)#end
```

The beauty of setting up DMVPN is that we can follow a simple checklist, with little variation – especially when setting up the spokes. As you can see, the commands we enter on Spoke-3 are identical to the ones we enter on Spoke-2.

With our tunnels up, it would be a good place for us to see what actually happens during the hub-to-spoke tunnel creation. To do this I started with all the routers switched off, so now would be a good time to save the configurations of the routers. I started by turning on

---

[2] http://www.cisco.com/c/en/us/td/docs/ios-xml/ios/ipaddr/command/ipaddr-cr-book/ipaddr-i4.html#wp2132052262

[3] http://www.cisco.com/c/en/us/td/docs/ios/12_4/ip_addr/configuration/guide/hadnhrp.html

Hub-1 and IGW, and enabled debugging on Hub-1. The console information was saved to a separate file. We will be debugging DMVPN and NHRP traffic, the commands for which are "debug dmvpn all all" and "debug nhrp":

```
Hub-1(config-if)#end
Hub-1#debug dmvpn ?
  all        enable all level debugging
  condition  conditional debugging for enabled
  detail     detailed reports
  error      error reports
  packet     packet level debugging

Hub-1#debug dmvpn all
% Incomplete command.

Hub-1#debug dmvpn all ?
  all     Enable NHRP/Tunnel Protection/Crypto debugs
  crypto  Enable Crypto IKE/IPSec debugs only
  nhrp    Enable NHRP debugs only
  socket  Enable Crypto Secure Socket debugs only
  tunnel  Enable Tunnel Protection debugs only

Hub-1#debug dmvpn all all
Hub-1#debug nhrp ?
  cache      NHRP cache operations
  condition  NHRP conditional debugging
  error      NHRP errors
  extension  NHRP extension processing
  group      NHRP groups
  packet     NHRP activity
  rate       NHRP rate limiting
  <cr>

Hub-1#debug nhrp
```

It is also a good idea to be able to view the traffic in Wireshark, so the traffic between Hub-1 and IGW was captured.

With our debugging turned on and our traffic being captured, we can start by turning on Spoke-1. Once we see the message stating that the tunnel is up, we can start Spoke-2 (purely because we can then compare the spoke routers), and once Spoke-2's tunnel is up, stop the Wireshark capture and turn off the debugging, using the command "un all".

Looking first at the Wireshark capture, which we can filter down, so that we can see just the NHRP traffic, we can see only a few entries:

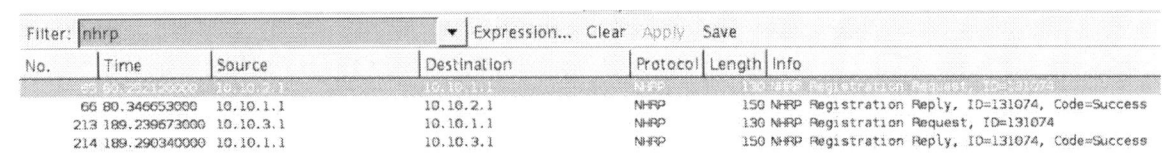

```
Filter: nhrp                              ▼ Expression... Clear Apply Save
No.     Time            Source      Destination   Protocol Length Info
    65 80.251000000    10.10.2.1    10.10.1.1     NHRP     130   NHRP Registration Request, ID=131074
    66 80.346653000    10.10.1.1    10.10.2.1     NHRP     150   NHRP Registration Reply, ID=131074, Code=Success
   213 189.239673000   10.10.3.1    10.10.1.1     NHRP     130   NHRP Registration Request, ID=131074
   214 189.290340000   10.10.1.1    10.10.3.1     NHRP     150   NHRP Registration Reply, ID=131074, Code=Success
```

Capture: 8

We have a registration request from both Spoke-1 and Spoke-2 and we have two registration replies from Hub-1 (one to each of the peer routers).

The interesting areas to mention, in the actual requests, are in the final layer – the Next Hop Resolution Protocol (NHRP Registration Request). In the NHRP Mandatory Part, we have the physical address and the tunnel addresses supplied by the Spoke router to the Hub router, along with the destination IP address of the Hub's tunnel.

```
▷ Frame 65: 130 bytes on wire (1040 bits), 130 bytes captured
▷ Ethernet II, Src: ca:02:04:2e:00:1c (ca:02:04:2e:00:1c), Dst:
▷ Internet Protocol Version 4, Src: 10.10.2.1 (10.10.2.1), Dst:
▷ Generic Routing Encapsulation (NHRP)
▽ Next Hop Resolution Protocol (NHRP Registration Request)
   ▷ NHRP Fixed Header
   ▽ NHRP Mandatory Part
        Source Protocol Len: 4
        Destination Protocol Len: 4
      ▷ Flags: 0x8002
        Request ID: 0x00020002 (131074)
        Source NBMA Address: 10.10.2.1 (10.10.2.1)
        Source Protocol Address: 192.168.1.2 (192.168.1.2)
        Destination Protocol Address: 192.168.1.1 (192.168.1.1)
      ▽ Client Information Entry
           Code: 0
           Prefix Length: 32
           Unused: 0
           Max Transmission Unit: 17916
           Holding Time (s): 7200
         ▷ Client Address Type/Len: NSAP format/0
         ▷ Client Sub Address Type/Len: NSAP format/0
           Client Protocol Length: 0
           CIE Preference Value: 0
```

Then, we have the NHRP Registration Reply, which is identical to the request, with the only difference being that the Code changes from a 0, to "Success" (for the Mandatory Part at least).

```
▷ Frame 66: 150 bytes on wire (1200 bits), 150 bytes captured
▷ Ethernet II, Src: ca:01:04:2d:00:1c (ca:01:04:2d:00:1c), Dst:
▷ Internet Protocol Version 4, Src: 10.10.1.1 (10.10.1.1), Dst:
▷ Generic Routing Encapsulation (NHRP)
▽ Next Hop Resolution Protocol (NHRP Registration Reply)
    ▷ NHRP Fixed Header
    ▽ NHRP Mandatory Part
        Source Protocol Len: 4
        Destination Protocol Len: 4
      ▷ Flags: 0x8002
        Request ID: 0x00020002 (131074)
        Source NBMA Address: 10.10.2.1 (10.10.2.1)
        Source Protocol Address: 192.168.1.2 (192.168.1.2)
        Destination Protocol Address: 192.168.1.1 (192.168.1.1)
      ▽ Client Information Entry
        Code: Success
        Prefix Length: 32
        Unused: 0
        Max Transmission Unit: 17916
        Holding Time (s): 7200
        ▷ Client Address Type/Len: NSAP format/0
        ▷ Client Sub Address Type/Len: NSAP format/0
        Client Protocol Length: 0
        CIE Preference Value: 0
```

There are a couple of other differences; we can see that we have more information in the Responder Address Extension field, containing the NBMA to tunnel IP address mapping for Hub-1

Let us now turn our attention to the debug logs from Hub-1. For the sake of brevity I have removed the dates and times, apart from the first one and last one of each registration request/reply pair.

The whole process takes two seconds, the caveat being that this is a non-production network under no discernable load, but even so, under normal network conditions there should not be a large degree of variation.

```
1. Hub-1#
2. *Dec  9 19:07:40.775:
3. NHRP: Receive Registration Request via Tunnel0 vrf 0, packet size:
   92
4. (F) afn: IPv4(1), type: IP(800), hop: 255, ver: 1
           shtl: 4(NSAP), sstl: 0(NSAP)
           pktsz: 92 extoff: 52
5. (M) flags: "unique nat ", reqid: 131074
```

```
                    src NBMA: 10.10.2.1
                    src protocol: 192.168.1.2, dst protocol: 192.168.1.1
6.  (C-1) code: no error(0)
                    prefix: 32, mtu: 17916, hd_time: 7200
                    addr_len: 0(NSAP), subaddr_len: 0(NSAP), proto_len: 0,
                    pref: 0
7.  Responder Address Extension(3):
8.  Forward Transit NHS Record Extension(4):
9.  Reverse Transit NHS Record Extension(5):
10. NAT address Extension(9):
11. (C-1) code: no error(0)
                    prefix: 32, mtu: 17916, hd_time: 0
                    addr_len: 4(NSAP), subaddr_len: 0(NSAP), proto_len: 4,
                    pref: 0
                    client NBMA: 10.10.1.1
                    client protocol: 192.168.1.1
12. NHRP: netid_in = 1, to_us = 1
13. NHRP: Tunnel0: Cache add for target 192.168.1.2/32 next-hop
    192.168.1.2
                    10.10.2.1
14. NHRP: Adding Tunnel Endpoints (VPN: 192.168.1.2, NBMA: 10.10.2.1)
15. NHRP: Successfully attached NHRP subblock for Tunnel Endpoints
    (VPN: 192.168.1.2, NBMA: 10.10.2.1)
16. NHRP: Inserted subblock node for cache: Target Inserted subblock
    node for cache: Target 192.168.1.2/32nhop 192.168.1.2
17. NHRP: Converted internal dynamic cache entry for 192.168.1.2/32
    interface Tunnel0 to external
18. NHRP: Tu0: Creating dynamic multicast mapping NBMA: 10.10.2.1
19. NHRP: Added dynamic multicast mapping for NBMA: 10.10.2.1
20. NHRP: Updating our cache with NBMA: 10.10.1.1, NBMA_ALT: 10.10.1.1
21. NHRP: New mandatory length: 32
22. NHRP: Attempting to send packet via DEST 192.168.1.2
23. NHRP: NHRP successfully resolved 192.168.1.2 to NBMA 10.10.2.1
24. NHRP: Encapsulation succeeded.  Tunnel IP addr 10.10.2.1
25. NHRP: Send Registration Reply via Tunnel0 vrf 0, packet size: 112
26. src: 192.168.1.1, dst: 192.168.1.2
27. (F) afn: IPv4(1), type: IP(800), hop: 255, ver: 1
                    shtl: 4(NSAP), sstl: 0(NSAP)
                    pktsz: 112 extoff: 52
28. (M) flags: "unique nat ", reqid: 131074
                    src NBMA: 10.10.2.1
                    src protocol: 192.168.1.2, dst protocol: 192.168.1.1
29. (C-1) code: no error(0)
                    prefix: 32, mtu: 17916, hd_time: 7200
                    addr_len: 0(NSAP), subaddr_len: 0(NSAP), proto_len: 0,
                    pref: 0
30. Responder Address Extension(3):
```

```
31. (C) code: no error(0)
            prefix: 32, mtu: 17916, hd_time: 7200
            addr_len: 4(NSAP), subaddr_len: 0(NSAP), proto_len: 4,
            pref: 0
            client NBMA: 10.10.1.1
            client protocol: 192.168.1.1
32. Forward Transit NHS Record Extension(4):
33. Reverse Transit NHS Record Extension(5):
34. NAT address Extension(9):
35. (C-1) code: no error(0)
            prefix: 32, mtu: 17916, hd_time: 0
            addr_len: 4(NSAP), subaddr_len: 0(NSAP), proto_len: 4,
            pref: 0
            client NBMA: 10.10.1.1
            client protocol: 192.168.1.1
36. NHRP: 136 bytes out Tunnel0
37. %DUAL-5-NBRCHANGE: EIGRP-IPv4 1: Neighbor 192.168.1.2 (Tunnel0) is
    up: new adjacency
38. NHRP: NHRP successfully resolved 192.168.1.2 to NBMA 10.10.2.1
39. *Dec  9 19:07:42.635:
40. Hub-1#
```

Breaking this output down, we can see that at line 3, Hub-1 receives a registration request through its tunnel 0 interface. Line 4 (F) is the Fixed Header portion of the packet. In line 5 (M being the mandatory part) we can see that the sources external and tunnel addresses are supplied, along with the destination address for the tunnel. In lines 13 through to 17 we start to add the data for the spoke to the NHRP cache.

Lines 18 and 19 are where we perform some dynamic mapping for Multicast traffic and lines 22 to 36 show the reply that Hub-1 sends back to Spoke 1. Finally in lines 37 and 38 we can see that our tunnel is healthy and we have formed an EIGRP adjacency across it.

The output for the registration request/reply between Hub-1 and Spoke-2 is no different (barring the obvious IP address differences), so we need not discuss those here, but it is worthwhile going through both outputs.

Let's start Spoke-3 and carry on, by confirming what the debug output has shown us.

We can start to confirm our EIGRP adjacencies and DMVPN network now. We can see that our EIGRP neighborships are up:

```
Hub-1#sh ip eigrp neigh
EIGRP-IPv4 Neighbors for AS(1)
H   Address          Interface   Hold Uptime   SRTT   RTO  Q   Seq
                                 (sec)         (ms)        Cnt Num
```

```
2   192.168.1.4   Tu0          13 00:00:52  147  1434  0  4
1   192.168.1.2   Tu0          12 00:00:56  128  1434  0  5
0   192.168.1.3   Tu0          13 00:00:57   87  1434  0  5
Hub-1#
```

We can also see how many NHRP clients are registered (either statically or dynamically) to our hub router:

```
Hub-1#sh ip nhrp summary
IP NHRP cache 3 entries, 984 bytes
    0 static   3 dynamic   0 incomplete
Hub-1#
```

We can also look at all our clients in greater detail:

```
Hub-1#sh ip nhrp
192.168.1.2/32 via 192.168.1.2
    Tunnel0 created 04:59:55, expire 01:34:05
    Type: dynamic, Flags: unique registered
    NBMA address: 10.10.2.1
192.168.1.3/32 via 192.168.1.3
    Tunnel0 created 04:59:53, expire 01:35:45
    Type: dynamic, Flags: unique registered
    NBMA address: 10.10.3.1
192.168.1.4/32 via 192.168.1.4
    Tunnel0 created 04:59:10, expire 01:36:05
    Type: dynamic, Flags: unique registered
    NBMA address: 10.10.4.1
Hub-1#
```

Or, even single out a particular client:

```
Hub-1#sh ip nhrp 192.168.1.2
192.168.1.2/32 via 192.168.1.2
    Tunnel0 created 04:59:47, expire 01:34:13
    Type: dynamic, Flags: unique registered
    NBMA address: 10.10.2.1
Hub-1#
```

We can also look at our DMVPN peers:

```
Hub-1#sh dmvpn
Legend: Attrb --> S - Static, D - Dynamic, I - Incomplete
        N - NATed, L - Local, X - No Socket
        # Ent --> Number of NHRP entries with same NBMA peer
        NHS Status: E --> Expecting Replies, R --> Responding,
```

```
        W --> Waiting
        UpDn Time --> Up or Down Time for a Tunnel
==================================================================

Interface: Tunnel0, IPv4 NHRP Details
Type:Hub, NHRP Peers:3,

 # Ent   Peer NBMA Addr  Peer Tunnel Add  State   UpDn Tm   Attrb
 -----   --------------  ---------------  -----   --------  -----
     1      10.10.2.1        192.168.1.2    UP    04:59:36    D
     1      10.10.3.1        192.168.1.3    UP    04:59:08    D
     1      10.10.4.1        192.168.1.4    UP    04:58:45    D

Hub-1#
```

On Hub-1 we can see that we have three dynamic peerings (D) and for each of these we can see the external IP address that they are connecting from, the internal address, the state of each of them and the connected time.

If we turn our attention to the spokes, we can start to look into how we can utilize the dynamic nature of DMVPN to easily create a meshed network as and when we need one.

Spoke-1 has a single DMVPN peer at the moment:

```
Spoke-1#sh dmvpn | b Interface
Interface: Tunnel0, IPv4 NHRP Details
Type:Spoke, NHRP Peers:1,

 # Ent   Peer NBMA Addr  Peer Tunnel Add  State   UpDn Tm   Attrb
 -----   --------------  ---------------  -----   --------  -----
     1      10.10.1.1        192.168.1.1    UP    05:04:45    S

Spoke-1#
```

This is our connection back to Hub-1. If we perform a traceroute to an address on one of the other routers in the network, then we can see that it first goes to Hub-1 before getting to the final destination:

```
Spoke-1#trace 3.3.3.3
Type escape sequence to abort.
Tracing the route to 3.3.3.3
VRF info: (vrf in name/id, vrf out name/id)
  1 192.168.1.1 88 msec 32 msec 20 msec
  2 192.168.1.3 56 msec 24 msec 16 msec
Spoke-1#
```

Similarly for a different destination:

```
Spoke-1#trace 4.4.4.4
Type escape sequence to abort.
Tracing the route to 4.4.4.4
VRF info: (vrf in name/id, vrf out name/id)
  1 192.168.1.1 72 msec 40 msec 56 msec
  2 192.168.1.4 100 msec 24 msec 28 msec
Spoke-1#
```

Now if we perform the same initial trace again, we can see that we get straight to the destination:

```
Spoke-1#trace 3.3.3.3
Type escape sequence to abort.
Tracing the route to 3.3.3.3
VRF info: (vrf in name/id, vrf out name/id)
  1 192.168.1.3 24 msec 36 msec 36 msec
Spoke-1#
```

What has happened here, is that Spoke-1 has queried Hub-1 and due to the information returned, built a tunnel (or tunnels in our case) on the fly:

```
Spoke-1#sh dmvpn | b Interface
Interface: Tunnel0, IPv4 NHRP Details
Type:Spoke, NHRP Peers:3,

 # Ent  Peer NBMA Addr Peer Tunnel Add State  UpDn Tm  Attrb
 -----  ------------- --------------- -----  -------- -----
     1      10.10.1.1     192.168.1.1    UP 05:06:04     S
     1      10.10.3.1     192.168.1.3    UP 00:00:55     D
     1      10.10.4.1     192.168.1.4    UP 00:00:47     D

Spoke-1#
```

Spoke-2 and Spoke-3 also have additional tunnels set up:

```
Spoke-2#sh dmvpn | b Interface
Interface: Tunnel0, IPv4 NHRP Details
Type:Spoke, NHRP Peers:2,

 # Ent  Peer NBMA Addr Peer Tunnel Add State  UpDn Tm  Attrb
 -----  ------------- --------------- -----  -------- -----
     1      10.10.1.1     192.168.1.1    UP 05:05:49     S
     1      10.10.2.1     192.168.1.2    UP 00:01:34     D
```

```
Spoke-2#

Spoke-3#sh dmvpn | b Interface
Interface: Tunnel0, IPv4 NHRP Details
Type:Spoke, NHRP Peers:2,

 # Ent   Peer NBMA Addr Peer Tunnel Add State  UpDn Tm Attrb
 -----   -------------- --------------- -----  -------- -----
     1      10.10.1.1      192.168.1.1    UP 05:05:23    S
     1      10.10.2.1      192.168.1.2    UP 00:01:40    D

Spoke-3#
```

We can look at these connections in greater detail:

```
Spoke-3#sh dmvpn detail | b Interface
Interface Tunnel0 is up/up, Addr. is 192.168.1.4, VRF ""
   Tunnel Src./Dest. addr: 10.10.4.1/MGRE, Tunnel VRF ""
   Protocol/Transport: "multi-GRE/IP", Protect ""
   Interface State Control: Disabled

IPv4 NHS:
10.10.1.1    E priority = 0 cluster = 0
192.168.1.1  RE priority = 0 cluster = 0
Type:Spoke, Total NBMA Peers (v4/v6): 3

#Ent Peer NBMA   Peer Tunnel  State UpDn Tm  Att   Target Network
---- ----------  -----------  ----- --------  ---  --------------
  1  10.10.1.1   192.168.1.1   UP   05:27:42   S   192.168.1.1/32
  1  10.10.2.1   192.168.1.2   UP   00:23:59   D   192.168.1.2/32
  1  10.10.4.1   192.168.1.4   UP   00:23:59  DLX  192.168.1.4/32


Crypto Session Details:
-----------------------------------------------------------------

Pending DMVPN Sessions:

Spoke-3#
```

For the sake of formatting, some of the column headings have been changed and spaces removed, such as "Peer NMBA" actually shows as "Peer NMBA Addr", "Peer Tunnel" is actually "Peer Tunnel Add", "Att" is actually "Attrb" and each entry is separated by a blank line.

We can see the traffic involved in setting up one of these dynamic tunnels, by capturing the traffic between Hub-1 and the IGW router.

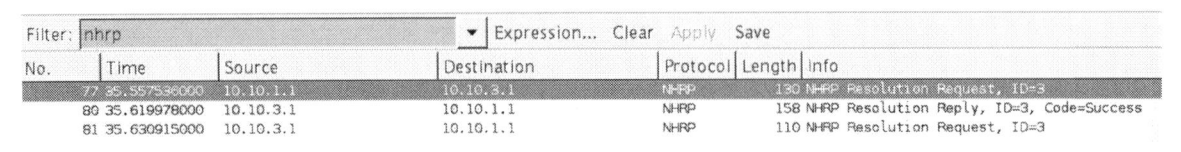

```
Filter: nhrp                                    ▼  Expression... Clear  Apply  Save
No.   Time           Source        Destination    Protocol  Length  Info
 77  35.557536000   10.10.1.1     10.10.3.1      NHRP       130  NHRP Resolution Request, ID=3
 80  35.619978000   10.10.3.1     10.10.1.1      NHRP       158  NHRP Resolution Reply, ID=3, Code=Success
 81  35.630915000   10.10.3.1     10.10.1.1      NHRP       110  NHRP Resolution Request, ID=3
```

Capture: 9

If we drill through the layers, we see that all the interesting details are in the NHRP Mandatory Part, which is in the final layer: Next Hop Resolution Protocol (NHRP Resolution Request). Here we have the source and destination details:

```
▽ Next Hop Resolution Protocol (NHRP Resolution Request)
   ▷ NHRP Fixed Header
   ▽ NHRP Mandatory Part
        Source Protocol Len: 4
        Destination Protocol Len: 4
      ▷ Flags: 0xc802
        Request ID: 0x00000003 (3)
        Source NBMA Address: 10.10.4.1 (10.10.4.1)
        Source Protocol Address: 192.168.1.4 (192.168.1.4)
        Destination Protocol Address: 192.168.1.3 (192.168.1.3)
      ▽ Client Information Entry
```

The second area of interest is the Forward Transit NHS Record Extension, which is used to build a list of the intermediate Next Hop Servers that sit between the source and destination. There is also the Reverse Transit NHS Record Extension, which works in the reverse direction, listing the NHSs between the destination and the source. This feature acts as a form of loop detection. We will cover this more when we look at how we can tweak NHRP and DMVPN.

```
▽ Forward Transit NHS Record Extension
        1... .... .... .... = Compulsory Flag: True
        ..00 0000 0000 0100 = Extension Type: 0x0004
        Extension length: 20
    ▽ Client Information Entry
        Code: Success
        Prefix Length: 32
        Unused: 0
        Max Transmission Unit: 17916
        Holding Time (s): 7200
        ▷ Client Address Type/Len: NSAP format/4
        ▷ Client Sub Address Type/Len: NSAP format/0
        Client Protocol Length: 4
        CIE Preference Value: 0
        Client NBMA Address: 10.10.1.1 (10.10.1.1)
        Client Protocol Address: 192.168.1.1 (192.168.1.1)
▽ Reverse Transit NHS Record Extension
        1... .... .... .... = Compulsory Flag: True
        ..00 0000 0000 0101 = Extension Type: 0x0005
        Extension length: 0
▷ Cisco NAT Address Extension
```

Before we jump ahead, though, let us look at the actual logic behind what is happening here.

Before the dynamic DMVPN tunnel is created, the router tries to forward a packet to the destination. It knows about the destination already because it has learnt about it through the dynamic routing protocol (EIGRP in our case). Because we have a route in the routing table, the router will try and find an NHRP mapping entry for that particular next hop IP address. As none exists, it triggers an NHRP resolution request, which is sent to the next-hop server. The NHS replies with the IP next-hop to the physical layer address mapping and thus, the tunnel is created. Now the client router has a one-hop route to the destination (or to be more correct, one or more hops *less*, than previous).

We can see this in action again, this time with the debugging enabled, by getting Spoke-3 to build a dynamic tunnel to Spoke 2. If you already have a dynamic tunnel and you want to follow along, then reload the routers.

We start by enabling debugging on the three routers:

```
Hub-1#debug nhrp
NHRP protocol debugging is on
Hub-1#
```

```
Spoke-2#debug nhrp
NHRP protocol debugging is on
Spoke-2#

Spoke-3#debug nhrp
NHRP protocol debugging is on
Spoke-3#
```

Spoke-3 has just the one tunnel at the moment:

```
Spoke-3#sh ip nhrp
192.168.1.1/32 via 192.168.1.1
   Tunnel0 created 00:32:05, never expire
   Type: static, Flags: used
   NBMA address: 10.10.1.1
Spoke-3#
```

So we begin by performing a traceroute to 3.3.3.3:

```
Spoke-3#trace 3.3.3.3
Type escape sequence to abort.
Tracing the route to 3.3.3.3
VRF info: (vrf in name/id, vrf out name/id)
  1 192.168.1.1 224 msec 76 msec 60 msec
  2 192.168.1.3 140 msec 48 msec 40 msec
Spoke-3#
```

Again, the debug output is listed without the date information, to save space and allow greater readability. We start with Spoke-3's output:

1. Spoke-3#
2. NHRP: NHRP could not map 192.168.1.3 to NBMA, cache entry not found
3. NHRP: MACADDR: if_in null netid-in 0 if_out Tunnel0 netid-out 1
4. NHRP: Sending packet to NHS 192.168.1.1 on Tunnel0
5. NHRP: NHRP successfully resolved 192.168.1.1 to NBMA 10.10.1.1
6. NHRP: Checking for delayed event /192.168.1.3 on list (Tunnel0).
7. NHRP: No node found.
8. NHRP: Adding Tunnel Endpoints (VPN: 192.168.1.3, NBMA: 10.10.1.1)
9. NHRP: Successfully attached NHRP subblock for Tunnel Endpoints (VPN: 192.168.1.3, NBMA: 10.10.1.1)
10. NHRP: Enqueued NHRP Resolution Request for destination: 192.168.1.3
11. NHRP: Checking for delayed event /192.168.1.3 on list (Tunnel0).
12. NHRP: No node found.
13. NHRP: Sending NHRP Resolution Request for dest: 192.168.1.3 to nexthop: 192.168.1.1 using our src: 192.168.1.4
14. NHRP: Attempting to send packet via DEST 192.168.1.1

```
15. NHRP: NHRP successfully resolved 192.168.1.1 to NBMA 10.10.1.1
16. NHRP: Encapsulation succeeded.  Tunnel IP addr 10.10.1.1
17. NHRP: Send Resolution Request via Tunnel0 vrf 0, packet size: 72
18.       src: 192.168.1.4, dst: 192.168.1.1
19. NHRP: 96 bytes out Tunnel0
20. NHRP: NHRP successfully resolved 192.168.1.3 to NBMA 10.10.1.1
21. NHRP: Receive Resolution Reply via Tunnel0 vrf 0, packet size: 140
22. NHRP: netid_in = 0, to_us = 1
23. NHRP: Checking for delayed event /192.168.1.3 on list (Tunnel0).
24. NHRP: No node found.
25. NHRP: No need to delay processing of resolution event nbma
    src:10.10.4.1 nbma dst:10.10.3.1
26. NHRP: Adding Tunnel Endpoints (VPN: 192.168.1.3, NBMA: 10.10.3.1)
27. NHRP: Cleanup up 0 stale cache entries
28. NHRP: Successfully attached NHRP subblock for Tunnel Endpoints (VPN:
    192.168.1.3, NBMA: 10.10.3.1)
29. NHRP: Receive Resolution Request via Tunnel0 vrf 0, packet size: 92
30. NHRP: netid_in = 1, to_us = 1
31. NHRP: nhrp_rtlookup yielded interface Tunnel0, prefixlen 24
32. NHRP: request was to us, responding with ouraddress
33. NHRP: Checking for delayed event 192.168.1.3/192.168.1.4 on list
    (Tunnel0).
34. NHRP: No node found.
35. NHRP: No need to delay processing of resolution event nbma
    src:10.10.4.1 nbma dst:10.10.3.1
36. NHRP: Attempting to send packet via DEST 192.168.1.3
37. NHRP: NHRP successfully resolved 192.168.1.3 to NBMA 10.10.3.1
38. NHRP: Encapsulation succeeded.  Tunnel IP addr 10.10.3.1
39. NHRP: Send Resolution Reply via Tunnel0 vrf 0, packet size: 120
40.       src: 192.168.1.4, dst: 192.168.1.3
41. NHRP: 144 bytes out Tunnel0
42. NHRP: NHRP successfully resolved 192.168.1.3 to NBMA 10.10.3.1
43. Spoke-3#un all
44. All possible debugging has been turned off
45. Spoke-3#
```

We can see that when we initiate the trace, Spoke-3 does a lookup in its NHRP cache (line 2) because it does not find one it sends a resolution request to its next hop server (line 13), the reply from this request comes back to us at line 21, in line 26 we start to add this information to our own NHRP cache.

It gets interesting at line 29, because here we actually get sent a resolution request, which we reply to on line 39.

If we look at the relevant lines from the debug log on Spoke-2, we can see that it goes through a similar process:

1. NHRP: NHRP could not map 192.168.1.4 to NBMA, cache entry not found
2. NHRP: Sending packet to NHS 192.168.1.1 on Tunnel0
3. NHRP: NHRP successfully resolved 192.168.1.1 to NBMA 10.10.1.1
4. NHRP: Adding Tunnel Endpoints (VPN: 192.168.1.4, NBMA: 10.10.1.1)
5. NHRP: Successfully attached NHRP subblock for Tunnel Endpoints (VPN: 192.168.1.4, NBMA: 10.10.1.1)
6. NHRP: Enqueued NHRP Resolution Request for destination: 192.168.1.4
7. NHRP: Receive Resolution Request via Tunnel0 vrf 0, packet size: 92
8. NHRP: request was to us, responding with our address
9. NHRP: Attempting to send packet via DEST 192.168.1.4
10. NHRP: NHRP successfully resolved 192.168.1.4 to NBMA 10.10.1.1
11. NHRP: Encapsulation succeeded. Tunnel IP addr 10.10.1.1
12. NHRP: Send Resolution Reply via Tunnel0 vrf 0, packet size: 120
          src: 192.168.1.3, dst: 192.168.1.4
13. NHRP: Sending NHRP Resolution Request for dest: 192.168.1.4 to nexthop: 192.168.1.1 using our src: 192.168.1.3
14. NHRP: Attempting to send packet via DEST 192.168.1.1
15. NHRP: NHRP successfully resolved 192.168.1.1 to NBMA 10.10.1.1
16. NHRP: Encapsulation succeeded. Tunnel IP addr 10.10.1.1
17. NHRP: Send Resolution Request via Tunnel0 vrf 0, packet size: 72
          src: 192.168.1.3, dst: 192.168.1.1
18. NHRP: NHRP successfully resolved 192.168.1.4 to NBMA 10.10.1.1
19. NHRP: Adding Tunnel Endpoints (VPN: 192.168.1.4, NBMA: 10.10.4.1)
20. NHRP: Cleanup up 0 stale cache entries
21. NHRP: Successfully attached NHRP subblock for Tunnel Endpoints (VPN: 192.168.1.4, NBMA: 10.10.4.1)
22. NHRP: NHRP successfully resolved 192.168.1.4 to NBMA 10.10.4.1

Now let us look at Hub-1, where all the magic happens:

1. Hub-1#
2. NHRP: NHRP successfully resolved 192.168.1.3 to NBMA 10.10.3.1
3. NHRP: Receive Resolution Request via Tunnel0 vrf 0, packet size: 72
4. NHRP: nhrp_cache_lookup_comp returned 0x69A01818
5. NHRP: Forwarding request due to authoritative request.
6. NHRP: Attempting to forward to destination: 192.168.1.3
7. NHRP: Forwarding: NHRP SAS picked source: 192.168.1.1 for destination: 192.168.1.3
8. NHRP: Attempting to send packet via DEST 192.168.1.3
9. NHRP: NHRP successfully resolved 192.168.1.3 to NBMA 10.10.3.1
10. NHRP: Encapsulation succeeded. Tunnel IP addr 10.10.3.1
11. NHRP: Forwarding Resolution Request via Tunnel0 vrf 0, packet size: 92
          src: 192.168.1.1, dst: 192.168.1.3

```
12. NHRP: Receive Resolution Reply via Tunnel0 vrf 0, packet size: 120
13. NHRP: Forwarding Resolution Reply to 192.168.1.4
14. NHRP: Attempting to forward to destination: 192.168.1.4
15. NHRP: Forwarding: NHRP SAS picked source: 192.168.1.1 for destination:
    192.168.1.4
16. NHRP: Attempting to send packet via DEST 192.168.1.4
17. NHRP: NHRP successfully resolved 192.168.1.4 to NBMA 10.10.4.1
18. NHRP: Encapsulation succeeded.  Tunnel IP addr 10.10.4.1
19. NHRP: Forwarding Resolution Reply via Tunnel0 vrf 0, packet size: 140
            src: 192.168.1.1, dst: 192.168.1.4
20. NHRP: Receive Resolution Request via Tunnel0 vrf 0, packet size: 72
21. NHRP: nhrp_cache_lookup_comp returned 0x69A016C0
22. NHRP: Forwarding request due to authoritative request.
23. NHRP: Attempting to forward to destination: 192.168.1.4
24. NHRP: Forwarding: NHRP SAS picked source: 192.168.1.1 for destination:
    192.168.1.4
25. NHRP: Attempting to send packet via DEST 192.168.1.4
26. NHRP: NHRP successfully resolved 192.168.1.4 to NBMA 10.10.4.1
27. NHRP: Encapsulation succeeded.  Tunnel IP addr 10.10.4.1
28. NHRP: Forwarding Resolution Request via Tunnel0
            vrf 0, packet size: 92
            src: 192.168.1.1, dst: 192.168.1.4
29. NHRP: 116 bytes out Tunnel0
30. NHRP: NHRP successfully resolved 192.168.1.3 to NBMA 10.10.3.1
31. Hub-1#un all
32. All possible debugging has been turned off
33. Hub-1#
```

We can see that Hub-1 does the brunt of the work. It receives resolution requests at lines 3 and 20. These are forwarded at lines 5-11 and 22-28.

Now our spokes have built the dynamic tunnels and each has full reachability. In order to maintain this reachability, phase 2 DMVPN does not modify the next-hop IP address. This means though, that each spoke must receive the full routing table and here we go back to one of the "issues" with Phase 2; in that we cannot use any form of summarization (and this only allows for one level of hubs). Whilst dual-hub topologies are not part of the CCIE Routing and Switching exam (and therefore will not be discussed here), we can look at summarization, and it will lead us nicely on to phase 3.

In the previous sentence I used the word "issues" in quotes, because it is only an issue sometimes. This is not like some of the other golden rules of networking, this is more of a "depending on what you are doing it may or may not work" type of scenario. So we will see it work and then we will step away from the topology and see what is actually meant by no summarization with phase 2.

We start by creating a number of loopback interfaces on our hub, and create a summary address within EIGRP:

```
Hub-1(config)#int lo1
Hub-1(config-if)#ip add 172.16.1.1 255.255.255.0
Hub-1(config-if)#int lo2
Hub-1(config-if)#ip add 172.16.2.2 255.255.255.0
Hub-1(config-if)#int lo3
Hub-1(config-if)#ip add 172.16.3.3 255.255.255.0
Hub-1(config-if)#router eigrp 1
Hub-1(config-router)#network 172.16.0.0 0.0.3.255
Hub-1(config-router)#int tun 0
Hub-1(config-if)#ip summary-address eigrp 1 172.16.0.0 255.255.252.0
Hub-1(config-if)#
```

Now, will we see this summarized route on the spokes, or not?

```
Spoke-1#sh ip route eigrp | b Gate
Gateway of last resort is 10.10.2.2 to network 0.0.0.0

      1.0.0.0/32 is subnetted, 1 subnets
D        1.1.1.1 [90/27008000] via 192.168.1.1, 00:10:02, Tun0
      3.0.0.0/32 is subnetted, 1 subnets
D        3.3.3.3 [90/28288000] via 192.168.1.3, 00:14:28, Tun0
      4.0.0.0/32 is subnetted, 1 subnets
D        4.4.4.4 [90/28288000] via 192.168.1.4, 00:21:03, Tun0
      172.16.0.0/22 is subnetted, 1 subnets
D        172.16.0.0 [90/27008000] via 192.168.1.1, 00:10:01, Tun0
Spoke-1#

Spoke-2#sh ip route 172.16.0.0
Routing entry for 172.16.0.0/22, 1 known subnets
  Redistributing via eigrp 1
D        172.16.0.0 [90/27008000] via 192.168.1.1, 00:10:23, Tun0
Spoke-2#

Spoke-3#sh ip route 172.16.0.0
Routing entry for 172.16.0.0/22, 1 known subnets
  Redistributing via eigrp 1
D        172.16.0.0 [90/27008000] via 192.168.1.1, 00:10:40, Tun0
Spoke-3#
```

We do. So this shows that summarization can actually work with Phase 2 DMVPN. Let's see where it does not work.

We have a much-simplified scenario with just three routers

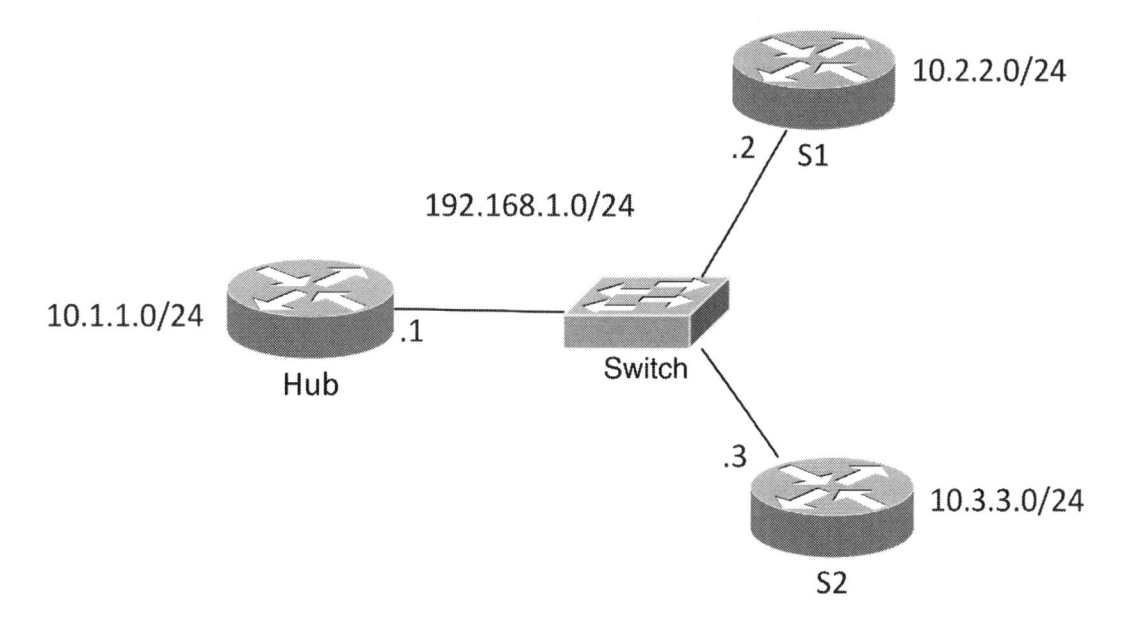

Each router is physically connected to a switch using an IP address in the 192.168.1.0/24 range. Our DMVPN network will be using the 172.16.1.0/24 range. The Hub router will have the final octet of all IP address as .1, S1 will use .2 and S2 will use .3. Each has a loopback interface; 10.1.1.1/24 for Hub, 10.2.2.2/24 for S1 and 10.3.3.3/24 for S2. The tunnel configuration is below:

```
Hub#sh run int tun 0 | b interface
interface Tunnel0
 ip address 172.16.1.1 255.255.255.0
 no ip redirects
 no ip next-hop-self eigrp 1
 ip nhrp map multicast dynamic
 ip nhrp network-id 1
 no ip split-horizon eigrp 1
 tunnel source GigabitEthernet1/0
 tunnel mode gre multipoint
end

Hub#

S1#sh run int tun 0 | b interface
interface Tunnel0
 ip address 172.16.1.2 255.255.255.0
 no ip redirects
```

```
  ip nhrp map 172.16.1.1 192.168.1.1
  ip nhrp map multicast 192.168.1.1
  ip nhrp network-id 1
  ip nhrp nhs 172.16.1.1
  tunnel source GigabitEthernet1/0
  tunnel mode gre multipoint
end

S1#

S2#sh run int tun 0 | b interface
interface Tunnel0
  ip address 172.16.1.3 255.255.255.0
  no ip redirects
  ip nhrp map multicast 192.168.1.1
  ip nhrp map 172.16.1.1 192.168.1.1
  ip nhrp network-id 1
  ip nhrp nhs 172.16.1.1
  tunnel source GigabitEthernet1/0
  tunnel mode gre multipoint
end

S2#
```

Let's go ahead and form our EIGRP adjacencies:

```
Hub(config)#router eigrp 1
Hub(config-router)#network 172.16.1.1 0.0.0.0
Hub(config-router)#network 10.1.1.1 0.0.0.0
Hub(config-router)#

S1(config-if)#router eigrp 1
S1(config-router)#network 172.16.1.2 0.0.0.0
S1(config-router)#network 10.2.2.2 0.0.0.0
S1(config-router)#

S2(config)#router eigrp 1
S2(config-router)#network 172.16.1.3 0.0.0.0
S2(config-router)#network 10.3.3.3 0.0.0.0
S2(config-router)#
```

With this in place we can see that we have the makings for a decent looking network.

```
Hub#sh ip route eigrp | b Gate
Gateway of last resort is not set
```

```
        10.0.0.0/8 is variably subnetted, 4 subnets, 2 masks
D       10.2.2.0/24 [90/27008000] via 172.16.1.2, 00:00:58, Tun0
D       10.3.3.0/24 [90/27008000] via 172.16.1.3, 00:00:21, Tun0
Hub#

S1#sh ip route EIGRP | b Gate
Gateway of last resort is not set

        10.0.0.0/8 is variably subnetted, 4 subnets, 2 masks
D       10.1.1.0/24 [90/27008000] via 172.16.1.1, 00:03:29, Tun0
D       10.3.3.0/24 [90/28288000] via 172.16.1.3, 00:02:39, Tun0
S1#

S1#trace 10.3.3.3
Type escape sequence to abort.
Tracing the route to 10.3.3.3
VRF info: (vrf in name/id, vrf out name/id)
  1 172.16.1.1 44 msec
    172.16.1.3 20 msec 20 msec
S1#trace 10.3.3.3
Type escape sequence to abort.
Tracing the route to 10.3.3.3
VRF info: (vrf in name/id, vrf out name/id)
  1 172.16.1.3 20 msec 32 msec *
S1#
```

All is working well with phase 2. So let's summarize the loopback networks into something a little more manageable.

```
Hub(config)#router eigrp 1
Hub(config-router)#network 10.0.0.0 0.0.0.255
Hub(config-router)#int tun 0
Hub(config-if)#ip summary-address eigrp 1 10.0.0.0 255.0.0.0
Hub(config-if)#
```

After a quick resync we have the new route entry, which has supressed the individual routes.

```
S1#sh ip route EIGRP | b Gate
Gateway of last resort is not set

        10.0.0.0/8 is variably subnetted, 3 subnets, 3 masks
D       10.0.0.0/8 [90/27008000] via 172.16.1.1, 00:00:18, Tun0
S1#

S2#sh ip route eigrp | b Gate
```

```
Gateway of last resort is not set

     10.0.0.0/8 is variably subnetted, 3 subnets, 3 masks
D       10.0.0.0/8 [90/27008000] via 172.16.1.1, 00:00:44, Tun0
S2#
```

So, we can have summarized routes and, as we can see below, these do not prevent the different nodes talking to each other. We will now look at why summarization is not a good idea in phase 2 DMVPN.

We still have connectivity from S1 to S2:

```
S1#sh ip nhrp
172.16.1.1/32 via 172.16.1.1
   Tunnel0 created 00:23:48, never expire
   Type: static, Flags: used
   NBMA address: 192.168.1.1
S1#ping 10.3.3.3
Type escape sequence to abort.
Sending 5, 100-byte ICMP Echos to 10.3.3.3
!!!!!
Success rate is 100 percent (5/5)
S1#sh ip nhrp
172.16.1.1/32 via 172.16.1.1
   Tunnel0 created 00:24:06, never expire
   Type: static, Flags: used
   NBMA address: 192.168.1.1
172.16.1.2/32 via 172.16.1.2
   Tunnel0 created 00:00:04, expire 01:59:56
   Type: dynamic, Flags: router unique local
   NBMA address: 192.168.1.2
     (no-socket)
172.16.1.3/32 via 172.16.1.3
   Tunnel0 created 00:00:04, expire 01:59:56
   Type: dynamic, Flags: router implicit used
   NBMA address: 192.168.1.3
S1#
```

As we have seen previously though, the beauty of phase 2 DMVPN is that, after an initial packet transfer, which initiates a request and reply sequence, our spokes can communicate directly with each other. However, due to the summarization we have just performed, this is now broken. Usually an initial traceroute will show two hops and after that we are down to one hop, but now this spoke-to-spoke tunnel never forms:

```
S1#trace 10.3.3.3 numeric
Type escape sequence to abort.
```

```
    Tracing the route to 10.3.3.3
    VRF info: (vrf in name/id, vrf out name/id)
      1 172.16.1.1 16 msec 20 msec 44 msec
      2 172.16.1.3 44 msec *  24 msec
    S1#trace 10.3.3.3 numeric
    Type escape sequence to abort.
    Tracing the route to 10.3.3.3
    VRF info: (vrf in name/id, vrf out name/id)
      1 172.16.1.1 12 msec 12 msec 12 msec
      2 172.16.1.3 20 msec *  12 msec
    S1#trace 10.3.3.3 numeric
    Type escape sequence to abort.
    Tracing the route to 10.3.3.3
    VRF info: (vrf in name/id, vrf out name/id)
      1 172.16.1.1 20 msec 12 msec 12 msec
      2 172.16.1.3 28 msec 500 msec
    S1#
```

This shows that although we have carefully constructed a phase 2 DMVPN network, designed for speed and with a reduced demand on our central hub, through the addition of one incorrect address summary, we can reduce this back down to, what is effectively, a phase 1 network, where all the traffic again goes through the hub. Strictly speaking, "incorrect" is the wrong term to use, misplaced would, perhaps, be more correct, as syntactically the summary address is correct, we just shouldn't use it here.

With this in mind, let us now move our DMVPN network up a notch and switch to phase 3. We will quickly go through this current topology, in order that we can see the benefits, before switching back to the main topology for a more in-depth discussion.

To switch to phase 3 requires only a couple of commands:

```
    Hub(config)#int tun 0
    Hub(config-if)#ip next-hop-self eigrp 1
    Hub(config-if)#ip nhrp redirect
    Hub(config-if)#

    S1(config)#int tun 0
    S1(config-if)#ip nhrp shortcut
    S1(config-if)#ip nhrp redirect
    S1(config-if)#

    S2(config)#int tun 0
    S2(config-if)#ip nhrp redirect
    S2(config-if)#ip nhrp shortcut
    S2(config-if)#
```

Our spoke has a number of tunnels and we still have the summarized address in our routing table:

```
S1#sh ip nhrp
172.16.1.1/32 via 172.16.1.1
   Tunnel0 created 00:28:23, never expire
   Type: static, Flags: used
   NBMA address: 192.168.1.1
172.16.1.2/32 via 172.16.1.2
   Tunnel0 created 00:04:21, expire 01:55:38
   Type: dynamic, Flags: router unique local
   NBMA address: 192.168.1.2
     (no-socket)
172.16.1.3/32 via 172.16.1.3
   Tunnel0 created 00:04:21, expire 01:55:38
   Type: dynamic, Flags: router implicit
   NBMA address: 192.168.1.3
S1#sh ip route eigrp | b Gate
Gateway of last resort is not set

     10.0.0.0/8 is variably subnetted, 3 subnets, 3 masks
D       10.0.0.0/8 [90/27008000] via 172.16.1.1, 00:01:18, Tun0
S1#
```

With Phase 3 running, we can have the summary-address and the spoke-to-spoke traffic:

```
S1#ping 10.3.3.3
Type escape sequence to abort.
Sending 5, 100-byte ICMP Echos to 10.3.3.3
!!!!!
Success rate is 100 percent (5/5)
S1#trace 10.3.3.3 num
Type escape sequence to abort.
Tracing the route to 10.3.3.3
VRF info: (vrf in name/id, vrf out name/id)
  1 172.16.1.3 40 msec *  20 msec
S1#sh ip nhrp
10.2.2.0/24 via 172.16.1.2
   Tunnel0 created 00:20:45, expire 01:39:14
   Type: dynamic, Flags: router unique local
   NBMA address: 192.168.1.2
     (no-socket)
10.3.3.0/24 via 172.16.1.3
   Tunnel0 created 00:21:50, expire 01:38:10
   Type: dynamic, Flags: router
```

```
        NBMA address: 192.168.1.3
    172.16.1.1/32 via 172.16.1.1
        Tunnel0 created 00:50:31, never expire
        Type: static, Flags: used
        NBMA address: 192.168.1.1
    172.16.1.2/32 via 172.16.1.2
        Tunnel0 created 00:26:29, expire 01:33:30
        Type: dynamic, Flags: router unique local
        NBMA address: 192.168.1.2
          (no-socket)
    172.16.1.3/32 via 172.16.1.3
        Tunnel0 created 00:26:29, expire 01:39:14
        Type: dynamic, Flags: router implicit
        NBMA address: 192.168.1.3
    S1#
```

We can see this in action again with S2:

```
    S2#trace 10.2.2.2
    Type escape sequence to abort.
    Tracing the route to 10.2.2.2
    VRF info: (vrf in name/id, vrf out name/id)
      1 172.16.1.1 48 msec 20 msec 20 msec
      2 172.16.1.2 36 msec 16 msec 492 msec
    S2#trace 10.2.2.2 num
    Type escape sequence to abort.
    Tracing the route to 10.2.2.2
    VRF info: (vrf in name/id, vrf out name/id)
      1 172.16.1.2 44 msec *  16 msec
    S2#
```

Therefore, with phase 3 we can have summarization and spoke-to-spoke traffic.

Let us return to our main topology, were we will look at phase 3 in greater detail.

4.4 Switching from Phase 2 to Phase 3

We start by enabling debugging on the hub and all of the spokes:

```
    Hub-1#debug nhrp
    NHRP protocol debugging is on
    Hub-1#

    Spoke-1#debug nhrp
    NHRP protocol debugging is on
```

```
Spoke-1#

Spoke-2#debug nhrp
NHRP protocol debugging is on
Spoke-2#

Spoke-3#debug nhrp
NHRP protocol debugging is on
Spoke-3#
```

We then remove the command "no ip next-hop-self eigrp 1" and add in the command "ip nhrp redirect" on the hub.

```
Hub-1(config)#int tun 0
Hub-1(config-if)#ip next-hop-self eigrp 1
Hub-1(config-if)#ip nhrp redirect
Hub-1(config-if)#end
```

> Note: If you get the following message:
>
> ```
> % NHRP-WARNING: 'ip nhrp redirect' failed to initialise
> % NHRP-WARNING: 'ipv6 nhrp redirect' failed to initialise
> ```
>
> Then this is most likely due to running a different IOS image

The Cisco guide[4] states that all the spokes should have ip nhrp shortcut and ip nhrp redirect, and that the hub just requires the ip nhrp redirect command. In reality the spokes just need the ip nhrp shortcut command. What do we do then, in an exam environment? This would probably be one of those times when you should ask the proctor. Exams do not necessarily test what we would do in real-life, so here might be a good time to put your hand up and ask. Be careful how you phrase the question as the proctor is not there to give you the answers – so don't say "Do I use redirect, or shortcut here?", instead say something along the lines of "The Cisco documentation states that the hub requires both the redirect and the shortcut commands, yet just the shortcut will work fine. Will I get penalized for not using the redirect command?". Alternatively, just follow the Cisco documentation.

---

[4] http://www.cisco.com/c/en/us/products/collateral/ios-nx-os-software/converged-vpn-solution-managed-services/prod_white_paper0900aecd8055c34e.html

I have used the redirect command as well on Spoke-2, just to prove that the shortcut command on its own (Spoke-1 and Spoke-3) works absolutely fine:

```
Spoke-1(config)#int tun 0
Spoke-1(config-if)#ip nhrp shortcut
Spoke-1(config-if)#end

Spoke-2(config)#int tun 0
Spoke-2(config-if)#ip nhrp shortcut
Spoke-2(config-if)#ip nhrp redirect
Spoke-2(config-if)#end

Spoke-3(config)#int tun 0
Spoke-3(config-if)#ip nhrp shortcut
Spoke-3(config-if)#end
```

Now, if we get Spoke-1 to set up a tunnel with Spoke-3, we can watch what happens in phase 3 DMVPN. Firstly we should make sure that we have the prefix in our routing table:

```
Spoke-1#sh ip route eigrp | b Gate
Gateway of last resort is 10.10.2.2 to network 0.0.0.0

      1.0.0.0/32 is subnetted, 1 subnets
D        1.1.1.1 [90/27008000] via 192.168.1.1, 00:17:09, Tun0
      3.0.0.0/32 is subnetted, 1 subnets
D        3.3.3.3 [90/28288000] via 192.168.1.1, 00:17:09, Tun0
      4.0.0.0/32 is subnetted, 1 subnets
D        4.4.4.4 [90/28288000] via 192.168.1.1, 00:17:09, Tun0
      172.16.0.0/22 is subnetted, 1 subnets
D        172.16.0.0 [90/27008000] via 192.168.1.1, 00:17:09, Tun0
Spoke-1#
```

Note here, that all our routes now point back to Hub-1 – this is because we are making ourselves the next-hop again. Please also note that the debug log has been truncated to just the pertinent lines, for ease of reading. I have also removed the packet size bits for the same reason.

We start the traceroute and immediately we can see that we start to query our next hop IP address. As in phase 2 we build up our resolution request and send it to the next-hop server

1. `Spoke-1#trace 4.4.4.4 numeric`
2. `NHRP: NHRP successfully resolved 192.168.1.1 to NBMA 10.10.1.1`
3. `NHRP: Enqueued NHRP Resolution Request for destination: 4.4.4.4`

4. NHRP: Sending NHRP Resolution Request for dest: 4.4.4.4 to nexthop: 192.168.1.1 using our src: 192.168.1.2
5. NHRP: Attempting to send packet via DEST 192.168.1.1
6. NHRP: NHRP successfully resolved 192.168.1.1 to NBMA 10.10.1.1
7. NHRP: Encapsulation succeeded. Tunnel IP addr 10.10.1.1
8. NHRP: Send Resolution Request via Tunnel0 vrf 0
       src: 192.168.1.2, dst: 192.168.1.1
9. NHRP: Receive Resolution Request via Tunnel0 vrf 0
10. NHRP: request was to us, responding with ouraddress
11. NHRP: No need to delay processing of resolution event nbma src:10.10.2.1 nbma dst:10.10.4.1
12. NHRP: Adding Tunnel Endpoints (VPN: 192.168.1.4, NBMA: 10.10.4.1)
13. NHRP: Successfully attached NHRP subblock for Tunnel Endpoints (VPN: 192.168.1.4, NBMA: 10.10.4.1)
14. NHRP: Attempting to send packet via DEST 192.168.1.4
15. NHRP: NHRP successfully resolved 192.168.1.4 to NBMA 10.10.4.1
16. NHRP: Encapsulation succeeded. Tunnel IP addr 10.10.4.1
17. NHRP: Send Resolution Reply via Tunnel0 vrf 0
       src: 192.168.1.2, dst: 192.168.1.4
18. NHRP: Receive Resolution Reply via Tunnel0 vrf 0
19. NHRP: Adding Tunnel Endpoints (VPN: 192.168.1.4, NBMA: 10.10.4.1)
20. NHRP: NHRP subblock already exists for Tunnel Endpoints (VPN: 192.168.1.4, NBMA: 10.10.4.1)
21. Spoke-1#

Looking at Hub-1, we can see a lot more information as to what is occurring:

1. NHRP: Receive Resolution Req
2. NHRP: Attempting to forward to destination: 4.4.4.4
3. NHRP: Forwarding: NHRP SAS picked source: 192.168.1.1 for destination: 4.4.4.4
4. NHRP: Attempting to send packet via DEST 4.4.4.4
5. NHRP: NHRP successfully resolved 192.168.1.4 to NBMA 10.10.4.1
6. NHRP: Encapsulation succeeded. Tunnel IP addr 10.10.4.1
7. NHRP: Forwarding Resolution Request via Tunnel0 vrf 0
         src: 192.168.1.1, dst: 4.4.4.4
8. NHRP: Attempting to Redirect, remote_nbma: 10.10.4.1
9. NHRP: inserting (10.10.4.1/192.168.1.2) in redirect table
10. NHRP: Pre-setting NBMA address in NHRP Traffic Indication to: 10.10.4.1
11. NHRP: Attempting to send packet via DEST 192.168.1.4
12. NHRP: Switching NHRP Packet using pre-set NBMA: 10.10.4.1
13. NHRP: Encapsulation succeeded. Tunnel IP addr 10.10.4.1
14. NHRP: Send Traffic Indication via Tunnel0 vrf 0
       src: 192.168.1.1, dst: 192.168.1.4
15. NHRP: Forwarding request due to authoritative request.

16. NHRP: Attempting to forward to destination: 192.168.1.2
17. NHRP: Forwarding: NHRP SAS picked source: 192.168.1.1 for destination: 192.168.1.2
18. NHRP: Attempting to send packet via DEST 192.168.1.2
19. NHRP: NHRP successfully resolved 192.168.1.2 to NBMA 10.10.2.1
20. NHRP: Encapsulation succeeded. Tunnel IP addr 10.10.2.1
21. NHRP: Forwarding Resolution Request via Tunnel0 vrf 0
        src: 192.168.1.1, dst: 192.168.1.2
22. NHRP: Receive Resolution Reply via Tunnel0 vrf 0
23. NHRP: Forwarding Resolution Reply to 192.168.1.2
24. NHRP: Attempting to forward to destination: 192.168.1.2
25. NHRP: Forwarding: NHRP SAS picked source: 192.168.1.1 for destination: 192.168.1.2
26. NHRP: Attempting to send packet via DEST 192.168.1.2
27. NHRP: NHRP successfully resolved 192.168.1.2 to NBMA 10.10.2.1
28. NHRP: Encapsulation succeeded. Tunnel IP addr 10.10.2.1
29. NHRP: Forwarding Resolution Reply via Tunnel0 vrf 0
        src: 192.168.1.1, dst: 192.168.1.2

The interesting line is 8, where we start to build a redirect message, which contains the NMBA to tunnel mapping (line 9). This is then sent at line 14 (the Traffic Indication), because as line 15 shows, we are authoritative. This redirect message is then sent back to Spoke-1 (lines 16 onwards).

The conversation between Hub-1 and Spoke-3 is actually a little easier to understand.

1. NHRP: NHRP could not map 192.168.1.2 to NBMA, cache entry not found
2. NHRP: Sending packet to NHS 192.168.1.1 on Tunnel0
3. NHRP: Sending NHRP Resolution Request for dest: 192.168.1.2 to nexthop: 192.168.1.1 using our src: 192.168.1.4
4. NHRP: Send Resolution Request via Tunnel0 vrf 0
        src: 192.168.1.4, dst: 192.168.1.1
5. NHRP: Receive Resolution Request via Tunnel0 vrf 0
6. NHRP: We are egress router for target 4.4.4.4, received via Tunnel0
7. NHRP: Redist mask now 1
8. NHRP: Send Resolution Reply via Tunnel0 vrf 0
        src: 192.168.1.4, dst: 192.168.1.2
9. NHRP: Receive Traffic Indication via Tunnel0 vrf 0
10. NHRP: Receive Resolution Reply via Tunnel0 vrf 0
11. NHRP: Adding Tunnel Endpoints (VPN: 192.168.1.2, NBMA: 10.10.2.1)
12. NHRP: Successfully attached NHRP subblock for Tunnel Endpoints (VPN: 192.168.1.2, NBMA: 10.10.2.1)

At line 1 we see that Spoke-3 does not have a mapping for 192.168.1.2, so it forwards a resolution request to Hub-1 (line 3), and builds the mapping with the contents of the reply from Hub-1. Because Hub-1 has already informed Spoke-1 of the NBMA to tunnel IP mapping for Spoke-3, Spoke-1 now sends a resolution request directly to Spoke-3, which is received by Spoke-3 in line 5. Spoke-3 already knows that it is the egress router for the target specified in the resolution request (line 6), so sends out its own resolution reply in line 8. Thus, our shortcut is created.

To see what shortcut entries we have, we need to look at the NHRP cache:

```
Spoke-1#sh ip nhrp 4.4.4.4
4.4.4.4/32 via 192.168.1.4
   Tunnel0 created 01:12:04, expire 00:47:56
   Type: dynamic, Flags: router used
   NBMA address: 10.10.4.1
Spoke-1#
```

Looking at the CEF table will only show us the routing table entry:

```
Spoke-1#sh ip cef 4.4.4.4
4.4.4.4/32
  nexthop 192.168.1.1 Tunnel0
Spoke-1#
```

If we return to the routing table, we can see that we are also over-riding the next hop:

```
Spoke-1#sh ip route eigrp | b Gate
Gateway of last resort is 10.10.2.2 to network 0.0.0.0

      1.0.0.0/32 is subnetted, 1 subnets
D        1.1.1.1 [90/27008000] via 192.168.1.1, 00:02:19, Tunnel0
      3.0.0.0/32 is subnetted, 1 subnets
D        3.3.3.3 [90/28288000] via 192.168.1.1, 00:02:20, Tunnel0
      4.0.0.0/32 is subnetted, 1 subnets
D  %     4.4.4.4 [90/28288000] via 192.168.1.1, 00:02:20, Tunnel0
      172.16.0.0/22 is subnetted, 1 subnets
D        172.16.0.0 [90/27008000] via 192.168.1.1, 00:02:19, Tunnel0
Spoke-1#
```

The % denotes that we are performing "next hop override". This is a good indication that our traffic is not traversing the hub:

```
Spoke-1#sh ip route eigrp | i %
      + - replicated route, % - next hop override
D  %    4.4.4.4 [90/28288000] via 192.168.1.1, 00:03:25, Tunnel0
Spoke-1#
```

So far, we have only looked at how DMVPN works with EIGRP. EIGRP is the preferred IGP, due to the scalability within DMVPN[5], yet we can run RIP, BGP and OSPF over DMVPN as well.

4.5 DMVPN and RIP

RIP does not need much tweaking to work with DMVPN; in fact all we need to do is to turn off the split horizon rule (no ip split horizon). Because it is so simplistic, we will skip over a practical example and move on to BGP over DMVPN.

4.6 DMVPN and BGP

BGP works very well with DMVPN, yet it can introduce a higher level of complexity. The beauty of DMVPN is that it can be very much a case of "fire and forget", the commands we need to use to get a working DMVPN environment up and running can be very minimal. Yet, once we start to introduce BGP, we can start to lose that ease of configuration.

We will start with Hub-1 and Spoke-1 and see what I mean by this. Let's start by clearing out our EIGRP configuration:

```
Hub-1(config)#no router eigrp 1
Hub-1(config)#do sh run int tun 0
Building configuration...

Current configuration : 213 bytes
!
interface Tunnel0
 ip address 192.168.1.1 255.255.255.0
 no ip redirects
 ip nhrp map multicast dynamic
 ip nhrp network-id 1
 ip nhrp redirect
 tunnel source GigabitEthernet1/0
 tunnel mode gre multipoint
end

Hub-1(config)#
```

Because "no router eigrp 1" removes all the configuration from the tunnel, we can just use the same command on the spokes:

---

[5] http://www.cisco.com/en/US/docs/solutions/Enterprise/WAN_and_MAN/DMVPN_1.html

```
Spoke-1(config)#no router eigrp 1

Spoke-2(config)#no router eigrp 1

Spoke-3(config)#no router eigrp 1
```

We start by creating the BGP process on Hub-1 and Spoke-1 in the traditional way:

```
Hub-1(config)#router bgp 100
Hub-1(config-router)#bgp router-id 1.1.1.1
Hub-1(config-router)#neigh 192.168.1.2 remote-as 100
Hub-1(config-router)#neigh 192.168.1.2 update-source tun 0
Hub-1(config-router)#neigh 192.168.1.2 ebgp-multihop 2
Hub-1(config-router)#network 1.1.1.1 mask 255.255.255.255
Hub-1(config-router)#

Spoke-1(config)#router bgp 100
Spoke-1(config-router)#neigh 192.168.1.1 remote-as 100
Spoke-1(config-router)#neigh 192.168.1.1 update-source tun 0
Spoke-1(config-router)#
%BGP-5-ADJCHANGE: neighbor 192.168.1.1 Up
Spoke-1(config-router)#neigh 192.168.1.1 ebgp-multihop 2
Spoke-1(config-router)#net 2.2.2.2 mask 255.255.255.255
Spoke-1(config-router)#
```

Technically we do not need to use ebgp-multihop, as we are running iBGP. However it doesn't hurt to put it in; it is one of those habits that will certainly help us when we implement eBGP.

Once the peering is up, we can check that the route advertised by Hub-1 is being received by Spoke-1 and we can advertise Spoke-1's loopback interface into BGP as well:

```
Spoke-1(config-router)#do sh ip route bgp | b Gate
Gateway of last resort is 10.10.2.2 to network 0.0.0.0

      1.0.0.0/32 is subnetted, 1 subnets
B        1.1.1.1 [200/0] via 192.168.1.1, 00:00:04
Spoke-1(config-router)#network 2.2.2.2 mask 255.255.255.255
Spoke-1(config-router)#
```

With this we can confirm we have reachability:

```
Hub-1(config-router)#do ping 2.2.2.2 so lo0
Type escape sequence to abort.
```

```
Sending 5, 100-byte ICMP Echos to 2.2.2.2:
Packet sent with a source address of 1.1.1.1
!!!!!
Success rate is 100 percent (5/5)
Hub-1(config-router)#
```

We know that all is working here, and we could go ahead and add the neighbor statements for Spoke-2 and Spoke-3 on to Hub-1 and create the routing process on those routers as well. In our environment, with the small number of routers that we have, this is not too arduous, yet, if we scaled this out, then we would have a very large number of neighbor commands on Hub-1. DMVPN can scale to hundreds, even thousands of spokes, so we can see that specifying neighbors individually will be time-consuming, will lead to a very large configuration on the router and also introduces a greater chance for error.

We can mitigate this in a couple of ways. Firstly, we can add our peers into a peer-group, in which we can specify that they are all in the same AS and that the update source is the tunnel interface. This would greatly reduce the configuration on the router, but would still leave the first neighbour command being required. The second method is to reintroduce a level of dynamism into the configuration, and use the BGP listen range command, which is what we will do now.

We start by removing the static neighbour command for Spoke-1:

```
Hub-1(config-router)#no neigh 192.168.1.2
%BGP_SESSION-5-ADJCHANGE: neighbor 192.168.1.2 IPv4 Unicast topology
base removed from session  Neighbor deleted
%BGP-5-ADJCHANGE: neighbor 192.168.1.2 Down Neighbor deleted
Hub-1(config-router)#do sh run | sec router bgp
router bgp 100
 bgp router-id 1.1.1.1
 bgp log-neighbor-changes
 network 1.1.1.1 mask 255.255.255.255
 network 192.168.1.1 mask 255.255.255.255
Hub-1(config-router)#
```

Now we can create a listen range, which will permit any router within the 192.168.1.0/24 network to peer with us. These peers will become a member of the peer-group "DMVPNPeers":

```
Hub-1(config-router)#bgp listen range 192.168.1.0/24 peer-group
DMVPNPeers
```

Next we set up the peer-group, ensuring that the peers are part of AS 100, and that the update source is tunnel 0:

```
Hub-1(config-router)#neighbor DMVPNPeers peer-group
Hub-1(config-router)#neighbor DMVPNPeers remote-as 100
Hub-1(config-router)#neighbor DMVPNPeers update-source tun 0
%BGP-5-ADJCHANGE: neighbor *192.168.1.2 Up
Hub-1(config-router)#
```

Spoke-1 now peers with Hub-1 again. We can continue and add the BGP configuration to Spoke-2 and to Spoke-3:

```
Spoke-2(config)#router bgp 100
Spoke-2(config-router)#neigh 192.168.1.1 remote-as 100
Spoke-2(config-router)#neigh 192.168.1.1 update-source tun 0
Spoke-2(config-router)#neigh 192.168.1.1 ebgp-multihop 2
Spoke-2(config-router)#network 3.3.3.3 mask 255.255.255.255
%BGP-5-ADJCHANGE: neighbor 192.168.1.1 Up
Spoke-2(config-router)#

Spoke-3(config)#router bgp 100
Spoke-3(config-router)#neigh 192.168.1.1 remote-as 100
Spoke-3(config-router)#neigh 192.168.1.1 update-source tun 0
Spoke-3(config-router)#neigh 192.168.1.1 ebgp-multihop 2
%BGP-5-ADJCHANGE: neighbor 192.168.1.1 Up
Spoke-3(config-router)#network 4.4.4.4 mask 255.255.255.255
Spoke-3(config-router)#
```

After a few moments, Hub-1 has all the advertised routes:

```
Hub-1(config-router)#do sh ip route bgp | b Gate
Gateway of last resort is not set

      2.0.0.0/32 is subnetted, 1 subnets
B        2.2.2.2 [200/0] via 192.168.1.2, 00:10:49
      3.0.0.0/32 is subnetted, 1 subnets
B        3.3.3.3 [200/0] via 192.168.1.3, 00:00:40
      4.0.0.0/32 is subnetted, 1 subnets
B        4.4.4.4 [200/0] via 192.168.1.4, 00:07:14
Hub-1(config-router)#
```

These routes are not propagated through to the spokes, though:

```
Spoke-1(config-router)#do sh ip route bgp | b Gate
Gateway of last resort is 10.10.2.2 to network 0.0.0.0
```

```
         1.0.0.0/32 is subnetted, 1 subnets
B        1.1.1.1 [200/0] via 192.168.1.1, 00:11:07
Spoke-1(config-router)#
```

We can remedy this easily, however, by adding our peers as route-reflector clients. This will cause the peers to reform their adjacencies:

```
Hub-1(config-router)#neighbor DMVPNPeers route-reflector-client
Hub-1(config-router)#
%BGP-5-ADJCHANGE: neighbor *192.168.1.2 Down RR client config change
%BGP_SESSION-5-ADJCHANGE: neighbor *192.168.1.2 IPv4 Unicast topology
base removed from session  RR client config change
%BGP-5-ADJCHANGE: neighbor *192.168.1.3 Down RR client config change
%BGP_SESSION-5-ADJCHANGE: neighbor *192.168.1.3 IPv4 Unicast topology
base removed from session  RR client config change
%BGP-5-ADJCHANGE: neighbor *192.168.1.4 Down RR client config change
%BGP_SESSION-5-ADJCHANGE: neighbor *192.168.1.4 IPv4 Unicast topology
base removed from session  RR client config change
Hub-1(config-router)#
%BGP-5-ADJCHANGE: neighbor *192.168.1.3 Up
%BGP-5-ADJCHANGE: neighbor *192.168.1.4 Up
%BGP-5-ADJCHANGE: neighbor *192.168.1.2 Up
Hub-1(config-router)#
```

When our peers are back up again, they have the full routing table:

```
Spoke-1(config-router)#
%BGP-5-ADJCHANGE: neighbor 192.168.1.1 Up
Spoke-1(config-router)#do sh ip route bgp | b Gate
Gateway of last resort is 10.10.2.2 to network 0.0.0.0

         1.0.0.0/32 is subnetted, 1 subnets
B        1.1.1.1 [200/0] via 192.168.1.1, 00:00:03
         3.0.0.0/32 is subnetted, 1 subnets
B        3.3.3.3 [200/0] via 192.168.1.3, 00:00:03
         4.0.0.0/32 is subnetted, 1 subnets
B        4.4.4.4 [200/0] via 192.168.1.4, 00:00:03
Spoke-1(config-router)#
```

We can confirm that we have reachability:

```
Spoke-1(config-router)#do ping 3.3.3.3 so lo0
Type escape sequence to abort.
Sending 5, 100-byte ICMP Echos to 3.3.3.3:
Packet sent with a source address of 2.2.2.2
!!!!!
```

```
Success rate is 100 percent (5/5)
Spoke-1(config-router)#
```

We can also confirm that we are running Phase 3 by looking at the traceroute output and seeing that although the first transits the hub, the second one does not:

```
Spoke-2(config-router)#do sh ip route bgp | b Gate
Gateway of last resort is 10.10.3.2 to network 0.0.0.0

      1.0.0.0/32 is subnetted, 1 subnets
B        1.1.1.1 [200/0] via 192.168.1.1, 00:01:22
      2.0.0.0/32 is subnetted, 1 subnets
B        2.2.2.2 [200/0] via 192.168.1.2, 00:01:19
      4.0.0.0/32 is subnetted, 1 subnets
B        4.4.4.4 [200/0] via 192.168.1.4, 00:01:20
Spoke-2(config-router)#do trace 4.4.4.4 so lo0
Type escape sequence to abort.
Tracing the route to 4.4.4.4
VRF info: (vrf in name/id, vrf out name/id)
  1 192.168.1.1 108 msec 80 msec 48 msec
  2 192.168.1.4 136 msec 128 msec 116 msec
Spoke-2(config-router)#do trace 4.4.4.4 so lo0
Type escape sequence to abort.
Tracing the route to 4.4.4.4
VRF info: (vrf in name/id, vrf out name/id)
  1 192.168.1.4 24 msec 36 msec 72 msec
Spoke-2(config-router)#
```

Our final look at the different IGPs will be OSPF.

4.7 DMVPN and OSPF

OSPF works well with DMVPN, yet due to scalability, EIGRP is preferred. With OSPF, the design rules state that we should limit the number of routers to between 50 and 100 per area. With more modern routers (which have upgraded CPUs and more memory) this is not so much of a requirement, but is still something that we should be aware of. With this in mind, let us look at OSPF.

We start by removing our BGP configuration

```
Hub-1(config-router)#exit
Hub-1(config)#no router bgp 100

Spoke-1(config-router)#exit
```

```
Spoke-1(config)#no router bgp 100

Spoke-2(config-router)#exit
Spoke-2(config)#no router bgp 100

Spoke-3(config-router)#exit
Spoke-3(config)#no router bgp 100
```

With our BGP configuration removed, we can now set up OSPF. Before we jump in though, it is important to talk about the differences between OSPF in phase 2 DMVPN and that of phase 3, as OSPF has different requirements depending on which phase we are running.

Let's switch back to phase 2 for a moment to walk through the differences properly:

```
Hub-1(config)#int tun 0
Hub-1(config-if)#no ip nhrp redirect
Hub-1(config-if)#

Spoke-1(config)#int tun 0
Spoke-1(config-if)#no ip nhrp shortcut
Spoke-1(config-if)#

Spoke-2(config)#int tun 0
Spoke-2(config-if)#no ip nhrp shortcut
Spoke-2(config-if)#no ip nhrp redirect
Spoke-2(config-if)#

Spoke-3(config)#int tun 0
Spoke-3(config-if)#no ip nhrp shortcut
Spoke-3(config-if)#
```

Our tunnels are still available, so we have a phase 2 design to work from:

```
Hub-1(config-if)#do sh ip nhrp
192.168.1.2/32 via 192.168.1.2
   Tunnel0 created 02:01:09, expire 01:59:09
   Type: dynamic, Flags: unique registered
   NBMA address: 10.10.2.1
192.168.1.3/32 via 192.168.1.3
   Tunnel0 created 02:01:09, expire 01:59:09
   Type: dynamic, Flags: unique registered
   NBMA address: 10.10.3.1
192.168.1.4/32 via 192.168.1.4
   Tunnel0 created 02:00:27, expire 01:59:09
   Type: dynamic, Flags: unique registered
```

```
     NBMA address: 10.10.4.1
 Hub-1(config-if)#
```

With phase 2 we need to set our ospf network type as broadcast, and we should make sure that the hello-interval on our hub and on our spokes match:

```
 Hub-1(config-if)#ip ospf network broadcast
 Hub-1(config-if)#ip ospf hello-interval 30

 Spoke-1(config-if)#ip ospf network broadcast
 Spoke-1(config-if)#ip ospf hello-interval 30

 Spoke-2(config-if)#ip ospf network broadcast
 Spoke-2(config-if)#ip ospf hello-interval 30

 Spoke-3(config-if)#ip ospf network broadcast
 Spoke-3(config-if)#ip ospf hello-interval 30
```

We require the network type to be broadcast so that we can elect a DR. Each spoke should also have an OSPF priority of 0 to prevent it from becoming the DR.

```
 Spoke-1(config-if)#ip ospf priority 0
 Spoke-1(config-if)#

 Spoke-2(config-if)#ip ospf pri 0
 Spoke-2(config-if)#

 Spoke-3(config-if)#ip ospf pri 0
 Spoke-3(config-if)#
```

With our foundation in place we can reintroduce a routing protocol to our DMVPN network. The temptation here would be to use OSPF process 1, yet if we do that we will have a lot of issues. We are already using this to connect Hub-1 to IGW, and, as such, we are advertising our public interface, which will cause route recursion within our tunnel (which we discussed earlier). Therefore we will be using OSPF process 2. I am keeping the spokes to also using process 2 for ease, rather than necessity.

```
 Hub-1(config-if)#router ospf 2
 Hub-1(config-router)#netw 1.1.1.1 0.0.0.0 area 0
 Hub-1(config-router)#netw 192.168.1.1 0.0.0.0 area 0
 Hub-1(config-router)#router-id 192.168.1.1
 Hub-1(config-router)#end

 Spoke-1(config-if)#router ospf 2
 Spoke-1(config-router)#net 2.2.2.2 0.0.0.0 area 0
```

```
Spoke-1(config-router)#net 192.168.1.2 0.0.0.0 area 0
Spoke-1(config-router)#
%OSPF-5-ADJCHG: Process 2, Nbr 172.16.3.3 on Tunnel0 from LOADING to
FULL, Loading Done
Spoke-1(config-router)#end

Spoke-2(config-if)#router ospf 2
Spoke-2(config-router)#net 3.3.3.3 0.0.0.0 area 0
Spoke-2(config-router)#net 192.168.1.3 0.0.0.0 area 0
Spoke-2(config-router)#
%OSPF-5-ADJCHG: Process 2, Nbr 172.16.3.3 on Tunnel0 from LOADING to
FULL, Loading Done
Spoke-2(config-router)#

Spoke-3(config)#router ospf 2
Spoke-3(config-router)#net 4.4.4.4 0.0.0.0 area 0
Spoke-3(config-router)#net 192.168.1.4 0.0.0.0 area 0
Spoke-3(config-router)#
%OSPF-5-ADJCHG: Process 2, Nbr 172.16.3.3 on Tunnel0 from LOADING to
FULL, Loading Done
Spoke-3(config-router)#
```

We can see that our tunnels are up:

```
Hub-1#sh ip nhrp
192.168.1.2/32 via 192.168.1.2
   Tunnel0 created 02:31:30, expire 01:28:47
   Type: dynamic, Flags: unique registered
   NBMA address: 10.10.2.1
192.168.1.3/32 via 192.168.1.3
   Tunnel0 created 02:31:30, expire 01:28:47
   Type: dynamic, Flags: unique registered
   NBMA address: 10.10.3.1
192.168.1.4/32 via 192.168.1.4
   Tunnel0 created 02:30:48, expire 01:28:48
   Type: dynamic, Flags: unique registered
   NBMA address: 10.10.4.1
Hub-1#
```

Out OSPF neighborships are healthy:

```
Hub-1#sh ip ospf neigh

Neighbor ID    Pri   State           Dead Time   Address         Interface
2.2.2.2          0   FULL/DROTHER    00:01:55    192.168.1.2     Tunnel0
```

```
3.3.3.3            0    FULL/DROTHER    00:01:55    192.168.1.3    Tunnel0
4.4.4.4            0    FULL/DROTHER    00:01:55    192.168.1.4    Tunnel0
10.10.10.10        1    FULL/DR         00:00:33    10.10.1.2      Gi1/0
Hub-1#
```

We can also see that we have reachability:

```
Hub-1#sh ip route ospf 2 | b Gate
Gateway of last resort is not set

      2.0.0.0/32 is subnetted, 1 subnets
O        2.2.2.2 [110/1001] via 192.168.1.2, 00:06:48, Tunnel0
      3.0.0.0/32 is subnetted, 1 subnets
O        3.3.3.3 [110/1001] via 192.168.1.3, 00:06:35, Tunnel0
      4.0.0.0/32 is subnetted, 1 subnets
O        4.4.4.4 [110/1001] via 192.168.1.4, 00:05:06, Tunnel0
Hub-1#ping 4.4.4.4
Type escape sequence to abort.
Sending 5, 100-byte ICMP Echos to 4.4.4.4:
!!!!!
Success rate is 100 percent (5/5)
Hub-1#
```

If we turn our attention to the spokes, we can see that we can set up dynamic spoke-to-spoke tunnels:

```
Spoke-1#sh ip route ospf | b Gate
Gateway of last resort is 10.10.2.2 to network 0.0.0.0

      1.0.0.0/32 is subnetted, 1 subnets
O        1.1.1.1 [110/1001] via 192.168.1.1, 00:07:33, Tunnel0
      3.0.0.0/32 is subnetted, 1 subnets
O        3.3.3.3 [110/1001] via 192.168.1.3, 00:07:10, Tunnel0
      4.0.0.0/32 is subnetted, 1 subnets
O        4.4.4.4 [110/1001] via 192.168.1.4, 00:05:40, Tunnel0
Spoke-1#trace 4.4.4.4 num
Type escape sequence to abort.
Tracing the route to 4.4.4.4
VRF info: (vrf in name/id, vrf out name/id)
  1 192.168.1.1 84 msec 44 msec 32 msec
  2 192.168.1.4 52 msec 44 msec 40 msec
Spoke-1#trace 4.4.4.4 num
Type escape sequence to abort.
Tracing the route to 4.4.4.4
VRF info: (vrf in name/id, vrf out name/id)
  1 192.168.1.4 32 msec 72 msec 40 msec
```

```
Spoke-1#sh ip nhrp
192.168.1.1/32 via 192.168.1.1
   Tunnel0 created 02:35:56, never expire
   Type: static, Flags: used
   NBMA address: 10.10.1.1
192.168.1.4/32 via 192.168.1.4
   Tunnel0 created 00:00:45, expire 01:59:15
   Type: dynamic, Flags: router
   NBMA address: 10.10.4.1
Spoke-1#
```

If you find that the OSPF adjacencies are not forming, then try shutting the tunnels on the spokes down, waiting for the notification that the interface is down, and then bringing the tunnels back up again.

All works well with our OSPF network running over phase 2 DMVPN.

With phase 3 the OSPF network type needs to be point-to-multipoint, but unlike phase 2 we do not need to change any priorities.

```
Hub-1(config)#int tun 0
Hub-1(config-if)#ip ospf network point-to-multipoint
Hub-1(config-if)#no ip ospf priority
Hub-1(config-if)#ip nhrp redirect
Hub-1(config-if)#

Spoke-1(config)#int tun 0
Spoke-1(config-if)#ip ospf network point-to-multipoint
Spoke-1(config-if)#no ip ospf priority
Spoke-1(config-if)#ip nhrp shortcut
Spoke-1(config-if)#

Spoke-2(config-router)#int tun 0
Spoke-2(config-if)#ip ospf network point-to-multipoint
Spoke-2(config-if)#no ip ospf priority
Spoke-2(config-if)#ip nhrp shortcut
Spoke-2(config-if)#

Spoke-3(config-router)#int tun 0
Spoke-3(config-if)#ip ospf network point-to-multipoint
Spoke-3(config-if)#no ip ospf priority
Spoke-3(config-if)#ip nhrp shortcut
Spoke-3(config-if)#
```

Now we can see that Phase 3 is working again:

```
Spoke-1(config-if)#do trace 4.4.4.4
Type escape sequence to abort.
Tracing the route to 4.4.4.4
VRF info: (vrf in name/id, vrf out name/id)
  1 192.168.1.1 20 msec 40 msec 16 msec
  2 192.168.1.4 48 msec 72 msec 16 msec
Spoke-1(config-if)#do trace 4.4.4.4
Type escape sequence to abort.
Tracing the route to 4.4.4.4
VRF info: (vrf in name/id, vrf out name/id)
  1 192.168.1.4 16 msec 20 msec 20 msec
Spoke-1(config-if)#do sh ip nhrp 4.4.4.4
4.4.4.4/32 via 192.168.1.4
    Tunnel0 created 00:00:46, expire 01:59:13
    Type: dynamic, Flags: router used
    NBMA address: 10.10.4.1
Spoke-1(config-if)#
```

We can also see that we do not have any "DROTHER" routers:

```
Hub-1(config-if)#do sh ip ospf neigh

Neighbor ID     Pri   State           Dead Time   Address        Int
4.4.4.4           0   FULL/  -        00:01:52    192.168.1.4    Tun0
3.3.3.3           0   FULL/  -        00:01:54    192.168.1.3    Tun0
2.2.2.2           0   FULL/  -        00:01:53    192.168.1.2    Tun0
10.10.10.10       1   FULL/DR         00:00:37    10.10.1.2      Gi1/0
Hub-1(config-if)#
```

Although OSPF has a couple of more "gotchas" than EIGRP, it is still relatively easy to set up.

Now that we have covered all the IGPs and DMVPN (apart from IS-IS, which does not work with DMVPN), let us turn our attention to protecting DMVPN.

4.8 Securing DMVPN

There are a couple of ways we can secure DMVPN. The first is through an authentication string, the second uses IPSec.

NHRP Authentication

We can specify an NHRP authentication string, which can be eight characters or less:

```
Hub-1(config-if)#ip nhrp authentication 802101.com
% Authentication string exceeds 8 character maximum
Hub-1(config-if)#ip nhrp authentication 802101
Hub-1(config-if)#
```

Setting this now will not cause our spokes to immediately cease working though; in fact we can still send and receive NHRP resolution queries without specifying the same authentication on the spoke:

```
Spoke-1(config-if)#do sh ip nhrp 4.4.4.4
4.4.4.4/32 via 192.168.1.4
   Tunnel0 created 00:00:46, expire 01:59:13
   Type: dynamic, Flags: router used
   NBMA address: 10.10.4.1
Spoke-1(config-if)#do sh ip nhrp
4.4.4.4/32 via 192.168.1.4
   Tunnel0 created 00:13:48, expire 01:46:11
   Type: dynamic, Flags: router
   NBMA address: 10.10.4.1
192.168.1.1/32 via 192.168.1.1
   Tunnel0 created 03:12:35, never expire
   Type: static, Flags: used
   NBMA address: 10.10.1.1
192.168.1.4/32 via 192.168.1.4
   Tunnel0 created 00:37:23, expire 01:22:36
   Type: dynamic, Flags: router
   NBMA address: 10.10.4.1
Spoke-1(config-if)#do ping 3.3.3.3
Type escape sequence to abort.
Sending 5, 100-byte ICMP Echos to 3.3.3.3
!!!!!
Success rate is 100 percent (5/5)
Spoke-1(config-if)#do sh ip nhrp 3.3.3.3
3.3.3.3/32 via 192.168.1.3
   Tunnel0 created 00:01:26, expire 01:58:33
   Type: dynamic, Flags: router
   NBMA address: 10.10.3.1
Spoke-1(config-if)#
```

Even if we shut and then no shut the tunnel interface on Spoke-1, we can still have a perfectly working tunnel, despite the authentication mismatch:

```
Spoke-1(config-if)#shut
Spoke-1(config-if)# '
%OSPF-5-ADJCHG: Process 2, Nbr 172.16.3.3 on Tunnel0 from FULL to
DOWN, Neighbor Down: Interface down or detached
```

```
Spoke-1(config-if)#
%LINK-5-CHANGED: Interface Tunnel0, changed state to administratively down
%LINEPROTO-5-UPDOWN: Line protocol on Interface Tunnel0, changed state to down
Spoke-1(config-if)#
Spoke-1(config-if)#no shut
Spoke-1(config-if)#
%LINK-3-UPDOWN: Interface Tunnel0, changed state to up
%LINEPROTO-5-UPDOWN: Line protocol on Interface Tunnel0, changed state to up
%OSPF-5-ADJCHG: Process 2, Nbr 172.16.3.3 on Tunnel0 from LOADING to FULL, Loading Done
Spoke-1(config-if)#
Spoke-1(config-if)#do sh ip nhrp
192.168.1.1/32 via 192.168.1.1
   Tunnel0 created 00:00:08, never expire
   Type: static, Flags: used
   NBMA address: 10.10.1.1
Spoke-1(config-if)#do sh ip route ospf | b Gate
Gateway of last resort is 10.10.2.2 to network 0.0.0.0

      1.0.0.0/32 is subnetted, 1 subnets
O        1.1.1.1 [110/1001] via 192.168.1.1, 00:00:16, Tun0
      3.0.0.0/32 is subnetted, 1 subnets
O        3.3.3.3 [110/2001] via 192.168.1.1, 00:00:16, Tun0
      4.0.0.0/32 is subnetted, 1 subnets
O        4.4.4.4 [110/2001] via 192.168.1.1, 00:00:16, Tun0
      192.168.1.0/24 is variably subnetted, 5 subnets, 2 masks
O        192.168.1.1/32 [110/1000] via 192.168.1.1, 00:00:16, Tun0
O        192.168.1.3/32 [110/2000] via 192.168.1.1, 00:00:16, Tun0
O        192.168.1.4/32 [110/2000] via 192.168.1.1, 00:00:16, Tun0
Spoke-1(config-if)#do trace 4.4.4.4
Type escape sequence to abort.
Tracing the route to 4.4.4.4
VRF info: (vrf in name/id, vrf out name/id)
  1 192.168.1.1 28 msec 76 msec 44 msec
  2 192.168.1.4 56 msec 72 msec 56 msec
Spoke-1(config-if)#do trace 4.4.4.4
Type escape sequence to abort.
Tracing the route to 4.4.4.4
VRF info: (vrf in name/id, vrf out name/id)
  1 192.168.1.4 32 msec 24 msec 48 msec
Spoke-1(config-if)#do sh run int tun 0 | i authen
Spoke-1(config-if)#
```

So even without the authentication on our spoke routers, all would appear to work well. We can add the authentication string though

```
Spoke-1(config-if)#ip nhrp authentication 802101
Spoke-1(config-if)#

Spoke-2(config-if)#ip nhrp authentication 802101
Spoke-2(config-if)#

Spoke-3(config-if)#ip nhrp authentication 802101
Spoke-3(config-if)#
```

There are a couple of issues with using the authentication string; it is not encrypted and from what we have seen so far, that a router without it can function as well as a router with it (even though the documentation states that all must share the same authentication string). There is a much more functional and secure way to protect our DMVPN network, and that is through IPSec. This is not to say that NHRP authentication does not work though – it did not work as advertised here, but we will see that it does work later on.

Tunnel protection using IPSec

We looked at using IPSec back in section 3.5, when we used it to secure our GRE tunnels. Now that our network has evolved to a phase 3 DMVPN infrastructure, we can use IPSec again to serve the same purposes. Using IPSec with DMVPN is very similar to how we implemented it earlier, with only minor, but important, changes.

We start with the ISAKMP configuration, creating our policy, which includes the encryption method, the authentication method, and the key, which is mapped to any IP address (0.0.0.0). Because we created an ISAKMP policy earlier on, our new one will be number 2:

```
Hub-1(config)#crypto isakmp policy 2
Hub-1(config-isakmp)#encryption 3des
Hub-1(config-isakmp)#authentication pre-share
Hub-1(config-isakmp)#group 2
Hub-1(config-isakmp)#exit
Hub-1(config)#crypto isakmp key 802-DMVPN address 0.0.0.0
Hub-1(config)#
```

Next we set up the IPSec configuration; first creating a transform set, which is given a name (802101-transform), and within it we specify the encryption and hashing settings. Within this transform set we specify a mode (transport).

```
Hub-1(config)#crypto ipsec transform-set 802-Trans esp-3des esp-sha-
hmac
Hub-1(cfg-crypto-trans)#mode ?
  transport  transport (payload encapsulation) mode
  tunnel     tunnel (datagram encapsulation) mode

Hub-1(cfg-crypto-trans)#mode transport
Hub-1(cfg-crypto-trans)#exit
```

The mode is very important and must be set to "transport" if we are behind a NAT device (which we will look at later on), but what does the mode signify? We spoke, briefly, about the mode back in section 3.5, when we created the transform set, but did not look at the options. Above we can see that we have two options for "mode"; transport and tunnel. Let's discuss these now.

Transport vs. Tunnel mode

Tunnel mode is the default mode with IOS. When we use tunnel mode IPSec protects the entire original IP packet. The original packet has an ESP header and ESP trailer added to it, along with a new IP header, and an ESP Auth block.

We use tunnel mode between two routers, or two firewalls. It will carry the data we define, in an access-list, from one side to another. This is the method we will use when we set up a site-to-site VPN in section 6, later on.

In tunnel mode, an ESP header is placed before the original IP header. A new IP header is placed at the beginning of the packet, and has an IP protocol ID of 50. If you look back at capture 3, then you can see the protocol within the IPv4 details.

Transport mode is used for end-to-end communication. Transport mode protects the payload, either using AH or ESP. The IPSec headers and trailer encapsulate the payload. The original IP header remains the same, apart from the protocol field is changed to match the type (ESP or AH). The original value is kept in the IPSec trailer, ready to be restored to the original packet, when it is decrypted.

Here we come to why transport mode is required here; we use it when another protocol, such as GRE or L2TP has already encapsulated the original packet. In our case GRE handles the encapsulation, whilst IPSec handles the encryption.

The packets created by tunnel mode differ to transport mode, in that with transport mode the original IP header is moved to the start of the packet. Because of this, transport mode does not provide the same level of protection, or encryption, as tunnel mode. The upshot, though, for transport mode is that it works well with NAT traversal, which we will look at in section 4.12.

A comparison of the end packets, in both tunnel and transport mode, is shown below:

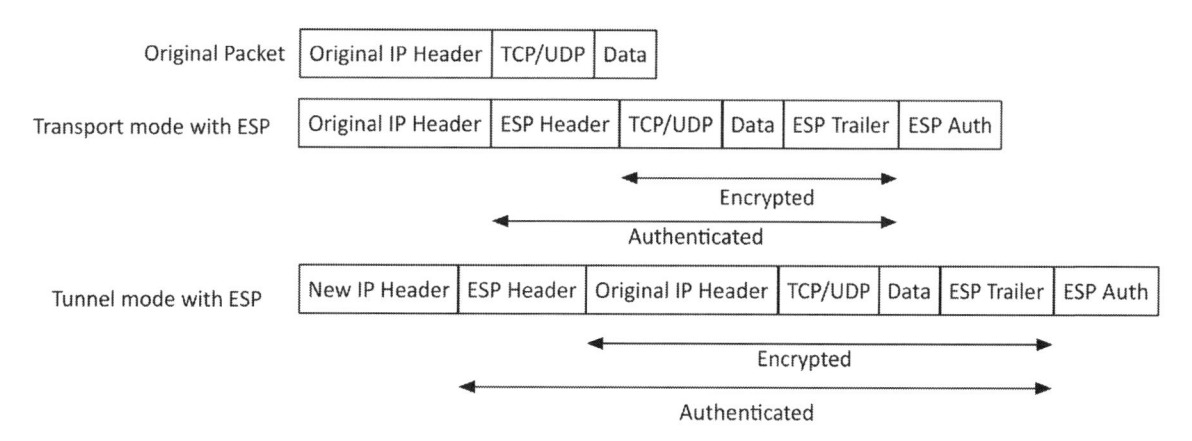

Original Packet	Original IP Header	TCP/UDP	Data		
Transport mode with ESP	Original IP Header	ESP Header	TCP/UDP	Data	ESP Trailer	ESP Auth
Tunnel mode with ESP	New IP Header	ESP Header	Original IP Header	TCP/UDP	Data	ESP Trailer	ESP Auth

We then move on to creating an IPSec profile. This profile references the transform set we created a moment ago:

```
Hub-1(config)#crypto ipsec profile DMVPN-Profile
Hub-1(ipsec-profile)#set transform-set 802-Trans
Hub-1(ipsec-profile)#exit
```

The final step is to associate all of this to our DMVPN tunnel using the "tunnel protection" command:

```
Hub-1(config)#int tun 0
Hub-1(config-if)#tunnel protection ipsec profile DMVPN-Profile
```

We should start to see some warnings on the console now:

```
Hub-1(config-if)#
%CRYPTO-4-RECVD_PKT_NOT_IPSEC: Rec'd packet not an IPSEC packet. (ip)
vrf/dest_addr= /10.10.1.1, src_addr= 10.10.3.1, prot= 47
Hub-1(config-if)#
%CRYPTO-4-RECVD_PKT_NOT_IPSEC: Rec'd packet not an IPSEC packet. (ip)
vrf/dest_addr= /10.10.1.1, src_addr= 10.10.2.1, prot= 47
Hub-1(config-if)#
%OSPF-5-ADJCHG: Process 2, Nbr 3.3.3.3 on Tunnel0 from FULL to DOWN,
Neighbor Down: Dead timer expired
Hub-1(config-if)#
```

Unlike the nhrp authentication string, a mismatch in the tunnel protection will be immediately noticeable. So let's put the same configuration on to our spokes. This is one of those times when cutting and pasting from notepad works very well, as there is no variation in the commands.

```
Spoke-1(config)#crypto isakmp policy 2
Spoke-1(config-isakmp)#encr 3des
Spoke-1(config-isakmp)#auth pre-share
Spoke-1(config-isakmp)#group 2
Spoke-1(config-isakmp)#exit
Spoke-1(config)#crypto isakmp key 802-DMVPN address 0.0.0.0
Spoke-1(config)#crypto ipsec transform-set 802-Trans esp-3des esp-sha-hmac
Spoke-1(cfg-crypto-trans)#mode transport
Spoke-1(cfg-crypto-trans)#exit
Spoke-1(config)#crypto ipsec profile DMVPN-Profile
Spoke-1(ipsec-profile)#set transform-set 802-Trans
Spoke-1(ipsec-profile)#exit
Spoke-1(config)#int tun 0
Spoke-1(config-if)#tunnel protection ipsec profile DMVPN-Profile
Spoke-1(config-if)#
%CRYPTO-6-ISAKMP_ON_OFF: ISAKMP is ON
Spoke-1(config-if)#

Spoke-2(config)#crypto isakmp policy 2
Spoke-2(config-isakmp)#encr 3des
Spoke-2(config-isakmp)#auth pre-share
Spoke-2(config-isakmp)#group 2
Spoke-2(config-isakmp)#exit
Spoke-2(config)#crypto isakmp key 802-DMVPN address 0.0.0.0
Spoke-2(config)#crypto ipsec transform-set 802-Trans esp-3des esp-sha-hmac
Spoke-2(cfg-crypto-trans)#mode transport
Spoke-2(cfg-crypto-trans)#exit
Spoke-2(config)#crypto ipsec profile DMVPN-Profile
Spoke-2(ipsec-profile)#set transform-set 802-Trans
Spoke-2(ipsec-profile)#exit
Spoke-2(config)#int tun 0
Spoke-2(config-if)#tunnel protection ipsec profile DMVPN-Profile
Spoke-2(config-if)#
%CRYPTO-6-ISAKMP_ON_OFF: ISAKMP is ON
Spoke-2(config-if)#
%OSPF-5-ADJCHG: Process 2, Nbr 172.16.3.3 on Tunnel0 from LOADING to FULL, Loading Done
Spoke-2(config-if)#

Spoke-3(config)#crypto isakmp policy 2
```

```
Spoke-3(config-isakmp)#encr 3des
Spoke-3(config-isakmp)#auth pre-share
Spoke-3(config-isakmp)#group 2
Spoke-3(config-isakmp)#exit
Spoke-3(config)#crypto isakmp key 802-DMVPN address 0.0.0.0
Spoke-3(config)#crypto ipsec transform-set 802-Trans esp-3des esp-sha-hmac
Spoke-3(cfg-crypto-trans)#mode transport
Spoke-3(cfg-crypto-trans)#exit
Spoke-3(config)#crypto ipsec profile DMVPN-Profile
Spoke-3(ipsec-profile)#set transform-set 802-Trans
Spoke-3(ipsec-profile)#exit
Spoke-3(config)#int tun 0
Spoke-3(config-if)#tunnel protection ipsec profile DMVPN-Profile
Spoke-3(config-if)#
%OSPF-5-ADJCHG: Process 2, Nbr 172.16.3.3 on Tunnel0 from LOADING to
FULL, Loading Done
Spoke-3(config-if)#
```

At this stage the spokes should start talking back to the Hub router.

```
Hub-1(config-if)#
%OSPF-5-ADJCHG: Process 2, Nbr 3.3.3.3 on Tunnel0 from LOADING to
FULL, Loading Done
Hub-1(config-if)#
%OSPF-5-ADJCHG: Process 2, Nbr 4.4.4.4 on Tunnel0 from LOADING to
FULL, Loading Done
Hub-1(config-if)#do sh ip ospf neigh

Neighbor ID     Pri   State       Dead Time   Address       Int
3.3.3.3           0   FULL/   -   00:01:54    192.168.1.3   Tun0
2.2.2.2           0   INIT/   -   00:01:52    192.168.1.2   Tun0
4.4.4.4           0   FULL/   -   00:01:42    192.168.1.4   Tun0
10.10.10.10       1   FULL/BDR    00:00:35    10.10.1.2     Gi1/0
Hub-1(config-if)#
```

Here we can see though that Spoke-1 is not forming an OSPF adjacency with the hub router (hopefully yours should be all ok). We start by checking NHRP:

```
Hub-1(config-if)#do sh ip nhrp
192.168.1.3/32 via 192.168.1.3
   Tunnel0 created 00:30:33, expire 01:47:56
   Type: dynamic, Flags: unique registered
   NBMA address: 10.10.3.1
192.168.1.4/32 via 192.168.1.4
   Tunnel0 created 00:29:10, expire 01:48:03
   Type: dynamic, Flags: unique registered
```

```
    NBMA address: 10.10.4.1
Hub-1(config-if)#
```

We can see that Spoke-1 has not registered with Hub-1. Although you may not be experiencing this issue, it's worthwhile us looking at it. We will set up some debugging on Hub-1. But just for Spoke-1, so, first of all, we need to shut down the tunnel interface on Spoke-1:

```
Spoke-1(config)#int tun 0
Spoke-1(config-if)#shut
Spoke-1(config-if)#
%CRYPTO-6-ISAKMP_ON_OFF: ISAKMP is OFF
Spoke-1(config-if)#
%LINK-5-CHANGED: Interface Tunnel0, changed state to administratively down
%LINEPROTO-5-UPDOWN: Line protocol on Interface Tunnel0, changed state to down
Spoke-1(config-if)#
```

Then we can set up very specific debugging on Hub-1, using the very handy "debug condition":

```
Hub-1#debug condition ip 192.168.1.2
Condition 1 set
Hub-1#debug nhrp
NHRP protocol debugging is on
Hub-1#
```

Now we have a very focused debug session, and can turn back on the tunnel interface on Spoke-1:

```
Spoke-1(config-if)#no shut
Spoke-1(config-if)#
```

The output has been limited to a few lines, so, once you have enough logs shown to make a diagnosis, remember to turn off the debugging:

```
NHRP: NHRP could not map 192.168.1.2 to NBMA, cache entry not found
NHRP: Send Resolution Request via Tunnel0 vrf 0, packet size: 86
      src: 192.168.1.1, dst: 192.168.1.2
NHRP: Encapsulation failed for destination 192.168.1.2 out Tunnel0
Hub-1#un all
All possible debugging has been turned off
Hub-1#
```

The clue here is that when Hub-1 tries to send a resolution request to Spoke-1, it fails to encapsulate it correctly – or more correctly, the encapsulation fails. It would be incorrect to read this as it failing on Hub-1, as we use the same configuration on the other spokes and they are fine.

```
Hub-1#sh ip nhrp 192.168.1.2
192.168.1.2/32
   Tunnel0 created 00:02:41, expire 00:00:23
   Type: incomplete, Flags: negative
   Cache hits: 7
Hub-1#
```

This turned out to be one of those misleading messages, but actually served a purpose. I won't go through all the ISAKMP and IPSec debugs that I looked at, as it turns out they were irrelevant. I ended up comparing the IPsec and ISAKMP configurations a couple of times, and finding no differences, compared the tunnel configuration of Spoke-1 to that of Spoke-2 and Spoke-3:

```
Spoke-1#sh run int tun 0 | b interf
interface Tunnel0
 ip address 192.168.1.2 255.255.255.0
 no ip redirects
 ip nhrp map 192.168.1.1 10.10.1.1
 ip nhrp map multicast 10.10.1.1
 ip nhrp network-id 1
 ip nhrp nhs 192.168.1.1
 ip nhrp shortcut
 ip ospf network point-to-multipoint
 tunnel source GigabitEthernet1/0
 tunnel mode gre multipoint
 tunnel protection ipsec profile DMVPN-Profile
end

Spoke-1#

Spoke-2#sh run int tun 0 | b interf
interface Tunnel0
 ip address 192.168.1.3 255.255.255.0
 no ip redirects
 ip nhrp authentication 802101
 ip nhrp map 192.168.1.1 10.10.1.1
 ip nhrp map multicast 10.10.1.1
 ip nhrp network-id 1
 ip nhrp nhs 192.168.1.1
```

```
  ip nhrp shortcut
  ip ospf network point-to-multipoint
  tunnel source GigabitEthernet1/0
  tunnel mode gre multipoint
  tunnel protection ipsec profile DMVPN-Profile
end

Spoke-2#
```

It turns out that Spoke-1 was missing the NHRP authentication command that was in place on the other spokes, most likely due to not saving the configuration from earlier. Once this was added, everything worked well again:

```
Spoke-1(config)#int tun 0
Spoke-1(config-if)#shut
Spoke-1(config-if)#ip nhrp authentication 802101
Spoke-1(config-if)#no shut
Spoke-1(config-if)#
%CRYPTO-6-ISAKMP_ON_OFF: ISAKMP is ON
Spoke-1(config-if)#
%LINK-3-UPDOWN: Interface Tunnel0, changed state to up
Spoke-1(config-if)#
%LINEPROTO-5-UPDOWN: Line protocol on Interface Tunnel0, changed state
to up
Spoke-1(config-if)#
%OSPF-5-ADJCHG: Process 2, Nbr 172.16.3.3 on Tunnel0 from LOADING to
FULL, Loading Done
Spoke-1(config-if)#end
Spoke-1#

Hub-1#sh ip nhrp 192.168.1.2
192.168.1.2/32 via 192.168.1.2
    Tunnel0 created 00:10:10, expire 01:49:50
    Type: dynamic, Flags: unique registered
    NBMA address: 10.10.2.1
Hub-1#sh ip ospf neigh

Neighbor ID     Pri   State        Dead Time   Address       Int
2.2.2.2           0   FULL/  -     00:01:49    192.168.1.2   Tun0
3.3.3.3           0   FULL/  -     00:01:39    192.168.1.3   Tun0
4.4.4.4           0   FULL/  -     00:01:48    192.168.1.4   Tun0
10.10.10.10       1   FULL/BDR     00:00:21    10.10.1.2     Gi1/0
Hub-1#
```

So here we can see a number of things; check the obvious, save your work, and that NHRP authentication does work and it works very well.

4.9 Tweaking DMVPN

We have a number of good reasons for tweaking DMVPN, these can be to enhance packet flow, provide better metric information for the higher-level protocols to make their routing decisions, or to reduce the CPU load on the router for NHRP. We will look at these now.

Packet fragmentation

When sending packets over any medium, we are bound to certain constraints, namely how much we can send before the data gets split into multiple packets. This is determined by the MTU – the Maximum Transfer Unit. Ethernet has an MTU of 1500 bytes. Once we start, as we have done so far, to encapsulate and protect our packets through GRE and IPSec we start to add bytes to the packets. GRE adds an additional 24 bytes (20 bytes IP header and 4 byte GRE header), which means that to ensure our packets don't get fragmented, we should be sending packets no larger than 1476 bytes (the effective tunnel size). If we add on IPSec then we stand to lose anything from 44 bytes to 73 bytes, depending on our encryption method, which means that our packet size (without fragmentation) needs to be in the region of 1432 to 1403.

We can use the interface command "ip mtu 1400" to reduce the chances of packet fragmentation.

```
Hub-1(config)#int tun 0
Hub-1(config-if)#ip mtu 1400
Hub-1(config-if)#

Spoke-1(config)#int tun 0
Spoke-1(config-if)#ip mtu 1400
Spoke-1(config-if)#

Spoke-2(config)#int tun 0
Spoke-2(config-if)#ip mtu 1400
Spoke-2(config-if)#

Spoke-3(config)#int tun 0
Spoke-3(config-if)#ip mtu 1400
Spoke-3(config-if)#
```

We can further control this by changing the TCP MSS (Maximum Segment Size), which defines the amount of data that a host is willing to accept in a single datagram, but does not count the TCP or IP headers. Generally, this is set to between 20 to 40 bytes lower than the MTU. Here we set the MSS to 40 bytes lower than the MTU:

```
Hub-1(config-if)#ip tcp adjust-mss 1360
Hub-1(config-if)#

Spoke-1(config-if)#ip tcp adjust-mss 1360
Spoke-1(config-if)#

Spoke-2(config-if)#ip tcp adjust-mss 1360
Spoke-2(config-if)#

Spoke-3(config-if)#ip tcp adjust-mss 1360
Spoke-3(config-if)#
```

Both the MTU and MSS settings should match on the hubs and the spokes in the network.

Interoperability with routing protocols

Because DMVPN relies on a routing protocol overlay, the metrics on the tunnel interface can, depending on the routing protocol, influence the paths taken on the network. Bandwidth and delay are two of these examples. By default, EIGRP will use 50% of the bandwidth, so it can, in effect, "starve" itself if the bandwidth is too small. Similarly delay is used in EIGRP calculations, by default for Ethernet this 1000us (tens of microseconds).

We can set the bandwidth (in kilobits) and delay using the commands below. Here we set the bandwidth to 10000 kilobits, or 100 megabytes, and we set the delay of 1000:

```
Hub-1(config-if)#bandwidth 100000
Hub-1(config-if)#delay 1000
Hub-1(config-if)#
```

NHRP tweaks

What can we do to tweak NHRP operations? Well, quite a lot really.

NHRP timers:

We can control how long a spoke sends registration messages to the next-hop server. By default these are sent every 1/3rd of its configured holdtime.

The holdtime can be set, in this case to 600 seconds, using the command:

```
Hub-1(config-if)#ip nhrp holdtime 600
```

We can change the registration timer (which is also in seconds), so that it is separate from the holdtime, using the command below.

```
Hub-1(config-if)#ip nhrp registration timeout 100
```

NHRP Caching:

We can set a router to be in "server-only" mode. If this is set the router cannot initiate NHRP resolution requests to establish NHRP shortcuts, but can only respond to NHRP resolution requests. We can supplement this further by specifying "non-caching", and if this is set then NHRP does not store the mapping information. The tunnel command for this is "ip nhrp server-only non-caching".

Controlling NHRP triggers:

We can control to whom and by what will trigger NHRP. We can do this on a per-destination basis, or by the number of packets that must be sent, or by a given traffic threshold.

Triggering NHRP on per-Destination basis:

Triggering NHRP on a per-destination is done through an access-list, and is called using the tunnel command "ip nhrp interest 101" (where 101 is the access list we have created to permit or deny our spokes).

Triggering NHRP on a packet count basis:

Using the tunnel interface command "ip nhrp use 5", if in the first minute 5 packets are sent to first destination and 5 are sent to a second destination then a single NHRP request is generated for the second destination.

Triggering NHRP based in traffic thresholds:

We can trigger NHRP based on traffic thresholds. This requires BGP and CEF, and will initiate SVCs (our dynamic spoke-to-spoke tunnels) once a configured traffic rate is reached. Imagine we are happy with traffic transiting the hub, but are bound to certain bandwidth costs. In times of high/bursting traffic, we can set up a temporary spoke-to-spoke tunnel and then drop the tunnel when the traffic falls below the threshold.

If the network is either CEF switched, or dCEF switched, then we need to use the global configuration command "ip cef accounting non-recursive" before we can implement this trigger.

Then we can set NHRP to trigger once the traffic reaches 100kbps, and to tear down the SVC if the traffic drops to 5kbps, using the command "ip nhrp trigger-svc 100 5".

This can also be used this with the per-destination method discussed previously.

Controlling the NHRP packet rate:

We can control the number of packets sent by NHRP. This can be used to protect the router from runaway NHRP processes (such as worms doing IP address scanning), using the command "ip nhrp max-send 10 every 10".

With this command we specify that a maximum of 10 NHRP packets can be sent from the interface every 10 seconds (which is twice the default rate).

Suppressing forward and reverse record options:

When we looked at the contents of the NHRP packet we saw that NHRP keeps route records in the request and reply packets, these were the Forward Transit NHS Record Extension and the Reverse Transit NHS Record Extension. These are used to detect link layer filtering and provide loop detection. The Route record contains the network and link layer addresses of all intermediate NHS between the source and destination (forward) and between the destination and the source (reverse). These are included by default. To turn off we use the command "no ip nhrp record".

Specifying the NHRP Responder IP Address

Finally we can specify which physical interface will be responding to NHRP requests. We can specify that the responder address will be the IP address of the loopback interface, using the command "ip nhrp responder loopback 0". When we do this, the NHS will put the primary IP address of the loopback interface in the NHRP reply packet. This can also be used for loop prevention, as if the reply contains the IP address of that server an error will be generated, the type of which is "NHRP Loop Detected", and the packet will be discarded.

We are not done with DMVPN yet, there is so much more we can do with it. We can implement QoS – which is a tweak, but deserves its own section, we can throw IPv6 traffic through it, we can hide behind a NAT device with no issues, and segregate traffic using VRFs. So let's look at those now.

4.10 DMVPN and QoS

When I started planning this series of books, I had a bit of a conundrum. Originally I planned to release the MPLS volume first, but this required a good understanding of BGP. So it made sense to write the BGP volume first, in order to lay the foundation, ready for the MPLS volume.

Here, we have the same scenario. Discussing DMVPN and QoS requires the reader to have an understanding of both, yet we have only discussed DMVPN. For this reason the explanation of QoS will be kept to a minimum, whilst the focus will be on how to implement QoS with DMVPN.

With QoS and DMVPN we can implement QoS on a per-tunnel basis. This is done via an NHRP group, and is set on the spoke (rather than the hub). The NHRP group is used to signal, to the hub, a spokes' group identity. The hub uses this information to place different QoS markings on different spokes, depending in their group membership.

We start by placing Spoke-1 and Spoke-2 into different nhrp groups:

```
Spoke-1(config)#int tun 0
Spoke-1(config-if)#ip nhrp group Spoke1
Spoke-1(config-if)#

Spoke-2(config)#int tun 0
Spoke-2(config-if)#ip nhrp group Spoke2
Spoke-2(config-if)#
```

On Hub-1 we create a couple of QoS policies. These are nothing fancy. We simply attach different DSCP settings (AF13 and AF11 respectively) to the different spokes:

```
Hub-1(config)#policy-map Spoke-1-QoS
Hub-1(config-pmap)#class class-default
Hub-1(config-pmap-c)#set dscp af13
Hub-1(config-pmap-c)#exit
Hub-1(config-pmap)#exit
Hub-1(config)#policy-map Spoke-2-QoS
Hub-1(config-pmap)#class class-default
Hub-1(config-pmap-c)#set dscp af11
Hub-1(config-pmap-c)#exit
Hub-1(config-pmap)#exit
```

Let's confirm our settings:

```
Hub-1(config)#do sh policy-map
  Policy Map Spoke-2-QoS
    Class class-default
      set dscp af11

  Policy Map Spoke-1-QoS
    Class class-default
      set dscp af13

Hub-1(config)#
```

We then map these policies, to the groups that we should be sent by the spokes.

```
Hub-1(config)#int tun 0
Hub-1(config-if)#ip nhrp map group Spoke1 service-policy output Spoke-1-QoS
Hub-1(config-if)#ip nhrp map group Spoke2 service-policy output Spoke-2-QoS
Hub-1(config-if)#end
```

If we clear NHRP (clear ip nhrp) we can see that Hub-1 sees the groups sent by Spoke-1 and Spoke-2:

```
Hub-1#sh ip nhrp
192.168.1.2/32 via 192.168.1.2
   Tunnel0 created 00:02:23, expire 01:57:36
   Type: dynamic, Flags: unique registered
   NBMA address: 10.10.2.1
   Group: Spoke1
```

```
  192.168.1.3/32 via 192.168.1.3
     Tunnel0 created 00:02:23, expire 01:57:36
     Type: dynamic, Flags: unique registered
     NBMA address: 10.10.3.1
     Group: Spoke2
  192.168.1.4/32 via 192.168.1.4
     Tunnel0 created 00:00:03, expire 01:59:56
     Type: dynamic, Flags: unique registered used
     NBMA address: 10.10.4.1
  Hub-1#
```

We can also sniff the traffic between Hub-1 and IGW, whilst sending ping packets to Spoke-1 and Spoke-2:

```
Hub-1#ping 192.168.1.2 rep 10
Type escape sequence to abort.
Sending 10, 100-byte ICMP Echos to 192.168.1.2:
!!!!!!!!!!
Success rate is 100 percent (10/10)
Hub-1#ping 192.168.1.3 rep 10
Type escape sequence to abort.
Sending 10, 100-byte ICMP Echos to 192.168.1.3:
!!!!!!!!!!
Success rate is 100 percent (10/10)
Hub-1#
```

Wireshark can then show us that we are correctly prioritising our traffic:

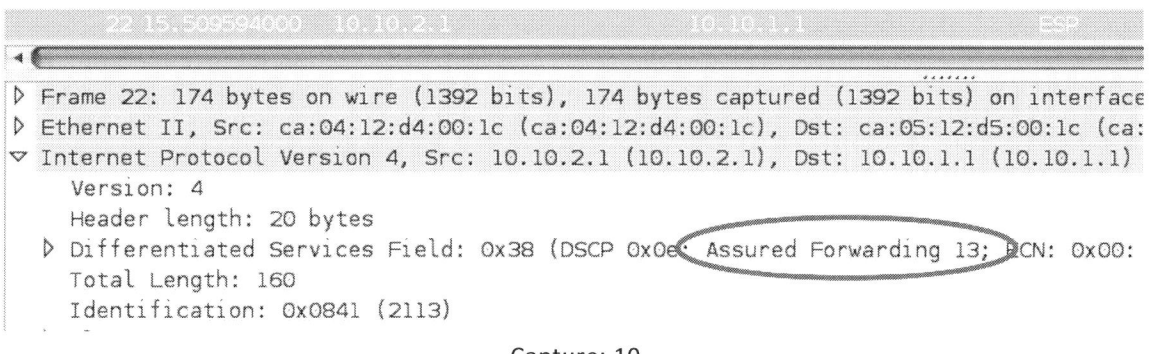

```
22 15.509594000    10.10.2.1              10.10.1.1              ESP

▷ Frame 22: 174 bytes on wire (1392 bits), 174 bytes captured (1392 bits) on interface
▷ Ethernet II, Src: ca:04:12:d4:00:1c (ca:04:12:d4:00:1c), Dst: ca:05:12:d5:00:1c (ca:
▽ Internet Protocol Version 4, Src: 10.10.2.1 (10.10.2.1), Dst: 10.10.1.1 (10.10.1.1)
     Version: 4
     Header length: 20 bytes
  ▷ Differentiated Services Field: 0x38 (DSCP 0x0e: Assured Forwarding 13; ECN: 0x00:
     Total Length: 160
     Identification: 0x0841 (2113)
```

Capture: 10

```
  37 20.040625000    10.10.3.1              10.10.1.1              ESP
```

▷ Frame 37: 174 bytes on wire (1392 bits), 174 bytes captured (1392 bits) on interface
▷ Ethernet II, Src: ca:04:12:d4:00:1c (ca:04:12:d4:00:1c), Dst: ca:05:12:d5:00:1c (ca:
▽ Internet Protocol Version 4, Src: 10.10.3.1 (10.10.3.1), Dst: 10.10.1.1 (10.10.1.1)
   Version: 4
   Header length: 20 bytes
   ▷ Differentiated Services Field: 0x28 (DSCP 0x0a: Assured Forwarding 11; ECN: 0x00:
   Total Length: 160
   Identification: 0x0478 (1144)

There is one section of the syllabus that does require a much deeper understanding of QoS, so for this reason we will go through the example and leave the explanation for the next volume. This is the idea of pre-classifying QoS. To implement this is actually extremely simple, but the explanation would run to several pages. If we want to pre-classify our QoS markings then under the tunnel interface we use the command "qos pre-classify":

```
Hub-1(config)#int tun 0
Hub-1(config-if)#qos pre-classify
```

As mentioned, we will return to DMVPN and QoS in the next volume and look at pre-classifying our QoS in greater detail. For the moment, let's crack on and look at IPv6!

4.11 DMVPN and IPv6

We can, without too much hard work or complication, use our existing DMVPN network to pass IPv6 traffic. None of the commands will be new to us by now, as we will see when we set up our Hub-1 router. We start by enabling the router for IPv6 traffic (which by default is disabled).

We will set up an IPv6 address on the tunnel interfaces of Hub-1, Spoke-1 and Spoke-3, and create a loopback interface (lo6) on each of them. The tunnel interface and the loopback interface will be advertised through EIGRPv6.

```
Hub-1(config)#ipv6 unicast-routing
Hub-1(config)#int tun 0
Hub-1(config-if)#ipv6 add fdd8:874b:eefc:ca68::1/64
Hub-1(config-if)#ipv6 mtu 1400
Hub-1(config-if)#ipv6 nhrp auth 802101
Hub-1(config-if)#ipv6 nhrp map multicast dynamic
Hub-1(config-if)#ipv6 nhrp network-id 10
Hub-1(config-if)#ipv6 nhrp holdtime 600
```

```
Hub-1(config-if)#ipv6 nhrp redirect
Hub-1(config-if)#ipv6 eigrp 6
Hub-1(config-if)#no ipv6 split-horizon eigrp 6
Hub-1(config-if)#int lo6
Hub-1(config-if)#ipv6 add 2001::1/64
Hub-1(config-if)#ipv6 eigrp 6
Hub-1(config-if)#router eigrp IPv6DMVPN
Hub-1(config-router)#address-family ipv6 autonomous-system 6
Hub-1(config-router-af)#
```

The commands on the hub do not vary between IPv4 and IPv6; the commands are the same, yet instead of "ip nhrp" we use "ipv6 nhrp". Our tunnel interface is assigned an IPv6 address, and assigned to an IPv6 EIGRP AS (6). We then create a loopback interface, with its own IPv6 address, and assign this to the same routing process. The last step is to create the routing process, which we do using EIGRP named mode.

The steps on the spoke routers are not all that different:

```
Spoke-1(config)#ipv6 unicast-routing
Spoke-1(config)#int tun 0
Spoke-1(config-if)#ipv6 add fdd8:874b:eefc:ca68::2/64
Spoke-1(config-if)#ipv6 mtu 1400
Spoke-1(config-if)#ipv6 nhrp auth 802101
Spoke-1(config-if)#ipv6 nhrp map fdd8:874b:eefc:ca68::/64 10.10.1.1
Spoke-1(config-if)#ipv6 nhrp map multicast 10.10.1.1
Spoke-1(config-if)#ipv6 nhrp nhs fdd8:874b:eefc:ca68::1 nbma 10.10.1.1
Spoke-1(config-if)#ipv6 nhrp network-id 10
Spoke-1(config-if)#ipv6 nhrp holdtime 600
Spoke-1(config-if)#ipv6 nhrp shortcut
Spoke-1(config-if)#ipv6 eigrp 6
Spoke-1(config)#router eigrp IPv6DMVPN
Spoke-1(config-router)#address-family ipv6 autonomous-system 6
Spoke-1(config-router-af)#
%DUAL-5-NBRCHANGE: EIGRP-IPv6 6: Neighbor FE80::C801:4FF:FE2D:8
(Tunnel0) is up: new adjacency
Spoke-1(config-router-af)#int lo6
Spoke-1(config-if)#ipv6 add 2002::2/128
Spoke-1(config-if)#ipv6 eigrp 6
Spoke-1(config-if)#
```

With the spoke routers we need to map the IPv6 tunnel address to the IPv4 NBMA address. Similarly, the multicast address we use is the same IPv4 external address. When we specify the next-hop server we use the IPv6 tunnel address, and specify the IPv4 NMBA address. Next we add the tunnel to an IPv6 routing process, which we then create.

Finally, we create a loopback interface, adding it to the same routing process. We then do the same on Spoke-3:

```
Spoke-3(config)#ipv6 unicast-routing
Spoke-3(config)#int lo6
Spoke-3(config-if)#ipv6 add 2004::4/128
Spoke-3(config-if)#ipv6 eigrp 6
Spoke-3(config-if)#int tun 0
Spoke-3(config-if)#ipv6 add fdd8:874b:eefc:ca68::4/64
Spoke-3(config-if)#ipv6 mtu 1400
Spoke-3(config-if)#ipv6 nhrp auth 802101
Spoke-3(config-if)#ipv6 nhrp map fdd8:874b:eefc:ca68::/64 10.10.1.1
Spoke-3(config-if)#ipv6 nhrp map multicast 10.10.1.1
Spoke-3(config-if)#ipv6 nhrp nhs fdd8:874b:eefc:ca68::1 nbma 10.10.1.1
Spoke-3(config-if)#ipv6 nhrp network-id 10
Spoke-3(config-if)#ipv6 nhrp holdtime 600
Spoke-3(config-if)#ipv6 nhrp shortcut
Spoke-3(config-if)#router eigrp IPv6DMVPN
Spoke-3(config-router)#address-family ipv6 auto 6
Spoke-3(config-router-af)#
%DUAL-5-NBRCHANGE: EIGRP-IPv6 6: Neighbor FE80::C801:4FF:FE2D:8
(Tunnel0) is up: new adjacency
Spoke-3(config-router-af)#
```

Now that the IPv6 portion of our tunnels has been completed, we should see the EIGRP adjacencies come up. We can confirm that we have the DMVPN peerings for IPv6 in the same way that we do for our IPv4 peers; using "sh dmvpn" and "sh ip nhrp", the only difference is that we use "sh dmvpn ipv6" and "sh ipv6 nhrp":

```
Hub-1(config-router-af)#do sh dmvpn ipv4 | b Interface
Interface: Tunnel0, IPv4 NHRP Details
Type:Hub, NHRP Peers:3,

 # Ent   Peer NBMA Addr  Peer Tunnel Add State  UpDn Tm  Attrb
 -----   --------------  --------------- -----  -------- -----
     1       10.10.2.1       192.168.1.2    UP 00:26:50    D
     1       10.10.3.1       192.168.1.3    UP 00:26:50    D
     1       10.10.4.1       192.168.1.4    UP 00:26:50    D

Hub-1(config-router-af)#do sh dmvpn ipv6 | b Interface
Interface: Tunnel0, IPv6 NHRP Details
Type:Hub, Total NBMA Peers (v4/v6): 2
   1.Peer NBMA Address: 10.10.2.1
      Tunnel IPv6 Address: FDD8:874B:EEFC:CA68::2
      IPv6 Target Network: FDD8:874B:EEFC:CA68::2/128
      # Ent: 1, Status: UP, UpDn Time: 00:16:53, Cache Attrib: D
```

```
    2.Peer NBMA Address: 10.10.4.1
        Tunnel IPv6 Address: FDD8:874B:EEFC:CA68::4
        IPv6 Target Network: FDD8:874B:EEFC:CA68::4/128
        # Ent: 1, Status: UP, UpDn Time: 00:02:57, Cache Attrib: D

Hub-1(config-router-af)#do sh ipv6 nhrp
FDD8:874B:EEFC:CA68::2/128 via FDD8:874B:EEFC:CA68::2
   Tunnel0 created 00:05:19, expire 01:54:40
   Type: dynamic, Flags: unique registered
   NBMA address: 10.10.2.1
FDD8:874B:EEFC:CA68::4/128 via FDD8:874B:EEFC:CA68::4
   Tunnel0 created 00:01:44, expire 01:58:15
   Type: dynamic, Flags: unique registered
   NBMA address: 10.10.4.1
FE80::C806:4FF:FE32:8/128 via FDD8:874B:EEFC:CA68::2
   Tunnel0 created 00:05:19, expire 01:54:40
   Type: dynamic, Flags: unique registered
   NBMA address: 10.10.2.1
FE80::C808:4FF:FE34:8/128 via FDD8:874B:EEFC:CA68::4
   Tunnel0 created 00:01:44, expire 01:58:15
   Type: dynamic, Flags: unique registered
   NBMA address: 10.10.4.1
Hub-1(config-router-af)#exit
Hub-1(config-router)#exit
Hub-1(config)#
```

If we look at the spokes we can see that we have visibility of, and reachability to, Hub-1:

```
Spoke-1(config-if)#do sh ipv6 route eigrp | e -
D    2001::/64 [90/27008000]
     via FE80::C801:4FF:FE2D:8, Tunnel0

Spoke-1(config-if)#do ping 2001::1
Type escape sequence to abort.
Sending 5, 100-byte ICMP Echos to 2001::1:
!!!!!
Success rate is 100 percent (5/5)
Spoke-1(config-if)#

Spoke-3(config-if)#do sh ipv6 route eigrp | e -
D    2001::/64 [90/27008000]
     via FE80::C801:4FF:FE2D:8, Tunnel0

Spoke-3(config-if)#do ping 2001::1
Type escape sequence to abort.
Sending 5, 100-byte ICMP Echos to 2001::1:
!!!!!
```

```
Success rate is 100 percent (5/5)
Spoke-3(config-router-af)#
```

The spokes do not, however, have visibility of each other. The lack of visibility is caused by the split-horizon rule, yet we used the command "no ipv6 split-horizon eigrp 6" when configuring the hub. So, what is the issue and how do we remedy this?

This is one of those little quirks with EIGRPv3 and to fix is relatively simple, we just need to look in the right place, and this is under "af-interface" within our EIGRP process:

```
Hub-1(config)#router eigrp IPv6DMVPN
Hub-1(config-router)#address-family ipv6 unicast auton 6
Hub-1(config-router-af)#af-interface tun 0
Hub-1(config-router-af-interface)#no split-horizon
Hub-1(config-router-af-interface)#
%DUAL-5-NBRCHANGE: EIGRP-IPv6 6: Neighbor FE80::C808:4FF:FE34:8
(Tunnel0) is resync: split horizon changed
%DUAL-5-NBRCHANGE: EIGRP-IPv6 6: Neighbor FE80::C806:4FF:FE32:8
(Tunnel0) is resync: split horizon changed
Hub-1(config-router-af-interface)#
```

This will trigger a resync of the peers, but once they come back up again, we can see that we have full visibility – Spoke-1 can see 2004::4, and Spoke-3 can see 2002::2:

```
Spoke-1(config-if)#do sh ipv6 route eigrp | e -
D   2001::/64 [90/27008000]
     via FE80::C801:4FF:FE2D:8, Tunnel0
D   2004::4/128 [90/27264000]
     via FE80::C801:4FF:FE2D:8, Tunnel0

Spoke-1(config-if)#

Spoke-3(config-router-af)#do sh ipv6 route eigrp | e -
D   2001::/64 [90/27008000]
     via FE80::C801:4FF:FE2D:8, Tunnel0
D   2002::2/128 [90/27264000]
     via FE80::C801:4FF:FE2D:8, Tunnel0

Spoke-3(config-router-af)#
```

More importantly, we have reachability:

```
Spoke-3#ping 2002::2 so lo6
Type escape sequence to abort.
Sending 5, 100-byte ICMP Echos to 2002::2:
```

```
Packet sent with a source address of 2004::4
!!!!!
Success rate is 100 percent (5/5)
Spoke-3#
```

Although IPv6 is easy to transport across an IPv4-based DMVPN infrastructure, it is not without its caveats, as we have seen. These quirks are, in general, more to do with the IGP running over the network, rather than DMVPN itself. DMVPN is a very flexible technology and in a way, is quite self-sufficient, as we will see as we move on to how it works in a NAT environment.

4.12 DMVPN and NAT

There are a number of reasons why we need to use NAT. The most obvious being that private addresses are not routable on the Internet and that public IPv4 addresses are in short supply. Here, we will look at how DMVPN operates with NAT.

We will set up Spoke-2 to be NAT'd through IGW's Gi 1/0 interface, which connects it to Hub-1.

We start with an access list to define our "interesting traffic":

```
IGW(config)#access-list 3 permit 10.10.3.0 0.0.0.255
```

Next, we set our inside and our outside interfaces:

```
IGW(config)#int gi 3/0
IGW(config-if)#ip nat inside

%LINEPROTO-5-UPDOWN: Line protocol on Interface NVI0, changed state to
up
IGW(config-if)#
IGW(config-if)#int gi 1/0
IGW(config-if)#ip nat outside
IGW(config-if)#exit
```

Finally we set up the NAT translation and confirm that it is behaving, as it should. I sent a ping from Spoke-2 to Hub-1's outside interface (10.10.1.1) to ensure that the translations were set up. You may see a packet drop as the translations are set up:

```
IGW(config)#ip nat inside source list 3 interf gi 1/0 overload

Spoke-2(config-if)#do ping 10.10.1.1
Type escape sequence to abort.
```

```
Sending 5, 100-byte ICMP Echos to 10.10.1.1:
!.!!!
Success rate is 80 percent (4/5)
Spoke-2(config-if)#

IGW(config)#do sh ip nat trans
Pro Inside global   Inside local   Outside local   Outside global
icmp 10.10.1.2:2    10.10.3.1:2    10.10.1.1:2     10.10.1.1:2
IGW(config)#
```

Soon after this you should start to see errors in the console of Hub-1:

```
Hub-1#
%CRYPTO-4-RECVD_PKT_INV_SPI: decaps: rec'd IPSEC packet has invalid
spi for destaddr=10.10.1.1, prot=50, spi=0xF71AA3E2(4145718242),
srcaddr=10.10.1.2, input interface=GigabitEthernet1/0
Hub-1#
%CRYPTO-4-IKMP_NO_SA: IKE message from 10.10.1.2 has no SA and is not
an initialization offer
Hub-1#
```

This shows that the NAT is working, but as the NHRP session is still active (at the moment) the errors will continue. We can either wait for the session to timeout, or shut down the tunnel on Spoke-2, clear the peering from Hub-1 and switch the tunnel back up:

```
Spoke-2(config-if)#int tun 0
Spoke-2(config-if)#shut
Spoke-2(config-if)#

Hub-1#clear ip nhrp 192.168.1.3
Hub-1#sh ip nhrp
192.168.1.2/32 via 192.168.1.2
   Tunnel0 created 00:43:09, expire 01:43:43
   Type: dynamic, Flags: unique registered
   NBMA address: 10.10.2.1
   Group: Spoke1
192.168.1.4/32 via 192.168.1.4
   Tunnel0 created 00:43:09, expire 01:53:07
   Type: dynamic, Flags: unique registered
   NBMA address: 10.10.4.1
Hub-1#

Spoke-2(config-if)#no sh
Spoke-2(config-if)#end
```

Once this has been done we can look at the NHRP record and see that the tunnel is active. We are registered dynamically with NHRP, our NBMA address has been correctly identified, but that we also have a "Claimed NBMA" address:

```
Hub-1#sh ip nhrp 192.168.1.3
192.168.1.3/32 via 192.168.1.3
   Tunnel0 created 00:00:13, expire 01:59:47
   Type: dynamic, Flags: unique registered used
   NBMA address: 10.10.1.2
   Group: Spoke2
     (Claimed NBMA address: 10.10.3.1)
Hub-1#
```

This claimed NBMA address is the address that Spoke-2 is translated to, by the IGW router. This tells us that the spoke router is behind a NAT device.

> Note: If you do not see the claimed address, but the IGW looks like it is correctly performing NAT, then this is likely to be due to a different IOS image. 15.2(4)M6 exhibits this behaviour, whilst 15.2(4)M4 works fine.

We can confirm that our DMVPN network is working correctly by checking our routing table and making sure that we have connectivity:

```
Spoke-2#sh ip route ospf | b Gate
Gateway of last resort is 10.10.3.2 to network 0.0.0.0

      1.0.0.0/32 is subnetted, 1 subnets
O        1.1.1.1 [110/1001] via 192.168.1.1, 00:02:30, Tun0
      2.0.0.0/32 is subnetted, 1 subnets
O        2.2.2.2 [110/1002] via 192.168.1.1, 00:02:30, Tun0
      4.0.0.0/32 is subnetted, 1 subnets
O        4.4.4.4 [110/1002] via 192.168.1.1, 00:02:30, Tun0
      192.168.1.0/24 is variably subnetted, 5 subnets, 2 masks
O        192.168.1.1/32 [110/1000] via 192.168.1.1, 00:02:30, Tun0
O        192.168.1.2/32 [110/1001] via 192.168.1.1, 00:02:30, Tun0
O        192.168.1.4/32 [110/1001] via 192.168.1.1, 00:02:30, Tun0
Spoke-2#ping 192.168.1.4
Type escape sequence to abort.
Sending 5, 100-byte ICMP Echos to 192.168.1.4:
!!!!!
Success rate is 100 percent (5/5)
Spoke-2#
```

This highlights one of the great aspects of DMVPN, we can be any number of hops away, we can be behind any number of NAT devices and still, we can have a vast network that is easy to set up and maintain.

4.13 DMVPN and VRFs

VRFs (Virtual Routing Forwarding) are a great way to provide separation of traffic, or to overcome the issue of IP address duplication.

Here we have a simple setup. DMVPNHUB connects the different offices of the RED and BLUE companies together. We have the "normal" connections of the left-hand side and DMVPN connections on the right-hand side. The DMVPN connections are using duplicate IP addresses as their "public" addresses.

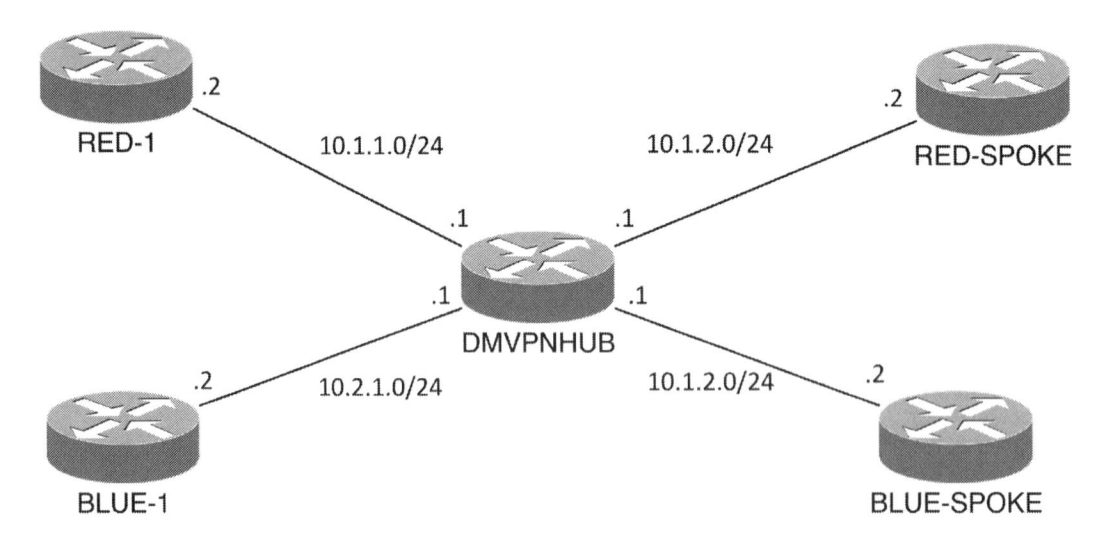

The initial setup is relatively simple. RED-1 and BLUE-1 have very standard configurations:

```
Router(config)#ho RED-1
RED-1(config)#int gi 1/0
RED-1(config-if)#ip add 10.1.1.2 255.255.255.0
RED-1(config-if)#no shut
RED-1(config-if)#

Router(config)#ho BLUE-1
BLUE-1(config)#int gi 1/0
BLUE-1(config-if)#ip add 10.2.1.2 255.255.255.0
BLUE-1(config-if)#no shut
```

```
BLUE-1(config-if)#
```

DMVPNHUB requires a couple of VRFs to be created. These are vrf RED and vrf BLUE, with RDs (Route Distinguishers) of 100:100 and 200:200 respectively. The interfaces connecting this router to RED-SPOKE and BLUE-SPOKE are assigned to these VRFs.

```
Router(config)#ho DMVPNHUB
DMVPNHUB(config)#ip vrf RED
DMVPNHUB(config-vrf)#rd 100:100
DMVPNHUB(config-vrf)#ip vrf BLUE
DMVPNHUB(config-vrf)#rd 200:200
DMVPNHUB(config-vrf)#int gi 1/0
DMVPNHUB(config-if)#desc Connection to RED-1
DMVPNHUB(config-if)#ip add 10.1.1.1 255.255.255.0
DMVPNHUB(config-if)#no shut
DMVPNHUB(config-if)#int gi 2/0
DMVPNHUB(config-if)#desc Connection to BLUE-1
DMVPNHUB(config-if)#ip add 10.2.1.1 255.255.255.0
DMVPNHUB(config-if)#no shut
DMVPNHUB(config-if)#int gi 3/0
DMVPNHUB(config-if)#ip vrf for RED
DMVPNHUB(config-if)#ip add 10.1.2.1 255.255.255.0
DMVPNHUB(config-if)#desc Connection to RED-SPOKE
DMVPNHUB(config-if)#no shut
DMVPNHUB(config-if)#int gi 4/0
DMVPNHUB(config-if)#ip vrf for BLUE
DMVPNHUB(config-if)#ip add 10.1.2.1 255.255.255.0
DMVPNHUB(config-if)#desc Connection to BLUE-SPOKE
DMVPNHUB(config-if)#no shut
DMVPNHUB(config-if)#
```

The configurations for RED-SPOKE and BLUE-SPOKE follow the same concept:

```
Router(config)#ho RED-SPOKE
RED-SPOKE(config)#ip vrf RED
RED-SPOKE(config-vrf)#rd 100:100
RED-SPOKE(config-vrf)#int gi 1/0
RED-SPOKE(config-if)#ip vrf for RED
RED-SPOKE(config-if)#ip add 10.1.2.2 255.255.255.0
RED-SPOKE(config-if)#no shut
RED-SPOKE(config-if)#

Router(config)#ho BLUE-SPOKE
BLUE-SPOKE(config)#ip vrf BLUE
BLUE-SPOKE(config-vrf)#rd 200:200
BLUE-SPOKE(config-vrf)#int gi 1/0
```

```
BLUE-SPOKE(config-if)#ip vrf for BLUE
BLUE-SPOKE(config-if)#ip add 10.1.2.2 255.255.255.0
BLUE-SPOKE(config-if)#no shut
BLUE-SPOKE(config-if)#
BLUE-SPOKE(config-if)#do ping vrf BLUE 10.1.2.1
Type escape sequence to abort.
Sending 5, 100-byte ICMP Echos to 10.1.2.1
.!!!!
Success rate is 80 percent (4/5)
BLUE-SPOKE(config-if)#
```

We will create our first tunnel, for the RED company:

```
DMVPNHUB(config-if)#int tunnel 100
DMVPNHUB(config-if)#
%LINEPROTO-5-UPDOWN: Line protocol on Interface Tunnel100, changed state to down
DMVPNHUB(config-if)#
DMVPNHUB(config-if)#ip add 10.100.100.1 255.255.255.0
DMVPNHUB(config-if)#ip nhrp map multicast dynamic
DMVPNHUB(config-if)#ip nhrp network-id 100
DMVPNHUB(config-if)#tun so gi 3/0
DMVPNHUB(config-if)#tun mode gre multi
DMVPNHUB(config-if)#

RED-SPOKE(config-if)#int tun 100
RED-SPOKE(config-if)#
%LINEPROTO-5-UPDOWN: Line protocol on Interface Tunnel100, changed state to down
RED-SPOKE(config-if)#
RED-SPOKE(config-if)#ip add 10.100.100.2 255.255.255.0
RED-SPOKE(config-if)#ip nhrp network-id 100
RED-SPOKE(config-if)#ip nhrp map 10.100.100.1 10.1.2.1
RED-SPOKE(config-if)#ip nhrp map multicast 10.1.2.1
RED-SPOKE(config-if)#ip nhrp nhs 10.100.100.1
RED-SPOKE(config-if)#tun so gi 1/0
RED-SPOKE(config-if)#tun mode gre multi
RED-SPOKE(config-if)#
%LINEPROTO-5-UPDOWN: Line protocol on Interface Tunnel100, changed state to up
RED-SPOKE(config-if)#
```

If we check our NHRP registrations, we see that the list is empty:

```
DMVPNHUB(config-if)#do sh ip nhrp
DMVPNHUB(config-if)#
```

We can treat our tunnel interface the same as our physical interfaces and assign it to the same VRF, which makes sense, so let's try that:

```
DMVPNHUB(config-if)#ip vrf for RED
DMVPNHUB(config-if)#ip add 10.100.100.1 255.255.255.0
DMVPNHUB(config-if)#

RED-SPOKE(config-if)#ip vrf for RED
RED-SPOKE(config-if)#ip add 10.100.100.2 255.255.255.0
RED-SPOKE(config-if)#
```

This alone is not enough:

```
DMVPNHUB(config-if)#do sh ip nhrp
DMVPNHUB(config-if)#
```

Under the "tunnel" command, we have an option to specify the VRF, so let's do that as well:

```
DMVPNHUB(config-if)#tunnel vrf RED
DMVPNHUB(config-if)#

RED-SPOKE(config-if)#tunnel vrf RED
RED-SPOKE(config-if)#
```

Now we have a dynamic NHRP registration:

```
DMVPNHUB(config-if)#do sh ip nhrp
10.100.100.2/32 via 10.100.100.2
   Tunnel100 created 00:00:22, expire 01:59:37
   Type: dynamic, Flags: unique registered used
   NBMA address: 10.1.2.2
DMVPNHUB(config-if)#
```

So, can we have just "tunnel vrf RED" on its own, or do we need that command and "ip vrf forwarding RED"?

```
DMVPNHUB(config-if)#no ip vrf for RED
% Interface Tunnel100 IPv4 disabled and address(es) removed due to disabling VRF
   DMVPNHUB(config-if)#ip add 10.100.100.1 255.255.255.0
DMVPNHUB(config-if)#do sh ip nhrp
```

```
DMVPNHUB(config-if)#

RED-SPOKE(config-if)#no ip vrf for RED
RED-SPOKE(config-if)#ip add 10.100.100.2 255.255.255.0
RED-SPOKE(config-if)#

DMVPNHUB(config-if)#do sh ip nhrp
DMVPNHUB(config-if)#
```

It would appear that we need both.

```
DMVPNHUB(config-if)#ip vrf for RED
DMVPNHUB(config-if)#ip add 10.100.100.1 255.255.255.0
DMVPNHUB(config-if)#

RED-SPOKE(config-if)#ip vrf forwarding RED
RED-SPOKE(config-if)#ip add 10.100.100.2 255.255.255.0
RED-SPOKE(config-if)#
```

If it doesn't come back up then do a "shut" and "no shut" on the spoke

```
DMVPNHUB(config-if)#do sh ip nhrp
10.100.100.2/32 via 10.100.100.2
   Tunnel100 created 00:00:09, expire 01:59:51
   Type: dynamic, Flags: unique registered used
   NBMA address: 10.1.2.2
DMVPNHUB(config-if)#
```

The command "ip vrf forwarding RED" is used to (in Cisco's terminology) "inject" the data packets inside the GRE tunnel into the MPLS VPN. This is "inner IP packet routing".

The command "tunnel vrf RED" is used to transport the actual GRE tunnel packets within the MPLS VPN. This is known as "outer IP packet routing"[6]. Because our tunnel endpoints are not in the global routing table, this command is required.

There is another distinction between the purposes of the two commands. Clear-text packets are sent using the "ip vrf forwarding" command, and encrypted packets are sent

---

[6] Ref: http://www.cisco.com/c/en/us/td/docs/ios-xml/ios/sec_conn_dmvpn/configuration/15-s/sec-conn-dmvpn-15-s-book/sec-conn-dmvpn.html#GUID-96BBE81D-EBF3-4CF0-8B7E-46754CACC338

using the "tunnel vrf" command. So, if we use encryption, can we remove the "ip vrf forwarding" command?

Let's set up some encryption and try this theory out.

For both DMVPNHUB and RED-SPOKE the steps are the same (again this is one of those times when using Notepad will really save some time). We create an ISAKMP policy, a crypto keyring, a transform et, an IPSec profile and lastly, we add this to our tunnel:

```
DMVPNHUB(config-if)#crypto isakmp policy 10
DMVPNHUB(config-isakmp)# encr aes
DMVPNHUB(config-isakmp)# authentication pre-share
DMVPNHUB(config-isakmp)# group 2
DMVPNHUB(config-isakmp)#
DMVPNHUB(config-isakmp)#crypto keyring DMVPN vrf RED
DMVPNHUB(conf-keyring)#pre-shared-key address 0.0.0.0 0.0.0.0 key 802101
DMVPNHUB(conf-keyring)#
DMVPNHUB(conf-keyring)#crypto ipsec transform-set DMVPN-TS esp-aes
DMVPNHUB(cfg-crypto-trans)# mode transport
DMVPNHUB(cfg-crypto-trans)#
DMVPNHUB(cfg-crypto-trans)#crypto ipsec profile DMVPNPROFILE
DMVPNHUB(ipsec-profile)# set transform-set DMVPN-TS
DMVPNHUB(ipsec-profile)#
DMVPNHUB(ipsec-profile)#int tun 100
DMVPNHUB(config-if)#tunnel prote
DMVPNHUB(config-if)#tunnel protection ipsec profile DMVPNPROFILE
DMVPNHUB(config-if)#
%CRYPTO-6-ISAKMP_ON_OFF: ISAKMP is ON
DMVPNHUB(config-if)#

RED-SPOKE(config-if)#crypto isakmp policy 10
RED-SPOKE(config-isakmp)# encr aes
RED-SPOKE(config-isakmp)# authentication pre-share
RED-SPOKE(config-isakmp)# group 2
RED-SPOKE(config-isakmp)#
RED-SPOKE(config-isakmp)#crypto keyring DMVPN vrf RED
RED-SPOKE(conf-keyring)#pre-shared-key address 0.0.0.0 0.0.0.0 key 802101
RED-SPOKE(conf-keyring)#
RED-SPOKE(conf-keyring)#crypto ipsec transform-set DMVPN-TS esp-aes
RED-SPOKE(cfg-crypto-trans)# mode transport
RED-SPOKE(cfg-crypto-trans)#
RED-SPOKE(cfg-crypto-trans)#crypto ipsec profile DMVPNPROFILE
RED-SPOKE(ipsec-profile)# set transform-set DMVPN-TS
RED-SPOKE(ipsec-profile)#int tun 100
```

```
RED-SPOKE(config-if)#tunnel protection ipsec profile DMVPNPROFILE
RED-SPOKE(config-if)#
%CRYPTO-6-ISAKMP_ON_OFF: ISAKMP is ON
RED-SPOKE(config-if)#
```

Because we are using GRE and now, IPSec, we really should fix our MTU and MSS, to avoid unwanted fragmentation:

```
RED-SPOKE(config-if)#ip mtu 1400
RED-SPOKE(config-if)#ip tcp adjust-mss 1360
RED-SPOKE(config-if)#

DMVPNHUB(config-if)#ip mtu 1400
DMVPNHUB(config-if)#ip tcp adjust-mss 1360
DMVPNHUB(config-if)#
```

Now we can now remove the command "ip vrf forwarding RED" from our hub and from our spoke:

```
DMVPNHUB(config-if)#no ip vrf for RED
% Interface Tunnel100 IPv4 disabled and address(es) removed due to disabling VRF
DMVPNHUB(config-if)#ip add 10.100.100.1 255.255.255.0
DMVPNHUB(config-if)#do sh ip nhrp
10.100.100.2/32 via 10.100.100.2
   Tunnel100 created 00:00:04, expire 01:59:55
   Type: dynamic, Flags: unique registered used
   NBMA address: 10.1.2.2
DMVPNHUB(config-if)#do ping vrf RED 10.100.100.2
Type escape sequence to abort.
Sending 5, 100-byte ICMP Echos to 10.100.100.2, timeout is 2 seconds:
.....
Success rate is 0 percent (0/5)
DMVPNHUB(config-if)#
```

Interestingly, our ping now fails. Regardless, let's go ahead and make the same changes to the spoke:

```
RED-SPOKE(config-if)#no ip vrf for RED
% Interface Tunnel100 IPv4 disabled and address(es) removed due to disabling VRF
RED-SPOKE(config-if)#ip add 10.100.100.2 255.255.255.0
RED-SPOKE(config-if)#do ping vrf RED 10.100.100.1
Type escape sequence to abort.
Sending 5, 100-byte ICMP Echos to 10.100.100.1:
```

```
.....
Success rate is 0 percent (0/5)
RED-SPOKE(config-if)#
```

Because we are no longer using the "ip vrf forwarding" command, we no longer need to specify the VRF when we are testing.

```
RED-SPOKE(config-if)#do ping 10.100.100.1
Type escape sequence to abort.
Sending 5, 100-byte ICMP Echos to 10.100.100.1:
!!!!.
Success rate is 80 percent (4/5)
RED-SPOKE(config-if)#

DMVPNHUB(config-if)#do ping 10.100.100.2
Type escape sequence to abort.
Sending 5, 100-byte ICMP Echos to 10.100.100.2:
!!!!!
Success rate is 100 percent (5/5)
DMVPNHUB(config-if)#
```

To prove that we don't need to specify a VRF for the routing on DMVPNHUB, let's set up "classic" EIGRP for the RED company:

```
RED-1(config)#router eigrp 100
RED-1(config-router)#net 10.1.1.0 0.0.0.255
RED-1(config-router)#

DMVPNHUB(config-if)#no ip split-horizon eigrp 100
DMVPNHUB(config-if)#no ip next-hop-self eigrp 100
DMVPNHUB(config-if)#router eigrp 100
DMVPNHUB(config-router)#network 10.1.1.0 0.0.0.255
DMVPNHUB(config-router)#network 10.100.100.0 0.0.0.255
%DUAL-5-NBRCHANGE: EIGRP-IPv4 100: Neighbor 10.1.1.2
(GigabitEthernet1/0) is up: new adjacency
DMVPNHUB(config-router)#

RED-SPOKE(config)#router eigrp 100
RED-SPOKE(config-router)#net 10.100.100.0 0.0.0.255
RED-SPOKE(config-router)#do sh ip eigrp neigh
EIGRP-IPv4 Neighbors for AS(100)
H   Address         Interface    Hold Uptime    SRTT   RTO    Q   Seq
                                 (sec)          (ms)          Cnt Num
0   10.100.100.1    Tu100          12 00:05:27  1542   5000   0   5
RED-SPOKE(config-router)#
```

```
DMVPNHUB(config-if)#do sh ip eigrp neigh
EIGRP-IPv4 Neighbors for AS(100)
H   Address         Interface    Hold Uptime    SRTT    RTO   Q   Seq
                                 (sec)          (ms)          Cnt Num
1   10.100.100.2    Tu100         10  00:07:31   96    1398   0   3
0   10.1.1.2        Gi1/0         13  00:07:46 1325    5000   0   3
DMVPNHUB(config-if)#

RED-SPOKE(config-router)#do sh ip route eigrp | b Gate
Gateway of last resort is not set

     10.0.0.0/8 is variably subnetted, 3 subnets, 2 masks
D       10.1.1.0/24 [90/26880256] via 10.100.100.1, 00:02:17, Tun100
RED-SPOKE(config-router)#do ping 10.1.1.2
Type escape sequence to abort.
Sending 5, 100-byte ICMP Echos to 10.1.1.2:
!!!!.
Success rate is 80 percent (4/5)
RED-SPOKE(config-router)#
```

Setting up the BLUE company is no different, however we can omit the "ip vrf forwarding command" straight away now. The only different is that we cannot use "crypto keyring DMVPN vrf BLUE", instead we must create a new keyring on DMVPNHUB.

```
DMVPNHUB(config-if)#int tun 200
DMVPNHUB(config-if)#ip add 10.200.200.1 255.255.255.0
DMVPNHUB(config-if)#no ip next-hop-self eigrp 200
DMVPNHUB(config-if)#no ip split-horizon eigrp 200
DMVPNHUB(config-if)#ip nhrp map multicast dynamic
DMVPNHUB(config-if)#ip nhrp network-id 200
DMVPNHUB(config-if)#ip mtu 1400
DMVPNHUB(config-if)#ip tcp adjust-mss 1360
DMVPNHUB(config-if)#tun so gi 4/0
DMVPNHUB(config-if)#tun mode gre multi
DMVPNHUB(config-if)#tunnel vrf BLUE
DMVPNHUB(config-if)#tunn pro ipsec prof DMVPNPROFILE
DMVPNHUB(config-if)#exit
DMVPNHUB(config)#crypto keyring DMVPN vrf BLUE
% can't change the VRF of a keyring on the fly. Remove & redefine
DMVPNHUB(config)#crypto keyring DMVPN-2 vrf BLUE
DMVPNHUB(conf-keyring)#pre-shared-key address 0.0.0.0 0.0.0.0 key 802101
DMVPNHUB(conf-keyring)#

BLUE-SPOKE(config)#crypto isakmp policy 10
BLUE-SPOKE(config-isakmp)# encr aes
```

```
BLUE-SPOKE(config-isakmp)# authentication pre-share
BLUE-SPOKE(config-isakmp)# group 2
BLUE-SPOKE(config-isakmp)#
BLUE-SPOKE(config-isakmp)#crypto keyring DMVPN vrf BLUE
BLUE-SPOKE(conf-keyring)#  pre-shared-key address 0.0.0.0 0.0.0.0 key
802101
BLUE-SPOKE(conf-keyring)#
BLUE-SPOKE(conf-keyring)#crypto ipsec transform-set DMVPN-TS esp-aes
BLUE-SPOKE(cfg-crypto-trans)# mode transport
BLUE-SPOKE(cfg-crypto-trans)#
BLUE-SPOKE(cfg-crypto-trans)#crypto ipsec profile DMVPNPROFILE
BLUE-SPOKE(ipsec-profile)# set transform-set DMVPN-TS
BLUE-SPOKE(ipsec-profile)#
BLUE-SPOKE(ipsec-profile)#ip vrf BLUE
BLUE-SPOKE(config-vrf)#rd 200:200
BLUE-SPOKE(config-vrf)#interface Tunnel200
BLUE-SPOKE(config-if)# ip address 10.200.200.2 255.255.255.0
BLUE-SPOKE(config-if)# no ip redirects
BLUE-SPOKE(config-if)# ip mtu 1400
BLUE-SPOKE(config-if)# ip nhrp map 10.200.200.1 10.1.2.1
BLUE-SPOKE(config-if)# ip nhrp map multicast 10.1.2.1
BLUE-SPOKE(config-if)# ip nhrp network-id 100
BLUE-SPOKE(config-if)# ip nhrp nhs 10.200.200.1
BLUE-SPOKE(config-if)# ip tcp adjust-mss 1360
BLUE-SPOKE(config-if)# tunnel source GigabitEthernet1/0
BLUE-SPOKE(config-if)# tunnel mode gre multipoint
BLUE-SPOKE(config-if)# tunnel vrf BLUE
BLUE-SPOKE(config-if)# tunnel protection ipsec profile DMVPNPROFILE
BLUE-SPOKE(config-if)#
BLUE-SPOKE(config-if)#
%LINEPROTO-5-UPDOWN: Line protocol on Interface Tunnel200, changed
state to up
%CRYPTO-6-ISAKMP_ON_OFF: ISAKMP is ON
BLUE-SPOKE(config-if)#
```

NHRP looks good:

```
DMVPNHUB(conf-keyring)#do sh ip nhrp
10.100.100.2/32 via 10.100.100.2
   Tunnel100 created 00:30:18, expire 01:29:41
   Type: dynamic, Flags: unique registered used
   NBMA address: 10.1.2.2
10.200.200.2/32 via 10.200.200.2
   Tunnel200 created 00:01:17, expire 01:58:42
   Type: dynamic, Flags: unique registered used
   NBMA address: 10.1.2.2
DMVPNHUB(conf-keyring)#
```

More importantly, our pings work:

```
DMVPNHUB(conf-keyring)#do ping 10.200.200.2
Type escape sequence to abort.
Sending 5, 100-byte ICMP Echos to 10.200.200.2:
!!!!!
Success rate is 100 percent (5/5)
DMVPNHUB(conf-keyring)#
```

Let's finish this off with a little EIGRP:

```
BLUE-1(config)#router eigrp 200
BLUE-1(config-router)#net 10.2.1.0 0.0.0.255
BLUE-1(config-router)#

BLUE-SPOKE(config-if)#router eigrp 200
BLUE-SPOKE(config-router)#net 10.200.200.0 0.0.0.255
BLUE-SPOKE(config-router)#

DMVPNHUB(conf-keyring)#router eigrp 200
DMVPNHUB(config-router)#net 10.2.1.0 0.0.0.255
DMVPNHUB(config-router)#
%DUAL-5-NBRCHANGE: EIGRP-IPv4 200: Neighbor 10.2.1.2
(GigabitEthernet2/0) is up: new adjacency
DMVPNHUB(config-router)#net 10.200.200.0 0.0.0.255
DMVPNHUB(config-router)#
%DUAL-5-NBRCHANGE: EIGRP-IPv4 200: Neighbor 10.200.200.2 (Tunnel200)
is up: new adjacency
DMVPNHUB(config-router)#
```

One last end-to-end check, and we are done:

```
BLUE-SPOKE(config-router)#do sh ip route eigrp | b Gate
Gateway of last resort is not set

      10.0.0.0/8 is variably subnetted, 3 subnets, 2 masks
D        10.2.1.0/24 [90/26880256] via 10.200.200.1, 00:01:17, Tun200
BLUE-SPOKE(config-router)#do ping 10.2.1.2
Type escape sequence to abort.
Sending 5, 100-byte ICMP Echos to 10.2.1.2:
!!!!!
Success rate is 100 percent (5/5)
BLUE-SPOKE(config-router)#
```

If we had a dual-hub dual-DMVPN topology then we could have more than one tunnel using the same source and destination. In this case, having the same IPSec SA to secure both would be preferable. Although it is beyond the scope of this volume, then we won't go into it in great depth, save to say that if we are using a shared IPSec SA, then instead of "tunnel protection ipsec profile <profilename>", we would use "tunnel protection ipsec profile <profilename> shared". The configuration would look something like this:

```
crypto ipsakmp policy 1
encrypt aes
auth pre-share
group 2
crypto isakmp key 802101 address 0.0.0.0 0.0.0.0
!
crypto ipsec transform-set TS-Set esp-aes esp-sha-hmac
 mode transport
!
crypto ipsec profile SharedDMVPNProfile
 set transform-set TS-Set
!
int tun 100
 <truncated>
 tunnel key 100
 tunnel protect ipsec profile SharedDMVPNProfile shared
!
int tun 200
 <truncated>
 tunnel key 200
 tunnel protect ipsec profile SharedDMVPNProfile shared
```

Hopefully, as you have seen, DMVPN is an easy to implement, scalable solution, with many benefits. There is, however, another solution, that offers a number of benefits above and beyond DMVPN and that is GETVPN.

5. GETVPN

Group Encrypted Transport VPN (GETVPN) features on the written exam portion of the CCIE Routing and Switching syllabus, it does not appear on the Service Provider syllabus, but does appear on both the CCIE Security written and lab. It is out of scope on the lab exam of the Routing and Switching track due to the infrastructure requirements that it has; therefore we will only briefly touch on this subject. These requirements are shared keys, a group SA and centralized policy and key management. It is this last part; the centralized policy and key management, that makes GETVPN suitable for a large scale deployment.

GETVPN is a highly scalable solution that has a number of benefits, these include:

- Simplification of communication – traffic can flow between sites without needing to pass through a central hub
- Security – GETVPN provides encryption for MPLS networks, whilst also allowing for meshing, QoS, and the site to site connectivity we have seen with DMVPN, yet unlike DMVPN it does not require a secondary overlay routing infrastructure.
- Ease of management – there is no longer a need for complex key management.
- Multicast support – packets can be replicated after encryption, so that multicast traffic can be replicated at the core, this is also helped by the fact that with GETVPN the original source and destination in the unencrypted packet are kept in the encrypted packet.

GETVPN has three components, these are:

Key Server (KS) – These distribute the encryption keys to all group members. A minimum of one KS is required in GETVPN. The KS will regenerate and distribute new IPSec SAs to the GMs, before the current SA expires, therefore ensuring no loss of functionality.

Group Member (GM) – these encrypt and decrypt the traffic. Because they all share the same key they can decrypt the traffic that was encrypted by another GM. The GM registers with the KS to get the current IPSec SA. It sends a group ID to the KS and in return gets the policy and key for that particular group.

Group Domain of Interpretation (GDOI) – this is the protocol used between the GM and the KS. We saw this as an option in section 3.5, when we looked at securing GRE with IPSec. A Phase 1 IKE SA protects GDOI and all participants must authenticate to the KS using IKE (See RFC 6407). GDOI uses two keys. One key is used to secure the control plane; this is called the Key Encryption Key (KEK). The other key is used to secure the data traffic, and is known as the Traffic Encryption Key (TEK).

Whilst GETVPN is a very interesting subject, because it is out of scope for the lab and only makes for a very small portion of the written exam, we won't go any deeper into it. There are some links at the end of this book on GETVPN, including a nice "minimalistic" set up that you may want to try at home, as well as the Cisco design guide for GETVPN.

Our last topic in this section of the book will look at "traditional" site to site VPNs.

6. Site-to-Site VPNs

So far all our DMVPN traffic is encrypted, through IPSec, yet this is only one of the topics on the CCIE syllabus. We have seen how we can create basic tunnels, protect them through IPSec, and build on them to create a DMVPN infrastructure. What we have not done, so far, is discuss a "standard" VPN. To finish this part of the book, we will look at how to create a site-to-site VPN, between Hub-1 and IGW. This is also referred to as a Lan-to-Lan (or L2L) VPN.

There is not much difference between how we have built our DMVPN infrastructure and a site-to-site VPN; they share many of the same components, as we will see as we start to set ours up.

We start by creating an ISAKMP policy. We could use an existing one, but let's start from scratch. We can either do a "sh run" and find an available policy number to use, or we can find it the easy way, and use "sh crypto isakmp policy":

```
Hub-1#sh crypto isakmp policy

Global IKE policy
Protection suite of priority 1
    encryption algorithm:   DES - (56 bit keys).
    hash algorithm:         Secure Hash Standard
    authentication method:  Pre-Shared Key
    Diffie-Hellman group:   #1 (768 bit)
    lifetime:               86400 seconds, no volume limit
Protection suite of priority 2
    encryption algorithm:   Three key triple DES
    hash algorithm:         Secure Hash Standard
    authentication method:  Pre-Shared Key
    Diffie-Hellman group:   #2 (1024 bit)
    lifetime:               86400 seconds, no volume limit
Hub-1#
```

Now we know we need to start with policy number 3. We will use triple-des for encryption and MD5 to hash. We will also use a pre-shared key, along with Diffie-Hellman group 2:

```
Hub-1(config)#crypto isakmp policy 3
Hub-1(config-isakmp)#encr 3des
Hub-1(config-isakmp)#hash md5
Hub-1(config-isakmp)#auth pre-share
Hub-1(config-isakmp)#group 2
Hub-1(config-isakmp)#exit
```

```
Hub-1(config)#crypto isakmp key HubToIGW address 10.10.1.2
```

We spoke about IKE Phase 1 (which we have just set up above) briefly, way back in section 3.5, and although IPSec VPNs are focused on more in the CCIE Security track, now would be a good time to go through this, and IKE Phase 2, in greater detail (without this turning into a Security track book).

As we mentioned, ISAKMP looks after a number of requirements needed by the IPSec part of the VPN, which is known as IKE Phase 2. Phase 1 is all about key exchange; both peers must authenticate with each other and a shared key must be exchanged.

Above, we have a number of components. We have set up an encryption method (3DES). This is used to encrypt and decrypt the secret keys, which are then transmitted using ESP.

The next component is the hashing algorithm (MD5). This is used to make sure that the message has not been altered in any way.

Next we have the authentication method, which can be PKI (Public Key Infrastructure) or PSK (pre-shared keys). Here we are using a pre-shared key of "HubToIGW".

Lastly, here, we have the Diffie-Hellman (DH) group. This is the Diffie-Hellman key exchange algorithm, which generates another shared secret key, adding an extra level of encryption. This results in an ISAKMP Security Association (SA).

This key exchange allows two routers (who may never have spoken to each other before) to establish a shared secret key, over an insecure network. This key is then used to encrypt subsequent communication.

With our policy set up, we then create the shared key for the two routers to use.

IKE phase 1 can occur in one of two modes; Main and Aggressive. Main mode has three two-way exchanges. In the first exchange, the algorithms and hashes to be used are agreed upon. The second exchange uses DH to generate a shared secret and in the final exchange, the routers verify the other site's identity (which is an encrypted version of the peers IP address). With Aggressive mode nearly everything is done within the first packet, which contains the DH public key, a "nonce" and an identity packet. The peer receives this and then sends back everything that is needed to complete the setup. Finally the initiator confirms the exchange. Aggressive mode is faster due to the fewer exchanges, but less secure as much of the communication takes place outside of a secure channel, so is more liable to eavesdropping and sniffing.

We can now move on to creating our IKE Phase 2 components. Phase 2 negotiates and establishes the IPSec SAs, which are protected by the existing IKE SA (from Phase 1). Phase 2 also will regenerate the IPSec SA to ensure security, as well as performing an additional DH exchange, though this last one is optional.

The requirements for Phase 2 are to define our "interesting traffic", which is the data we want to protect. This will be the communication between the 10.10.100.0/24 network on Hub-1 and the 10.10.200.0/24 network on IGW (which we will create in the form of loopback interfaces):

```
Hub-1(config)#ip access-list extended IGW-Traffic
Hub-1(config-ext-nacl)#permit ip 10.10.100.0 0.0.0.255 10.10.200.0 0.0.0.255
Hub-1(config-ext-nacl)#exit
```

We then create a transform set, again this is for encryption and hashing, note that we are accepting the default mode of tunnel:

```
Hub-1(config)#crypto ipsec transform-set HubToIGW esp-3des esp-md5-hmac
Hub-1(cfg-crypto-trans)#exit
```

Next comes the crypto map, which links our peer to the transform set, and to the interesting traffic:

```
Hub-1(config)#crypto map HubToIGW 10 ipsec-isakmp
% NOTE: This new crypto map will remain disabled until a peer
        and a valid access list have been configured.
Hub-1(config-crypto-map)#set peer 10.10.1.2
Hub-1(config-crypto-map)#set transform-set HubToIGW
Hub-1(config-crypto-map)#match address IGW-Traffic
Hub-1(config-crypto-map)#exit
```

The very last step in creating the VPN is to apply the crypto map to the correct interface:

```
Hub-1(config)#int gi 1/0
Hub-1(config-if)#crypto map HubToIGW
Hub-1(config-if)#
```

Because we have defined our interesting traffic to be a completely new subnet, we will go ahead and create a loopback interface to simulate these networks:

```
Hub-1(config-if)#int lo10
Hub-1(config-if)#ip add 10.10.100.1 255.255.255.0
```

The final step is to make sure that the router knows where to go to for this network:

```
Hub-1(config-if)#router ospf 1
Hub-1(config-router)#redis conn subnets route-map MyLo10
Hub-1(config-router)#route-map MyLo10
Hub-1(config-route-map)#match interface loopback 10
Hub-1(config-route-map)#exi
Hub-1(config)#end
```

The steps on IGW are very similar. The only differences are in IP addressing. The ISAKMP policy settings are the same:

```
IGW(config)#crypto isakmp policy 3
IGW(config-isakmp)#encr 3des
IGW(config-isakmp)#hash md5
IGW(config-isakmp)#auth pre-share
IGW(config-isakmp)#group 2
IGW(config-isakmp)#exit
IGW(config)#crypto isakmp key HubToIGW address 10.10.1.1
```

The interesting traffic is the same, although we do need to swap the source and destination networks around:

```
IGW(config)#ip access-list extended IGW-Traffic
IGW(config-ext-nacl)#permit ip 10.10.200.0 0.0.0.255 10.10.100.0 0.0.0.255
IGW(config-ext-nacl)#exit
```

The transform set is the same:

```
IGW(config)#crypto ipsec transform-set HubToIGW esp-3des esp-md5-hmac
IGW(cfg-crypto-trans)#exit
```

The crypto map is the same:

```
IGW(config)#crypto map HubToIGW 10 ipsec-isakmp
% NOTE: This new crypto map will remain disabled until a peer
        and a valid access list have been configured.
IGW(config-crypto-map)#set peer 10.10.1.1
IGW(config-crypto-map)#set transform-set HubToIGW
IGW(config-crypto-map)#match address IGW-Traffic
IGW(config-crypto-map)#exit
IGW(config)#int gi 1/0
IGW(config-if)#crypto map HubToIGW
```

```
IGW(config-if)#
```

Finally we create the network and static route on IGW:

```
IGW(config-if)#int lo10
IGW(config-if)#ip add 10.10.200.1 255.255.255.0
IGW(config-if)#exit
IGW(config)#ip route 10.10.100.0 255.255.255.0 10.10.1.1
```

Now we can establish our VPN, by pinging between the new networks:

```
IGW(config)#do ping 10.10.100.1 so lo10
Type escape sequence to abort.
Sending 5, 100-byte ICMP Echos to 10.10.100.1:
Packet sent with a source address of 10.10.200.1
.!!!!
Success rate is 80 percent (4/5)
IGW(config)#end
```

Note that we do lose the initial ping, as the VPN is not yet up. The next four pings are successful and we can use the command "sh crypto session" to confirm that the VPN is up:

```
IGW#sh crypto session
Crypto session current status

Interface: GigabitEthernet1/0
Session status: UP-ACTIVE
Peer: 10.10.1.1 port 500
  IKEv1 SA: local 10.10.1.2/500 remote 10.10.1.1/500 Active
  IPSEC FLOW: permit ip 10.10.200.0/255.255.255.0
10.10.100.0/255.255.255.0
        Active SAs: 2, origin: crypto map

IGW#
```

Because we have made a change to the network, we should confirm that we still have reachability to our DMVPN spokes and to the protected network on IGW from Hub-1:

```
Hub-1#ping 192.168.1.4
Type escape sequence to abort.
Sending 5, 100-byte ICMP Echos to 192.168.1.4:
!!!!!
Success rate is 100 percent (5/5)
Hub-1#ping 10.10.200.1 so lo10
```

```
Type escape sequence to abort.
Sending 5, 100-byte ICMP Echos to 10.10.200.1:
Packet sent with a source address of 10.10.100.1
!!!!!
Success rate is 100 percent (5/5)
Hub-1#
```

If we look at the crypto sessions on IGW, we have entries for our site-to-site VPN as well as our DMVPN peers. Note that we have one tunnel using a different port (4500 instead of 500), this is due to NAT traversal (NAT-T), which we will look at in the next part:

```
Hub-1#sh crypto session
Crypto session current status

Interface: GigabitEthernet1/0
Session status: UP-ACTIVE
Peer: 10.10.1.2 port 500
  IKEv1 SA: local 10.10.1.1/500 remote 10.10.1.2/500 Active
  IPSEC FLOW: permit ip 10.10.100.0/255.255.255.0
10.10.200.0/255.255.255.0
        Active SAs: 2, origin: crypto map

Interface: Tunnel0
Session status: UP-ACTIVE
Peer: 10.10.1.2 port 4500
  IKEv1 SA: local 10.10.1.1/4500 remote 10.10.1.2/4500 Active
  IPSEC FLOW: permit 47 host 10.10.1.1 host 10.10.1.2
        Active SAs: 2, origin: crypto map

Interface: Tunnel0
Session status: UP-ACTIVE
Peer: 10.10.2.1 port 500
  IKEv1 SA: local 10.10.1.1/500 remote 10.10.2.1/500 Active
  IPSEC FLOW: permit 47 host 10.10.1.1 host 10.10.2.1
        Active SAs: 2, origin: crypto map

Interface: Tunnel0
Session status: UP-ACTIVE
Peer: 10.10.4.1 port 500
  IKEv1 SA: local 10.10.1.1/500 remote 10.10.4.1/500 Active
  IPSEC FLOW: permit 47 host 10.10.1.1 host 10.10.4.1
        Active SAs: 2, origin: crypto map

Hub-1#
```

With our site-to-site VPN in place, we have actually introduced a problem into our network. The console of Hub-1 now shows:

```
Hub-1#
%CRYPTO-4-IKMP_BAD_MESSAGE: IKE message from 10.10.1.2 failed its
sanity check or is malformed
Hub-1#
```

If you do not see this error, then shut down the tunnel interface on Spoke-2, clear it from nhrp on Hub-1 (clear ip nhrp 192.168.1.3) and bring the tunnel interface back up again.

Our site-to-site VPN has broken Spoke-2! Which can only mean, almost as if it were planned, that it's a good time to look at NAT in greater detail.

Part 2: NAT

7. Network Address Translation

NAT allows a network using private IP addresses to access the Internet using public addresses. Private addresses are not routable over the Internet, so a router will act as a gateway to the Internet for the private network, translating their private addresses to its public address (or to a pool of public addresses).

There are a few requirements for NAT. We need to define the public address. Most commonly this is using the interface command "ip nat outside", which we have already seen. We also need to specify what is going to be translated, most commonly this is done using the interface command "ip nat inside" – again we have already used this. The final step is to define the translation rules.

We have configured these before, when we created a NAT on IGW for Spoke-2, but we did not discuss the mechanics of what actually occurs when this is set up. We will look at this now.

How NAT works depends on the direction in which the traffic is flowing and this is the NAT Order of Operations. If a packet is flowing from the inside to the outside, then NAT occurs after routing, if the packet is going in the opposite direction (outside to inside), then the translation occurs before routing.

In our first example, we set up a translation for the 10.10.3.0/24 network to be translated to the "outside" interface of IGW. Spoke-2's 10.10.3.1 IP address became 10.10.1.2. The configuration for which looked like this:

```
int gi 1/0
  ip nat outside
int gi 3/0
  ip nat inside
!
ip nat inside source list 3 interface gi 1/0 overload
!
access-list 3 permit 10.10.3.0 0.0.0.255
```

For our requirements, this was probably more complicated than it needed to be. What we have done is mapped an entire network (for which we have just one host), to IGWs interface connecting to Hub-1 and enabled port-address translation, therefore allowing for potentially thousands of hosts to be translated. Really, all we needed was a static one-to-one translation, which we will look at in a moment. It did, however, give us all the components we need to look at.

Cisco's terminology for NAT can be slightly confusing, as they use the concept of "inside local", "inside global", "outside local" and "outside global", when referring to the different interfaces and IP addresses used. Because GigabitEthernet 1/0 (on IGW) is our Internet-facing interface, it is designated the "outside" interface. This becomes our "inside global" address. The network we are "hiding", the one sitting behind Gi 3/0 (our "inside" interface), becomes our "inside local" address. Similarly, if we were communicating with another network behind another router, the public interface of the other router would be the "outside global" (such as Hub-1's 10.10.1.1 address). The network behind it (such as Hub-1's 1.1.1.0/24 network) would be the "outside local" address.

The Cisco definition of these terms is:

Inside local – "*the IP address assigned to a host on the inside network*".
Inside global – "*a legitimate IP address assigned by the NIC or service provider*".
Outside local – "*The IP address of an outside host as it appears to the inside network*".
Outside global – "*The IP address assigned to a host on the outside network by the host owner*".

By Cisco's own admission these "definitions still leave a lot to be interpreted".[7]

The configuration we have at the moment is a form of Dynamic NAT, whereby, we have a group of inside local addresses (10.10.3.0/24) mapped to a inside global address (10.10.1.2) yet, because we have used the keyword "overload", we are actually using PAT.

The "overload" keyword instructs the router to perform PAT, or Port Address Translation. This allows us to have a much larger number of hosts on the inside and each UDP or TCP session is given its own port number. These port numbers will be taken from the ranges 0-511, 512-1023 and 1024-65535. Therefore, we can have thousands of translations on one router without any issue. These translations will be generated and flushed depending on the traffic.

We will look at the different NAT types in a moment, but we should return to Spoke-2 now.

Before we fix Spoke-2 we should investigate why it is not working. We start by setting up a debug condition and then by enabling debugging of ISAKMP:

---

[7] http://www.cisco.com/c/en/us/support/docs/ip/network-address-translation-nat/4606-8.html

```
%CRYPTO-4-IKMP_BAD_MESSAGE: IKE message from 10.10.1.2 failed its
sanity check or is malformed
Hub-1#debug condition ip 10.10.1.2
Condition 1 set
Hub-1#debug crypto isakmp
Crypto ISAKMP debugging is on
Hub-1#
```

Without pasting all the logs, we will have a look at a truncated, but pertinent, version of the debug output:

1. Hub-1#
2. ISAKMP (0): received packet from 10.10.1.2 dport 500 sport 500 Global (N) NEW SA
3. ISAKMP: Created a peer struct for 10.10.1.2, peer port 500
4. ISAKMP: New peer created peer = 0x69C32854 peer_handle = 0x8000009E
5. ISAKMP: Locking peer struct 0x69C32854, refcount 1 for crypto_isakmp_process_block
6. ISAKMP: local port 500, remote port 500
7. ISAKMP:(0):insert sa successfully sa = 69C45428
8. ISAKMP:(0):Input = IKE_MESG_FROM_PEER, IKE_MM_EXCH
9. ISAKMP:(0):Old State = IKE_READY New State = IKE_R_MM1
10. ISAKMP:(0): processing SA payload. message ID = 0
11. ISAKMP:(0):found peer pre-shared key matching 10.10.1.2
12. ISAKMP:(0): local preshared key found
13. ISAKMP:(0):Checking ISAKMP transform 1 against priority 1 policy
14. ISAKMP: encryption 3DES-CBC
15. ISAKMP: hash SHA
16. ISAKMP: default group 2
17. ISAKMP: auth pre-share
18. ISAKMP: life type in seconds
19. ISAKMP: life duration (VPI) of 0x0 0x1 0x51 0x80
20. ISAKMP:(0):Encryption algorithm offered does not match policy!
21. ISAKMP:(0):atts are not acceptable. Next payload is 0
22. ISAKMP:(0):Checking ISAKMP transform 1 against priority 2 policy
23. ISAKMP: encryption 3DES-CBC
24. ISAKMP: hash SHA
25. ISAKMP: default group 2
26. ISAKMP: auth pre-share
27. ISAKMP: life type in seconds
28. ISAKMP: life duration (VPI) of 0x0 0x1 0x51 0x80
29. ISAKMP:(0):atts are acceptable. Next payload is 0
30. Hub-1#

From the output we can see that (in line 11) Hub-1 finds a pre-shared key that matches 10.10.1.2. Now, clearly, when we set up the site-to-site VPN we entered a very specific pre-shared key for IGW, which Hub-1 now sees as being the source of Spoke-2's DMVPN connection attempts. We need to change the NAT for Spoke-2, so that we are using a different address to that of the outside interface. We can do this using a static NAT.

7.1 Static NAT

We will now change the NAT statement on IGW, so that instead of mapping the subnet that Spoke-2 resides on to the same outside interface that we use for our site-to-site VPN to Hub-1, we will map Spoke-2's outside address (10.10.3.1) to a completely different address (10.10.1.3). This is an example of a static NAT, in which there is always a 1:1 relationship between the original address and the translated address.

We start by removing the existing NAT:

```
IGW(config)#no ip nat inside source list 3 interface
GigabitEthernet1/0 overload

Dynamic mapping in use, do you want to delete all entries? [no]: yes
IGW(config)#
IGW(config)#ip nat inside source static 10.10.3.1 10.10.1.3
IGW(config)#do sh ip nat trans
Pro   Inside global    Inside local     Outside local    Outside global
icmp  10.10.1.3:0      10.10.3.1:0      10.10.1.1:0      10.10.1.1:0
udp   10.10.1.3:500    10.10.3.1:500    10.10.1.1:500    10.10.1.1:500
udp   10.10.1.3:4500   10.10.3.1:4500   10.10.1.1:4500   10.10.1.1:4500
---   10.10.1.3        10.10.3.1        ---              ---
IGW(config)#
```

We can now send some traffic from Spoke-2 (in order that the translation be properly formed), and our tunnel should come up:

```
Spoke-2#ping 10.10.1.1
Type escape sequence to abort.
Sending 5, 100-byte ICMP Echos to 10.10.1.1:
.!!!!
Success rate is 80 percent (4/5)
Spoke-2#
%OSPF-5-ADJCHG: Process 2, Nbr 1.1.1.1 on Tunnel0 from LOADING to
FULL, Loading Done
Spoke-2#
```

We can see that we have an OSPF adjacency again, so if we go back to Hub-1 we should be able to see a healthy NHRP peering:

```
Hub-1#sh ip nhrp
192.168.1.2/32 via 192.168.1.2
   Tunnel0 created 03:24:19, expire 01:03:12
   Type: dynamic, Flags: unique registered
   NBMA address: 10.10.2.1
   Group: Spoke1
192.168.1.3/32 via 192.168.1.3
   Tunnel0 created 00:01:14, expire 01:58:45
   Type: dynamic, Flags: unique registered
   NBMA address: 10.10.1.3
   Group: Spoke2
     (Claimed NBMA address: 10.10.3.1)
192.168.1.4/32 via 192.168.1.4
   Tunnel0 created 03:24:20, expire 01:03:22
   Type: dynamic, Flags: unique registered
   NBMA address: 10.10.4.1
Hub-1#
```

Here we can see that Spoke-2 has registered with NHRP and the NBMA address is the static translation we set up (10.10.1.3).

With static NAT we can also map port numbers, so keeping with Spoke-2, we could make its telnet port (23) accessible through a different port number (2323):

```
IGW(config)#ip nat inside source static tcp 10.10.3.1 23 10.10.1.3 2323
IGW(config)#
```

We can then try telnetting through to the new port (once we have set a password on Spoke-2):

```
Spoke-2(config)#line vty 0 4
Spoke-2(config-line)#password cisco
Spoke-2(config-line)#

Hub-1#telnet 10.10.1.3 2323
Trying 10.10.1.3, 2323 ... Open


User Access Verification

Password:
Spoke-2>exit

[Connection to 10.10.1.3 closed by foreign host]
Hub-1#
```

We can see this in the translations table:

```
IGW#sh ip nat trans
Pro Inside global    Inside local    Outside local      Outside global
tcp 10.10.1.3:2323   10.10.3.1:23    10.10.1.1:27580    10.10.1.1:27580
tcp 10.10.1.3:2323   10.10.3.1:23    ---                ---
udp 10.10.1.3:4500   10.10.3.1:4500  10.10.1.1:4500     10.10.1.1:4500
--- 10.10.1.3        10.10.3.1       ---                ---
IGW#
```

There is a lot we can do with static NAT and we will have a look at some of these now. In order to do this we should set up our Services router and add some loopback interfaces to it. Because we do not want to set up multiple static routes, we will join it with Hub-1 using OSPF. Feel free to save and turn off the Spoke routers, as we do not need these at this stage.

```
Hub-1(config)#int gi 2/0
Hub-1(config-if)#ip add 10.250.1.1 255.255.255.0
Hub-1(config-if)#desc Link to ISP-1
Hub-1(config-if)#no sh
Hub-1(config-if)#int gi 3/0
Hub-1(config-if)#ip add 10.250.2.1 255.255.255.0
Hub-1(config-if)#desc Link to ISP-2
Hub-1(config-if)#no shu
Hub-1(config-if)#router ospf 1
Hub-1(config-router)#net 10.250.1.0 0.0.0.255 a 0
Hub-1(config-router)#net 10.250.2.0 0.0.0.255 a 0
Hub-1(config-router)#

ISP-1 (config)#int gi 1/0
ISP-1 (config-if)#ip add 10.250.1.2 255.255.255.0
ISP-1 (config-if)#desc Link to Hub-1
ISP-1 (config-if)#no sh
ISP-1 (config-if)#int gi 2/0
ISP-1 (config-if)#ip add 10.251.1.2 255.255.255.0
ISP-1 (config-if)#desc Link to Services
ISP-1 (config-if)#no sh
ISP-1 (config-if)#router ospf 1
ISP-1 (config-router)#net 10.250.1.0 0.0.0.255 a 0
ISP-1 (config-router)#net 10.251.1.0 0.0.0.255 a 0
ISP-1 (config-router)#exit
ISP-1(config)#end

ISP-2(config)#int gi 1/0
ISP-2(config-if)#ip add 10.250.2.2 255.255.255.0
```

```
ISP-2(config-if)#desc Link to Hub-1
ISP-2(config-if)#no sh
ISP-2(config-if)#int gi 2/0
ISP-2(config-if)#ip add 10.251.2.2 255.255.255.0
ISP-2(config-if)#desc Link to Services
ISP-2(config-if)#no sh
ISP-2(config-if)#router ospf 1
ISP-2(config-router)#net 10.250.2.0 0.0.0.255 a 0
ISP-2(config-router)#net 10.251.2.0 0.0.0.255 a 0
ISP-2(config-router)#end

Services(config)#int gi 1/0
Services(config-if)#ip add 10.251.1.1 255.255.255.0
Services(config-if)#desc Link to ISP-1
Services(config-if)#no sh
Services(config-if)#int gi 2/0
Services(config-if)#ip add 10.251.2.1 255.255.255.0
Services(config-if)#desc Link to ISP-2
Services(config-if)#no sh
Services(config-if)#router ospf 1
Services(config-router)#net 10.251.1.0 0.0.0.255 a 0
Services(config-router)#net 10.251.2.0 0.0.0.255 a 0
Services(config-router)#
Services(config-router)#do sh ip route ospf | b Gate
Gateway of last resort is not set

      10.0.0.0/8 is variably subnetted, 7 subnets, 2 masks
O        10.10.1.0/24 [110/3] via 10.251.2.2, 00:00:05, Gi2/0
                      [110/3] via 10.251.1.2, 00:00:15, Gi1/0
O        10.250.1.0/24 [110/2] via 10.251.1.2, 00:00:15, Gi1/0
O        10.250.2.0/24 [110/2] via 10.251.2.2, 00:00:05, Gi2/0
Services(config-router)#
Services(config-router)#int lo0
Services(config-if)#ip add 10.250.10.1 255.255.255.0
Services(config-if)#int lo1
Services(config-if)#ip add 10.250.11.1 255.255.255.0
Services(config-if)#int lo2
Services(config-if)#ip add 10.250.12.1 255.255.255.0
Services(config-if)#
```

Now that we have something to work with, we can have a look, firstly, at static NAT with route-maps.

Static NAT with route-maps

Route-maps are very powerful and we can use them to have very granular control over our routing.

Consider our topology as it stands at the moment. If Hub-1 wants to communicate with one of Services' loopback interfaces (and let's focus on loopback 0 for the moment), it can take two routes; either through ISP-1, or through ISP-2. So what happens if we implement NAT on Services? We introduce an new IP address of 10.251.1.15, which logic would dictate, Hub-1 would reach through its closest interface (Gi2/0). If however, Hub-1 loses the connection to ISP-1, then we could end up with sub-optimal routing and Hub-1 would try and reach it by going through ISP-2. This is not so much an issue in our small environment, yet on a larger scale, this could be very problematic.

Using route-maps, we can have the same inside source address mapped to different outside addresses, depending on what interface our traffic is going through. We can make ISP-1 and ISP-2 access Services Lo0 interface through different addresses.

We start by defining our inside and outside interfaces:

```
Services(config-if)#int gi 1/0
Services(config-if)#ip nat outside

%LINEPROTO-5-UPDOWN: Line protocol on Interface NVI0, changed state to up
Services(config-if)#
Services(config-if)#int gi 2/0
Services(config-if)#ip nat outside
Services(config-if)#int lo0
Services(config-if)#ip nat inside
Services(config-if)#exit
```

Next we set up two NAT statements, each specifying a route-map:

```
Services(config)#ip nat inside source static 10.250.10.1 10.251.1.15 route-map ToISP-1
Services(config)#ip nat inside source static 10.250.10.1 10.251.2.15 route-map ToISP-2
Services(config)#
```

Lastly, we create the route-maps and all we do here is match the nearest outside interface:

```
Services(config)#route-map ToISP-1 permit 10
```

```
Services(config-route-map)#match interface gi 1/0
Services(config-route-map)#exit
Services(config)#route-map ToISP-2 permit 10
Services(config-route-map)#match interface gi 2/0
Services(config-route-map)#exit
Services(config)#
```

So now, if all is working, we should be able to get to 10.250.10.1 through two different addresses. We can now ping this address from ISP-1 and see the translations being created:

```
ISP-1#ping 10.251.1.15
Type escape sequence to abort.
Sending 5, 100-byte ICMP Echos to 10.251.1.15:
!!!!!
Success rate is 100 percent (5/5)
ISP-1#

Services(config)#do sh ip nat trans
Pro Inside global      Inside local     Outside local    Outside global
icmp 10.251.1.15:1     10.250.10.1:1    10.251.1.2:1     10.251.1.2:1
--- 10.251.1.15        10.250.10.1      ---              ---
--- 10.251.2.15        10.250.10.1      ---              ---
Services(config)#
```

When we do the same from ISP-2, we see another translation get created:

```
ISP-2#ping 10.251.2.15
Type escape sequence to abort.
Sending 5, 100-byte ICMP Echos to 10.251.2.15:
!!!!!
Success rate is 100 percent (5/5)
ISP-2#

Services(config)#do sh ip nat trans
Pro Inside global      Inside local     Outside local    Outside global
icmp 10.251.2.15:1     10.250.10.1:1    10.251.2.2:1     10.251.2.2:1
icmp 10.251.1.15:2     10.250.10.1:2    10.251.1.2:2     10.251.1.2:2
--- 10.251.1.15        10.250.10.1      ---              ---
--- 10.251.2.15        10.250.10.1      ---              ---
Services(config)#
```

The translations table shows us the 1:1 mapping of the real IP address to NAT IP address. However, as we know, we also require a layer 2 mapping, otherwise we would have no connectivity. This is achieved using the Alias table, which is highly important, as we will see next.

Static NAT with IP aliasing

As well as keeping the translation table, IOS also keeps an alias table, which is used for ARP. IP aliasing is automatic. We can see the generated aliases using the command "sh ip alias":

```
Services(config)#do sh ip aliases
Address Type            IP Address      Port
Interface               10.250.10.1
Interface               10.250.11.1
Interface               10.250.12.1
Interface               10.251.1.1
Dynamic                 10.251.1.15
Interface               10.251.2.1
Dynamic                 10.251.2.15
Services(config)#
```

This means that the Services router can perform ARP from the outside:

```
Services(config)#do sh arp
Protocol   Address          Age (min)  Hardware Addr   Type  Interface
Internet   10.251.1.1              -   ca03.042f.001c  ARPA  Gi1/0
Internet   10.251.1.2             22   ca04.0430.0038  ARPA  Gi1/0
Internet   10.251.1.15             -   ca03.042f.001c  ARPA  Gi1/0
Internet   10.251.2.1              -   ca03.042f.0038  ARPA  Gi2/0
Internet   10.251.2.2             20   ca05.0431.0038  ARPA  Gi2/0
Internet   10.251.2.15             -   ca03.042f.0038  ARPA  Gi2/0
Services(config)#
```

If, for any reason we do not want this to occur, we can disable it using the keyword "no-alias":

```
Services(config)#ip nat inside source static 10.250.10.1 10.251.2.15 route-map ToISP-2 no-alias
```

> If you want to stop the commands being truncated (replaced with a $) on the console, do the following:
>
> ```
> Services(config)#line console 0
> Services(config-line)#width 512
> Services(config-line)#exit
> Services(config)#
> ```

Let's go ahead and create some more loopbacks on Hub-1, and advertise them into OSPF:

```
Hub-1(config-router)#int lo4
Hub-1(config-if)#ip add 172.16.4.1 255.255.255.0
Hub-1(config-if)#int lo5
Hub-1(config-if)#ip add 172.16.5.1 255.255.255.0
Hub-1(config-if)#router ospf 1
Hub-1(config-router)#net 172.16.5.0 0.0.0.255 a 0
Hub-1(config-router)#net 172.16.4.0 0.0.0.255 a 0
Hub-1(config-router)#
```

Now, if we do a trace through to Hub-1, we can see there is no entry for 10.251.2.15.

```
Services(config)#do trace 172.16.4.1 so lo0
Type escape sequence to abort.
Tracing the route to 172.16.4.1
VRF info: (vrf in name/id, vrf out name/id)
  1 10.251.1.2 36 msec
    10.251.2.2 44 msec
    10.251.1.2 12 msec
  2 10.250.2.1 56 msec
    10.250.1.1 52 msec
    10.250.2.1 20 msec
Services(config)#do sh ip alias
Address Type              IP Address         Port
Interface                 10.250.10.1
Interface                 10.250.11.1
Interface                 10.250.12.1
Interface                 10.251.1.1
Dynamic                   10.251.1.15
Interface                 10.251.2.1
Services(config)#
```

We do not have an ARP entry for it either:

```
Services(config)#do sh arp
Protocol  Address        Age (min)  Hardware Addr    Type   Interface
Internet  10.251.1.1          -     ca03.042f.001c   ARPA   Gi1/0
Internet  10.251.1.2         38     ca04.0430.0038   ARPA   Gi1/0
Internet  10.251.1.15         -     ca03.042f.001c   ARPA   Gi1/0
Internet  10.251.2.1          -     ca03.042f.0038   ARPA   Gi2/0
Internet  10.251.2.2         36     ca05.0431.0038   ARPA   Gi2/0
Services(config)#
```

To see the actual effect that this has, we need to look at ISP-2. If it has an arp entry for 10.251.2.15 then clear it using the command "clear arp 10.251.2.15", it may take a few moments for the entry to clear, or you may have to run it again:

```
ISP-2#clear arp 10.251.2.15
ISP-2#sh arp
Protocol   Address         Age (min)  Hardware Addr   Type   Interface
Internet   10.250.2.1           50    ca01.042d.0054  ARPA   Gi1/0
Internet   10.250.2.2            -    ca05.0431.001c  ARPA   Gi1/0
Internet   10.251.2.1           48    ca03.042f.0038  ARPA   Gi2/0
Internet   10.251.2.2            -    ca05.0431.0038  ARPA   Gi2/0
Internet   10.251.2.15          37    ca03.042f.0038  ARPA   Gi2/0
ISP-2#sh arp
Protocol   Address         Age (min)  Hardware Addr   Type   Interface
Internet   10.250.2.1           50    ca01.042d.0054  ARPA Gi1/0
Internet   10.250.2.2            -    ca05.0431.001c  ARPA Gi1/0
Internet   10.251.2.1           48    ca03.042f.0038  ARPA Gi2/0
Internet   10.251.2.2            -    ca05.0431.0038  ARPA Gi2/0
ISP-2#
```

With the entry now gone, try pinging it:

```
ISP-2#ping 10.251.2.15
Type escape sequence to abort.
Sending 5, 100-byte ICMP Echos to 10.251.2.15:
.....
Success rate is 0 percent (0/5)
ISP-2#
```

It will fail. Because Services is no longer providing aliasing for this particular NAT, it does not generate an ARP entry on ISP-2, and the ping fails. We can fix this by adding a static ARP entry on ISP-2 (note that you may not have the exact same MAC address as the output above):

```
ISP-2#conf t
ISP-2(config)#arp 10.251.2.15 ca03.042f.0038 arpa
ISP-2(config)#do ping 10.251.2.15
Type escape sequence to abort.
Sending 5, 100-byte ICMP Echos to 10.251.2.15:
!!!!!
Success rate is 100 percent (5/5)
ISP-2(config)#
```

Alternatively, we can turn on the alias again and watch the ping succeed:

```
Services(config)#ip nat inside source static 10.250.10.1 10.251.2.15
route-map ToISP-2
Services(config)#

ISP-2(config)#no arp 10.251.2.15 ca03.042f.0038 arpa
ISP-2(config)#do sh arp
Protocol   Address          Age (min)   Hardware Addr    Type    Interface
Internet   10.250.2.1            65     ca01.042d.0054   ARPA    Gi1/0
Internet   10.250.2.2             -     ca05.0431.001c   ARPA    Gi1/0
Internet   10.251.2.1            65     ca03.042f.0038   ARPA    Gi2/0
Internet   10.251.2.2             -     ca05.0431.0038   ARPA    Gi2/0
ISP-2(config)#do ping 10.251.2.15
Type escape sequence to abort.
Sending 5, 100-byte ICMP Echos to 10.251.2.15:
.!!!!
Success rate is 80 percent (4/5)
ISP-2(config)#
```

A third alternative would be to use proxy-arp, but our network is not well suited to this.

Policy-based NAT

With policy-based NAT we can have one inside host with two different global addresses, depending on whom we are talking to. In this example we will give Services' Lo1 interface different IP addresses, depending on which of Hub-1's loopback interfaces (either Lo4 or Lo5) it is talking to.

We start with a couple of extended access-lists to match our Lo1 interface to the different loopbacks on Hub-1:

```
Services(config)#ip access-list extended Hub-1-lo4
Services(config-ext-nacl)#permit ip host 10.250.11.1 host 172.16.4.1
Services(config-ext-nacl)#exit
Services(config)#ip access-list extended Hub-1-lo5
Services(config-ext-nacl)#permit ip host 10.250.11.1 host 172.16.5.1
Services(config-ext-nacl)#exit
```

We then create a route-map to match these access-lists:

```
Services(config)#route-map lo1-to-hub-1-lo4 permit 10
Services(config-route-map)#match ip address Hub-1-lo4
Services(config-route-map)#exit
Services(config)#route-map lo1-to-hub-1-lo5 permit 10
Services(config-route-map)#match ip address Hub-1-lo5
Services(config-route-map)#exit
```

Services(config)#

Lastly, we create the NAT objects, referencing the route-maps we just created:

```
Services(config)#int lo1
Services(config-if)#ip nat inside
Services(config-if)#ip nat inside source static 10.250.11.1
10.251.1.24 route-map lo1-to-hub-1-lo4
Services(config)#ip nat inside source static 10.250.11.1 10.251.1.25
route-map lo1-to-hub-1-lo5
Services(config)#
```

We have an issue, however. Our Lo1 traffic is only working one way. Pings from Lo1 do not work. Pings do work if we omit the source, so we know basic connectivity is working:

```
Services(config)#do ping 172.16.4.1 so lo1
Type escape sequence to abort.
Sending 5, 100-byte ICMP Echos to 172.16.4.1:
Packet sent with a source address of 10.250.11.1
.....
Success rate is 0 percent (0/5)
Services(config)#do ping 172.16.5.1 so lo1
Type escape sequence to abort.
Sending 5, 100-byte ICMP Echos to 172.16.5.1:
Packet sent with a source address of 10.250.11.1
.....
Success rate is 0 percent (0/5)
Services(config)#do ping 172.16.5.1
Type escape sequence to abort.
Sending 5, 100-byte ICMP Echos to 172.16.5.1:
!!!!!
Success rate is 100 percent (5/5)
Services(config)#do ping 172.16.4.1
Type escape sequence to abort.
Sending 5, 100-byte ICMP Echos to 172.16.4.1:
!!!!!
Success rate is 100 percent (5/5)
Services(config)#
```

Hub-1 can access the correct IP addresses, as required:

```
Hub-1(config-router)#do ping 10.251.1.24 so lo4
Type escape sequence to abort.
Sending 5, 100-byte ICMP Echos to 10.251.1.24:
Packet sent with a source address of 172.16.4.1
!!!!!
```

```
Success rate is 100 percent (5/5)
Hub-1(config-router)#do ping 10.251.1.25 so lo5
Type escape sequence to abort.
Sending 5, 100-byte ICMP Echos to 10.251.1.25:
Packet sent with a source address of 172.16.5.1
!!!!!
Success rate is 100 percent (5/5)
Hub-1(config-router)#
```

We can also see that the translations are working properly when the traffic is inbound:

```
Services(config)#do sh ip nat trans
Pro Inside global    Inside local    Outside local   Outside global
icmp 10.251.1.24:0   10.250.11.1:0   172.16.4.1:0    172.16.4.1:0
icmp 10.251.1.25:1   10.250.11.1:1   172.16.5.1:1    172.16.5.1:1
---  10.251.1.15     10.250.10.1     ---             ---
---  10.251.1.24     10.250.11.1     ---             ---
---  10.251.1.25     10.250.11.1     ---             ---
---  10.251.2.15     10.250.10.1     ---             ---
Services(config)#
```

Hopefully, some debugging will help us here:

```
Services(config)#do debug ip nat
IP NAT debugging is on
Services(config)#do ping 172.16.4.1 so lo1
Type escape sequence to abort.
Sending 5, 100-byte ICMP Echos to 172.16.4.1:
Packet sent with a source address of 10.250.11.1
.....
Success rate is 0 percent (0/5)
Services(config)#
```

Not much there. Let's go a bit deeper:

```
Services(config)#do debug ip nat detailed
IP NAT detailed debugging is on
Services(config)#do ping 172.16.4.1 so lo1
Type escape sequence to abort.
Sending 5, 100-byte ICMP Echos to 172.16.4.1:
Packet sent with a source address of 10.250.11.1

*Jan  8 21:56:55.499: NAT: map match ToISP-2.
*Jan  8 21:56:57.499: NAT: map match ToISP-2.
*Jan  8 21:56:59.499: NAT: map match ToISP-2.
*Jan  8 21:57:01.499: NAT: map match ToISP-2.
```

```
*Jan  8 21:57:03.499: NAT: map match ToISP-2.
Success rate is 0 percent (0/5)
Services(config)#
```

Now we are getting somewhere. Our very broad route-map (ToISP-2), which we set up a while ago, is set to match on interface only. So we need to add another clause to this route-map, so that it matches the interface AND the source address:

```
Services(config)#ip access-list extended MyLo0
Services(config-ext-nacl)#permit ip host 10.250.10.1 any
Services(config-ext-nacl)#exit
Services(config)#route-map ToISP-2 permit 10
Services(config-route-map)#match ip address MyLo0
Services(config-route-map)#exit
Services(config)#
```

We can confirm that the route-map looks like it should (that we have both the match clauses):

```
Services(config)#do sh route-map ToISP-2
route-map ToISP-2, permit, sequence 10
  Match clauses:
    ip address (access-lists): MyLo0
    interface GigabitEthernet2/0
  Set clauses:
  Policy routing matches: 0 packets, 0 bytes
Services(config)#
```

Does it work now?

```
Services(config)#do ping 172.16.4.1 so lo1
Type escape sequence to abort.
Sending 5, 100-byte ICMP Echos to 172.16.4.1:
Packet sent with a source address of 10.250.11.1
.....
Success rate is 0 percent (0/5)
Services(config)#do ping 172.16.5.1 so lo1
Type escape sequence to abort.
Sending 5, 100-byte ICMP Echos to 172.16.5.1:
Packet sent with a source address of 10.250.11.1

*Jan  8 22:02:13.795: NAT: map match ToISP-1.
*Jan  8 22:02:15.795: NAT: map match ToISP-1.
*Jan  8 22:02:17.795: NAT: map match ToISP-1.
*Jan  8 22:02:19.795: NAT: map match ToISP-1.
*Jan  8 22:02:21.795: NAT: map match ToISP-1.
```

```
Success rate is 0 percent (0/5)
Services(config)#
```

No, it does not. Testing the other NAT rule, we can see that we need to perform the same actions for the route-map ToISP-1.

> Note that the order in which we need to edit the route-maps may differ – in my first test ToISP-1 was shown in the first debug. In my third test the ping actually worked fine. If it works for you then please do still edit the other route-map!

We do not need to create another access-list, we can just reference the one we just created (MyLo0):

```
Services(config)#route-map ToISP-1 permit 10
Services(config-route-map)#match ip address MyLo0
Services(config-route-map)#exit
```

Let's give it a shot now:

```
Services(config)#do ping 172.16.4.1 so lo1
Type escape sequence to abort.
Sending 5, 100-byte ICMP Echos to 172.16.4.1:
Packet sent with a source address of 10.250.11.1
!!!!!
Success rate is 100 percent (5/5)
Services(config)#
   NAT: map match lo1-to-hub-1-lo4
      mapping pointer available mapping:0
   NAT: New entry added to map hash table
   NAT: i: icmp (10.250.11.1, 23) -> (172.16.4.1, 23) [115]
   NAT: s=10.250.11.1->10.251.1.24, d=172.16.4.1 [115]
   NAT*: o: icmp (172.16.4.1, 23) -> (10.251.1.24, 23) [115]
   NAT*: s=172.16.4.1, d=10.251.1.24->10.250.11.1 [115]
   NAT: i: icmp (10.250.11.1, 23) -> (172.16.4.1, 23) [116]
   NAT: s=10.250.11.1->10.251.1.24, d=172.16.4.1 [116]
   NAT*: o: icmp (172.16.4.1, 23) -> (10.251.1.24, 23) [116]
   NAT*: s=172.16.4.1, d=10.251.1.24->10.250.11.1 [116]
   NAT: i: icmp (10.250.11.1, 23) -> (172.16.4.1, 23) [117]
   NAT: s=10.250.11.1->10.251.1.24, d=172.16.4.1 [117]
   NAT*
Services(config)#
```

That looks better!

```
Services(config)#do ping 172.16.5.1 so lo1
Type escape sequence to abort.
Sending 5, 100-byte ICMP Echos to 172.16.5.1:
Packet sent with a source address of 10.250.11.1
!!!!
   NAT: map match lo1-to-hub-1-lo5
     mapping pointer available mapping:0
   NAT: New entry added to map hash table
   NAT: i: icmp (10.250.11.1, 24) -> (172.16.5.1, 24) [120]
   NAT: s=10.250.11.1->10.251.1.25, d=172.16.5.1 [120]
   NAT*: o: icmp (172.16.5.1, 24) -> (10.251.1.25, 24) [120]
   NAT*: s=172.16.5.1, d=10.251.1.25->10.250.11.1 [120]
   NAT: i: icmp (10.250.11.1, 24) -> (172.16.5.1, 24) [121]
   NAT: s=10.250.11.1->10.251.1.25, d=172.16.5.1 [121]!
Success rate is 100 percent (5/5)
Services(config)#
```

We can now see that the translations are working as expected.

```
Services(config)#do sh ip nat trans
Pro Inside global      Inside local    Outside local   Outside global
icmp 10.251.1.24:23    10.250.11.1:23  172.16.4.1:23   172.16.4.1:23
icmp 10.251.1.25:24    10.250.11.1:24  172.16.5.1:24   172.16.5.1:24
---  10.251.1.15       10.250.10.1     ---             ---
---  10.251.1.24       10.250.11.1     ---             ---
---  10.251.1.25       10.250.11.1     ---             ---
---  10.251.2.15       10.250.10.1     ---             ---
Services(config)#
```

> If you still do not get the correct translations check back over the object naming and how they are cross-referenced. Can you spot the mistake I made?
>
> ```
> ip nat inside source static 10.250.11.1 10.251.1.24 route-map
> lo1-to-hub-1-lo4
> !
> ip access-list extended Hub-1-lo4
>   permit ip host 10.250.11.1 host 172.16.4.1
> !
> route-map lo1-to-hub1-lo4 permit 10
>   match ip address Hub-1-lo4
> !
> ```
>
> The missing hyphen in the route-map name cost me quite some time in troubleshooting (and again when I went through a second time and missed the upper-case H in the match statement). The lesson here is to pick a naming convention that works for you, one that minimizes the chances of making simple mistakes (which can cost you valuable time, especially in an 8 hour exam!).

Static NAT with Load distribution

One of the nice features with Cisco IOS, is that when everything is created equally, it will happily load-share without requiring manual intervention.

Using one of the loopback interfaces on Hub-1 we can see that load-sharing and NAT happily co-exist. Because the Services router knows about the new path through two different interfaces and because the metrics are all equal, we will use both paths:

```
Services(config)#do sh ip route 172.16.4.1
Routing entry for 172.16.4.1/32
  Known via "ospf 1", distance 110, metric 3, type intra area
  Last update from 10.251.1.2 on Gi1/0, 00:01:01 ago
  Routing Descriptor Blocks:
  * 10.251.2.2, from 192.168.1.1, 00:01:01 ago, via Gi2/0
      Route metric is 3, traffic share count is 1
    10.251.1.2, from 192.168.1.1, 00:01:01 ago, via Gi1/0
      Route metric is 3, traffic share count is 1
Services(config)#do trace 172.16.4.1
Type escape sequence to abort.
Tracing the route to 172.16.4.1
```

```
    VRF info: (vrf in name/id, vrf out name/id)
      1 10.251.1.2 44 msec
        10.251.2.2 32 msec
        10.251.1.2 16 msec
      2 10.250.2.1 16 msec
        10.250.1.1 40 msec
        10.250.2.1 36 msec
    Services(config)#
```

Because we were not performing NAT here, our translation table will be empty:

```
    Services(config)#do sh ip nat trans
    Pro Inside global    Inside local     Outside local    Outside global
    --- 10.251.1.15      10.250.10.1      ---              ---
    --- 10.251.2.15      10.250.10.1      ---              ---
    Services(config)#
```

If we perform the same trace, but specify Lo0 as our source, this will be NATed, and we can see the translations across both paths in the translations table. Please note that to prevent column wrapping and making the output harder to read, I have removed the first three digits of the translated port. For the Inside global and Inside local these are 491, and for the Outside they are 334.

```
    Services(config)#do trace 172.16.4.1 so lo0
    Type escape sequence to abort.
    Tracing the route to 172.16.4.1
    VRF info: (vrf in name/id, vrf out name/id)
      1 10.251.1.2 36 msec
        10.251.2.2 24 msec
        10.251.1.2 20 msec
      2 10.250.2.1 20 msec
        10.250.1.1 60 msec
        10.250.2.1 24 msec
    Services(config)#do sh ip nat trans
    Pro Inside global    Inside local     Outside local    Outside global
    udp 10.251.1.15:61   10.250.10.1:61   172.16.4.1:34    172.16.4.1:34
    udp 10.251.2.15:62   10.250.10.1:62   172.16.4.1:35    172.16.4.1:35
    udp 10.251.1.15:63   10.250.10.1:63   172.16.4.1:36    172.16.4.1:36
    udp 10.251.2.15:64   10.250.10.1:64   172.16.4.1:37    172.16.4.1:37
    udp 10.251.1.15:65   10.250.10.1:65   172.16.4.1:38    172.16.4.1:38
    udp 10.251.2.15:66   10.250.10.1:66   172.16.4.1:39    172.16.4.1:39
    --- 10.251.1.15      10.250.10.1      ---              ---
    --- 10.251.2.15      10.250.10.1      ---              ---
    Services(config)#
```

We can load-balance as well. An easy way to see this is to set up multiple IP addresses on one interface and using the rotary keyword, instruct the router to use each in turn.

We start by setting up some more IP addresses on Lo2, and enabling it for NAT:

```
Services(config)#int lo2
Services(config-if)#ip nat inside
Services(config-if)#ip add 10.250.12.2 255.255.255.0 sec
Services(config-if)#ip add 10.250.12.3 255.255.255.0 sec
Services(config-if)#ip add 10.250.12.4 255.255.255.0 sec
Services(config-if)#ip add 10.250.12.5 255.255.255.0 sec
Services(config-if)#exit
```

We then create a rotary pool for all of the addresses on Lo2. Next, we create an access-list – this contains our NAT address, and finally, we create a NAT statement that ties these all together:

```
Services(config)#ip nat pool Lo2-pool 10.250.12.1 10.250.12.5 prefix-len 24 type rotary
Services(config)#access-list 1 permit host 10.251.1.215
Services(config)#ip nat inside destination list 1 pool Lo2-pool
```

At the moment, we do not have any additional entries in the translation table, so let's generate some traffic and see what happens.

```
Services(config)#do sh ip nat trans
Pro Inside global      Inside local      Outside local     Outside global
--- 10.251.1.15        10.250.10.1       ---               ---
--- 10.251.1.24        10.250.11.1       ---               ---
--- 10.251.1.25        10.250.11.1       ---               ---
--- 10.251.2.15        10.250.10.1       ---               ---
Services(config-if)#

Hub-1#telnet 10.251.1.215
Trying 10.251.1.215 ...
% Connection timed out; remote host not responding

Hub-1#
```

It fails. If we look at our alias table, we see that there is no alias generated. As we have seen before this is very important!

```
Services(config-if)#do sh ip alias
Address Type            IP Address         Port
Interface               10.250.10.1
```

```
Interface                10.250.11.1
Interface                10.250.12.1
Interface                10.250.12.2
Interface                10.250.12.3
Interface                10.250.12.4
Interface                10.250.12.5
Interface                10.251.1.1
Dynamic                  10.251.1.15
Dynamic                  10.251.1.24
Dynamic                  10.251.1.25
Interface                10.251.2.1
Dynamic                  10.251.2.15
Services(config-if)#
```

Instead of creating a static ARP entry, like we did last time, we will create a static alias instead:

```
Services(config-if)#exit
Services(config)#ip alias 10.251.1.215 ?
  <1-65535>  IP port number

Services(config)#ip alias 10.251.1.215 23
Services(config)#
```

Now we can see the entry:

```
Services(config)#do sh ip alias
Address Type             IP Address       Port
Interface                10.250.10.1
Interface                10.250.11.1
Interface                10.250.12.1
Interface                10.250.12.2
Interface                10.250.12.3
Interface                10.250.12.4
Interface                10.250.12.5
Interface                10.251.1.1
Dynamic                  10.251.1.15
Dynamic                  10.251.1.24
Dynamic                  10.251.1.25
Alias                    10.251.1.215     23
Interface                10.251.2.1
Dynamic                  10.251.2.15
Services(config)#
```

Because of this, our telnet works:

```
Hub-1#telnet 10.251.1.215
Trying 10.251.1.215 ... Open


Password required, but none set

[Connection to 10.251.1.215 closed by foreign host]
Hub-1#
```

Do this five times in all and we should be able to see that each address in our pool is used, consecutively – we are load-balancing the traffic.

```
Services(config)#do sh ip nat trans
Pro Inside global      Inside local       Outside local      Outside global
tcp 10.251.1.215:23    10.250.12.1:23     10.250.1.1:19318   10.250.1.1:19318
tcp 10.251.1.215:23    10.250.12.2:23     10.250.1.1:32309   10.250.1.1:32309
tcp 10.251.1.215:23    10.250.12.3:23     10.250.1.1:42493   10.250.1.1:42493
tcp 10.251.1.215:23    10.250.12.4:23     10.250.1.1:16121   10.250.1.1:16121
tcp 10.251.1.215:23    10.250.12.5:23     10.250.1.1:27106   10.250.1.1:27106
--- 10.251.1.15        10.250.10.1        ---                ---
--- 10.251.1.24        10.250.11.1        ---                ---
--- 10.251.1.25        10.250.11.1        ---                ---
--- 10.251.2.15        10.250.10.1        ---                ---
Services(config)#
```

So far, all our translations have been from inside-to-outside, so let's see what happens when it is from outside-to-inside.

NAT order of Operation

At the start of this part, we spoke briefly about the NAT "Order of Operation", where the order in which NAT operations are performed, is dependent on which way the traffic is flowing. In the previous example, we saw that we can have NAT traffic working one way only (inbound), so in this case the order of operation will differ to traffic headed out from us.

There is a clearer way to see this though, which we will set up now.

```
Services(config)#ip nat outside source static 172.16.6.1 10.250.13.1
```

In the above statement we are performing NAT from the outside towards the inside. We will now set up Hub-1 to have this new address:

```
Hub-1(config)#int lo6
```

```
Hub-1(config-if)#ip add 172.16.6.1 255.255.255.0
Hub-1(config-if)#router ospf 1
Hub-1(config-router)#net 172.16.6.0 0.0.0.255 a 0

Hub-1(config)#do ping 10.251.1.15 so lo6
Type escape sequence to abort.
Sending 5, 100-byte ICMP Echos to 10.251.1.15:
Packet sent with a source address of 172.16.6.1
.....
Success rate is 0 percent (0/5)
Hub-1(config)#
```

Although the ping fails, it is enough for the translation to succeed:

```
Services(config)#
   NAT: o: icmp (172.16.6.1, 21) -> (10.251.1.15, 21) [106]
   NAT: s=172.16.6.1->10.250.13.1, d=10.251.1.15 [106]
   NAT: s=10.250.13.1, d=10.251.1.15->10.250.10.1 [106]
Services(config)#
Services(config)#do sh ip nat trans
Pro Inside global    Inside local    Outside local   Outside global
--- ---              ---             10.250.13.1     172.16.6.1
icmp 10.251.1.15:21 10.250.10.1:21 10.250.13.1:21 172.16.6.1:21
--- 10.251.1.15      10.250.10.1     ---             ---
--- 10.251.1.24      10.250.11.1     ---             ---
--- 10.251.1.25      10.250.11.1     ---             ---
--- 10.251.2.15      10.250.10.1     ---             ---
Services(config)#
```

If we enable detailed debugging, we can start to see the order of events. The debugging used here will generate a lot of events, including all the OSPF flows, so here is just the relevant data:

1. Services(config)#do debug ip packet detail
2. IP packet debugging is on (detailed)
3. Services(config)#
4. Services(config)#
5. NAT*: o: icmp (172.16.6.1, 23) -> (10.251.1.15, 23) [115]
6. NAT*: s=172.16.6.1->10.250.13.1, d=10.251.1.15 [115]
7. NAT*: s=10.250.13.1, d=10.251.1.15->10.250.10.1 [115]
8. IP: s=10.250.13.1 (GigabitEthernet1/0), d=10.250.10.1, len 100, input feature
9. FIBipv4-packet-proc: route packet from GigabitEthernet1/0 src 10.250.13.1 dst 10.250.10.1
10. FIBfwd-proc: Default:10.250.10.1/32 receive entry
11. FIBipv4-packet-proc: packet routing failed

```
12. IP: tableid=0, s=10.250.13.1 (GigabitEthernet1/0), d=10.250.10.1
    (Loopback0), routed via RIB
13. IP: s=10.250.13.1 (GigabitEthernet1/0), d=10.250.10.1 (Loopback0), len
    100, output feature
```

Repeat the ping from Hub-1 after setting up the debug in line 1. At line 5, our packet comes in from Hub-1 and is translated on line 6, from 172.16.6.1 to 10.250.13.1, with the destination being 10.251.1.15. A reverse translation is set up on the next line (line 7) mapping 10.251.1.15 to 10.250.10.1. On line 11, we can see that the packet routing fails. This was evident from Hub-1 when the pings failed. We can fix this though, through the addition of one keyword:

```
Services(config)#ip nat outside source static 172.16.6.1 10.250.13.1
add-route
Services(config)#end
```

The addition of the "add-route" keyword creates an entry in the routing table for the translation:

```
Services#sh ip route | i 10.250.13.1
S        10.250.13.1/32 [1/0] via 172.16.6.1
Services#
Services#sh ip route 10.250.13.1
Routing entry for 10.250.13.1/32
  Known via "static", distance 1, metric 0
  Routing Descriptor Blocks:
  * 172.16.6.1
      Route metric is 0, traffic share count is 1
Services#
```

Now, if we try and ping again from Hub-1, the ping succeeds:

```
Hub-1(config)#do ping 10.251.1.15 so lo6
Type escape sequence to abort.
Sending 5, 100-byte ICMP Echos to 10.251.1.15:
Packet sent with a source address of 172.16.6.1
!!!!!
Success rate is 100 percent (5/5)
Hub-1(config)#
```

Because the traffic is translated from the outside to the inside, the order of events differs from traffic going from the inside to the outside. Most of the steps are the same, but there is a slight variation:

1	If IPSec is being used, then check input access lists	
2	Decryption	
3	Check input access lists	
4	Check input rate limits	
5	Input accounting	
6	Redirect to web cache	
	Inside-to-Outside	**Outside-to-Inside**
7	Policy routing	NAT Outside to Inside (Global to Local)
8	Routing	Policy Routing
9	NAT Inside to Outside (Local to Global)	Routing
10	Crypto (Check map and mark from encryption)	
11	Check output access list	
12	Inspect CBAC	
13	TCP intercept	
14	Encryption	
15	Queuing	

If we compare the debug logs from our outside-in now to those of inside-out, we should be able to see a difference:

```
Services#ping 172.16.6.1 so lo0 rep 2
Type escape sequence to abort.
Sending 2, 100-byte ICMP Echos to 172.16.6.1:
Packet sent with a source address of 10.250.10.1
!!
Success rate is 100 percent (2/2)
Services#
 1. IP: s=10.251.2.1 (local), d=224.0.0.5 (GigabitEthernet2/0), len 80,
    local feature, NAT(2), rtype 0, forus FALSE, sendself FALSE, mtu 0,
    fwdchk FALSE
 2. IP: s=10.250.10.1 (local), d=172.16.6.1, len 100, local feature,
    NAT(2), rtype 0, forus FALSE, sendself FALSE, mtu 0, fwdchk FALSE
 3. NAT: map match ToISP-1
 4. mapping pointer available mapping:0
 5. NAT: Existing entry found in the global tree,updating it to point
    to the latest node passed
 6. NAT: New entry added to map hash table
 7. NAT: i: icmp (10.250.10.1, 18) -> (172.16.6.1, 18) [70]
 8. NAT: s=10.250.10.1->10.251.1.15, d=172.16.6.1 [70]
 9. NAT*: o: icmp (172.16.6.1, 18) -> (10.251.1.15, 18) [70]
10. NAT*: s=172.16.6.1, d=10.251.1.15->10.250.10.1 [70]
11. IP: s=10.250.10.1 (local), d=172.16.6.1, len 100, loc
Services#
```

We have captured enough to see what is going on. If we compare the outside-to-inside log against the one above, we can see the order of operation is different. The first output shows that the NAT (lines 5-7) occurs before the routing (the IP entries on lines 8, 12 and 13), the second show that routing (lines 1 and 2) occurs before NAT (lines 3 to 11).

Static Extendable NAT

When we looked at policy-based NAT, we had one host with different addresses, depending on whom we were talking to. We can, though, have one host with two different addresses, no matter whom we are talking to.

If we try to enter two NAT statements, each with different inside global addresses, we get denied:

```
Services(config)#ip nat inside source static 10.250.14.1 10.251.1.141
Services(config)#ip nat inside source static 10.250.14.1 10.251.1.142
% 10.250.14.1 already mapped (10.250.14.1 -> 10.251.1.141)
Services(config)#
```

To overcome this, we can use the "extendable" keyword, which is needed on both statements:

```
Services(config)#ip nat inside source static 10.250.14.1 10.251.1.141 extendable
Services(config)#ip nat inside source static 10.250.14.1 10.251.1.142 extendable
Services(config)#
```

Let's create a loopback with this IP address and see this in action:

```
Services(config)#int lo4
Services(config-if)#ip add 10.250.14.1 255.255.255.0
Services(config-if)#end
Services#sh ip nat trans
Pro Inside global     Inside local    Outside local    Outside global
--- ---                ---              10.250.13.1      172.16.6.1
--- 10.251.1.141      10.250.14.1      ---              ---
--- 10.251.1.15       10.250.10.1      ---              ---
--- 10.251.1.24       10.250.11.1      ---              ---
--- 10.251.1.25       10.250.11.1      ---              ---
--- 10.251.1.142      10.250.14.1      ---              ---
--- 10.251.2.15       10.250.10.1      ---              ---
Services#
```

```
Hub-1#ping 10.251.1.141
Type escape sequence to abort.
Sending 5, 100-byte ICMP Echos to 10.251.1.141:
!!!!!
Success rate is 100 percent (5/5)
Hub-1#ping 10.251.1.142
Type escape sequence to abort.
Sending 5, 100-byte ICMP Echos to 10.251.1.142:
!!!!!
Success rate is 100 percent (5/5)
Hub-1#
```

Now we have two connections to the same host, using different global addresses.

```
Services#sh ip nat trans
Pro Inside global    Inside local   Outside local Outside global
--- ---              ---            10.250.13.1   172.16.6.1
icmp 10.251.1.141:10 10.250.14.1:10 10.250.1.1:10 10.250.1.1:10
icmp 10.251.1.142:11 10.250.14.1:11 10.250.1.1:11 10.250.1.1:11
--- 10.251.1.141     10.250.14.1    ---           ---
--- 10.251.1.15      10.250.10.1    ---           ---
--- 10.251.1.24      10.250.11.1    ---           ---
--- 10.251.1.25      10.250.11.1    ---           ---
--- 10.251.1.142     10.250.14.1    ---           ---
--- 10.251.2.15      10.250.10.1    ---           ---
Services#
```

NAT ALG

NAT ALG (Application Layer Gateway) is a way of supporting those applications that separate the control and data parts – such as FTP, where the control (the commands used to transfer) occurs over port 21, and the actual data transfer uses port 20. This method of splitting the traffic into two distinct streams is also used heavily in SIP traffic, as well as TOR, and messaging clients, where voice, video and file transfer occur over different ports.

ALG is on by default, and this is referred to as "fixups". If we want to turn it off we would use the keyword "no-payload". There are not many resources or guides, as to how and when to use the "no-payload" option, but those that can be found are usually written with DNS in mind. The example NAT statement would be:

```
Services(config)#ip nat inside source static tcp 10.250.14.1 53 10.251.1.141 53 no-payload
```

From the Cisco documentation this "Prohibits the translation of an embedded address or port in the payload". In the context of DNS and to give a scenario in which the usage of the "no-payload" command would be applicable, then imagine that we have a DNS server behind a router performing NAT. The client sends a DNS lookup to the server, the server replies, with the correct data, but the NAT router sends an ICMP Destination Unreachable back to the client. The "no-payload" option fixes this issue.

The scenarios where this is required are very specific and in most probability, over-kill for our needs for the exam.

It is time to leave static NAT, and move on to dynamic NAT.

7.2 Dynamic NAT

We start, as always, with some loopback interfaces to play with. Note, we are using /32 subnets, so that we can have them as individual hosts, in order that we can use a /24 supernet later on:

```
Services(config)#int lo5
Services(config-if)#ip add 10.250.15.1 255.255.255.255
Services(config-if)#int lo6
Services(config-if)#ip add 10.250.15.2 255.255.255.255
Services(config-if)#int lo7
Services(config-if)#ip add 10.250.15.3 255.255.255.255
```

Next, we set up an access-list to match our new subnet (10.250.15.0/24).

```
Services(config-if)#access-list 10 permit 10.250.15.0 0.0.0.255
```

We then create a NAT pool, with an address range of 10.251.1.20 – 10.251.1.25:

```
Services(config)#ip nat pool loopbacks-pool 10.251.1.20 10.251.1.25 netmask 255.255.255.0
```

The final step is to create a NAT statement, which matches the access-list (10) to our NAT pool (loopbacks-pool):

```
Services(config)#ip nat inside source list 10 pool loopbacks-pool
Services(config)#
```

To test this out, we can send some packets from each of the new loopback addresses to the same destination, though using the same destination is not a requirement, it just makes this easier to interpret in our example:

```
Services(config)#do ping 172.16.4.1 so lo5
Type escape sequence to abort.
Sending 5, 100-byte ICMP Echos to 172.16.4.1:
Packet sent with a source address of 10.250.15.1
.!!!!
Success rate is 80 percent (4/5)
Services(config)#do ping 172.16.4.1 so lo6
Type escape sequence to abort.
Sending 5, 100-byte ICMP Echos to 172.16.4.1:
Packet sent with a source address of 10.250.15.2
!!!!!
Success rate is 100 percent (5/5)
Services(config)#do ping 172.16.4.1 so lo7
Type escape sequence to abort.
Sending 5, 100-byte ICMP Echos to 172.16.4.1:
Packet sent with a source address of 10.250.15.3
!!!!!
Success rate is 100 percent (5/5)
Services(config)#
```

These pings each create a NAT translation, starting with the first IP address in our range (10.251.1.20) and incrementing in a one-to-one basis:

```
Services(config)#do sh ip nat trans
Pro Inside global      Inside local       Outside local    Outside global
--- ---                ---                10.250.13.1      172.16.6.1
--- 10.251.1.141       10.250.14.1        ---              ---
icmp 10.251.1.20:22    10.250.15.1:22     172.16.4.1:22    172.16.4.1:22
--- 10.251.1.20        10.250.15.1        ---              ---
icmp 10.251.1.21:23    10.250.15.2:23     172.16.4.1:23    172.16.4.1:23
--- 10.251.1.21        10.250.15.2        ---              ---
icmp 10.251.1.22:24    10.250.15.3:24     172.16.4.1:24    172.16.4.1:24
--- 10.251.1.22        10.250.15.3        ---              ---
--- 10.251.1.15        10.250.10.1        ---              ---
--- 10.251.1.24        10.250.11.1        ---              ---
--- 10.251.1.25        10.250.11.1        ---              ---
--- 10.251.1.142       10.250.14.1        ---              ---
--- 10.251.2.15        10.250.10.1        ---              ---
Services(config)#
```

A nice feature of dynamic NAT is that we can, under certain situations, match the host portion of the inside address to the host portion of the translated global address. So, if our inside local range had been 10.250.15.20 – 10.250.15.22 then at the moment, the first host to initiate traffic would get 10.251.1.20, the next one would get 10.251.1.21 and so on. If we added the keyword "type match-host" then 10.250.15.20 would get 10.251.1.20, 10.250.15.21 would get 10.251.1.21 and so on.

Let's see this in action:

```
Services(config)#int lo5
Services(config-if)#ip add 10.250.15.20 255.255.255.255
Services(config-if)#int lo6
Services(config-if)#ip add 10.250.15.21 255.255.255.255
Services(config-if)#int lo7
Services(config-if)#ip add 10.250.15.22 255.255.255.255
```

If we try and add the "match-host" keyword, we find that we cannot change a pool that is in use. We, also, cannot delete a pool that is in use, so we must clear the translations. Once this is done, we can delete the pool and recreate it, using the keyword:

```
Services(config)#ip nat pool loopbacks-pool 10.251.1.20 10.251.1.25 netmask 255.255.255.0 type match-host
%Pool loopbacks-pool in use, cannot redefine
Services(config)#no ip nat pool loopbacks-pool 10.251.1.20 10.251.1.25 netmask 255.255.255.0
%Pool loopbacks-pool in use, cannot destroy
Services(config)#do clear ip nat trans *
Services(config)#no ip nat pool loopbacks-pool 10.251.1.20 10.251.1.25 netmask 255.255.255.0
Services(config)#ip nat pool loopbacks-pool 10.251.1.20 10.251.1.25 netmask 255.255.255.0 type match-host
Services(config)#
```

Now, we have matching host IDs!

```
Services(config)#do ping 172.16.4.1 so lo5
Type escape sequence to abort.
Sending 5, 100-byte ICMP Echos to 172.16.4.1:
Packet sent with a source address of 10.250.15.20
!!!!!
Success rate is 100 percent (5/5)
Services(config)#do ping 172.16.4.1 so lo6
Type escape sequence to abort.
Sending 5, 100-byte ICMP Echos to 172.16.4.1:
Packet sent with a source address of 10.250.15.21
!!!!!
Success rate is 100 percent (5/5)
```

```
Services(config)#do ping 172.16.4.1 so lo7
Type escape sequence to abort.
Sending 5, 100-byte ICMP Echos to 172.16.4.1:
Packet sent with a source address of 10.250.15.22
!!!!!
Success rate is 100 percent (5/5)
Services(config)#do sh ip nat trans
Pro Inside global      Inside local       Outside local    Outside global
--- ---                ---                10.250.13.1      172.16.6.1
--- 10.251.1.141       10.250.14.1        ---              ---
icmp 10.251.1.20:25    10.250.15.20:25    172.16.4.1:25    172.16.4.1:25
--- 10.251.1.20        10.250.15.20       ---              ---
icmp 10.251.1.21:26    10.250.15.21:26    172.16.4.1:26    172.16.4.1:26
--- 10.251.1.21        10.250.15.21       ---              ---
icmp 10.251.1.22:27    10.250.15.22:27    172.16.4.1:27    172.16.4.1:27
--- 10.251.1.22        10.250.15.22       ---              ---
--- 10.251.1.15        10.250.10.1        ---              ---
--- 10.251.1.24        10.250.11.1        ---              ---
--- 10.251.1.25        10.250.11.1        ---              ---
--- 10.251.1.142       10.250.14.1        ---              ---
--- 10.251.2.15        10.250.10.1        ---              ---
Services(config)#
```

As you can see, whilst dynamic NAT works well, it does have limitations – we can only NAT as many local addresses as we have global addresses. If we extended our example here to include three more loopback interfaces and if all tried to access the outside at the same time, the last one would fail. We would have run out of global addresses to use, and they would have to wait until the others went quiet and the translations timed out.

Thankfully, there is a solution to this and that is Port Address Translation.

7.3 PAT (Port Address Translation)

As we have already seen, one keyword can solve all our problems. We saw an issue with dynamic NAT, in that the number of inside hosts we can perform NAT for, is only as good as the number of global addresses we have - due to the one-to-one relationship that gets created as we work our way through the pool.

PAT changes things; we can have multiple hosts hidden behind one IP address. This allows (potentially) thousands of hosts to share one IP address.

In this example we will reduce our pool size to one, and see how PAT works with this.

Firstly, lets see the effect if we try to NAT two hosts to one IP address without using PAT. We start by reducing the pool:

```
Services(config)#no ip nat pool loopbacks-pool
%Pool loopbacks-pool in use, cannot destroy
Services(config)#do clear ip nat trans *
Services(config)#no ip nat pool loopbacks-pool
Services(config)#ip nat pool loopbacks-pool 10.251.1.20 10.251.1.20 ?
  netmask        Specify the network mask
  prefix-length  Specify the prefix length

Services(config)#ip nat pool loopbacks-pool 10.251.1.20 10.251.1.20 pref 24
Services(config)#
```

Here I have used the "prefix-length" option instead of the netmask option. Now, if we ping Hub-1 from the same subnet as before (i.e. anything in the 10.250.15.0/24 range), then we can see the first connection will succeed, but subsequent attempts will fail:

```
Services(config)#do ping 172.16.4.1 so lo5 rep 2
Type escape sequence to abort.
Sending 2, 100-byte ICMP Echos to 172.16.4.1:
Packet sent with a source address of 10.250.15.1
!!
Services(config)#do ping 172.16.4.1 so lo6 rep 2
Type escape sequence to abort.
Sending 2, 100-byte ICMP Echos to 172.16.4.1:
Packet sent with a source address of 10.250.15.2
..
Success rate is 0 percent (0/2)
Services(config)#
```

Our translation table shows us exactly what we would expect to see:

```
Services(config)#do sh ip nat trans
Pro Inside global      Inside local       Outside local      Outside global
--- ---                ---                10.250.13.1        172.16.6.1
--- 10.251.1.141       10.250.14.1        ---                ---
icmp 10.251.1.20:28    10.250.15.20:28    172.16.4.1:28      172.16.4.1:28
--- 10.251.1.20        10.250.15.20       ---                ---
--- 10.251.1.15        10.250.10.1        ---                ---
--- 10.251.1.24        10.250.11.1        ---                ---
--- 10.251.1.25        10.250.11.1        ---                ---
--- 10.251.1.142       10.250.14.1        ---                ---
--- 10.251.2.15        10.250.10.1        ---                ---
Services(config)#
```

If we enable debugging, we can get a good idea of what is occurring:

```
1.  Services(config)#do debug ip nat det
2.  IP NAT detailed debugging is on
3.  Services(config)#do ping 172.16.4.1 so lo5 rep 2
4.  Type escape sequence to abort.
5.  Sending 2, 100-byte ICMP Echos to 172.16.4.1:
6.  Packet sent with a source address of 10.250.15.1
7.  !!
8.  Services(config)#
9.  NAT: i: icmp (10.250.15.1, 10) -> (172.16.4.1, 10) [41]
10. NAT: s=10.250.15.1->10.251.1.20, d=172.16.4.1 [41]
11. NAT*: o: icmp (172.16.4.1, 10) -> (10.251.1.20, 10) [41]
12. NAT*: s=172.16.4.1, d=10.251.1.20->10.250.15.1 [41]
13. NAT: i: icmp (10.250.15.1, 10) -> (172.16.4.1, 10) [42]
14. NAT: s=10.250.15.1->10.251.1.20, d=172.16.4.1 [42]
15. NAT*: o: icmp (172.16.4.1, 10) -> (10.251.1.20, 10) [42]
16. NAT*: s=172.16.4.1, d=10.251.1.20->10.250.15.1 [42]
17. Services(config)#do ping 172.16.4.1 so lo6 rep 2
18. Type escape sequence to abort.
19. Sending 2, 100-byte ICMP Echos to 172.16.4.1:
20. Packet sent with a source address of 10.250.15.2
21. NAT: failed to allocate address for 10.250.15.2, list/map 10
22. mapping pointer available mapping:0
23. NAT: translation failed (A), dropping packet s=10.250.15.2
    d=172.16.4.1.
24. NAT: failed to allocate address for 10.250.15.2, list/map 10
25. mapping pointer available mapping:0
26. NAT: translation failed (A), dropping packet s=10.250.15.2
    d=172.16.4.1.
27. Success rate is 0 percent (0/2)
28. Services(config)#
```

The debug tells us that the first NAT translation works (lines 9 to 16), but the second fails. Line 21 tells us why; we are unable to allocate a pool address for the IP address 10.250.15.2, which was mapped by access list 10. Because of this, the packet is dropped at line 23. We can fix this by using PAT instead.

We can switch to PAT just by adding the keyword "overload". Doing this tears down the NAT, and builds a new PAT rule:

```
Services(config)#ip nat inside source list 10 pool loopbacks-pool
overload
%Dynamic mapping in use, cannot change
```

```
Services(config)#do clear ip nat trans *
Services(config)# ip nat inside source list 10 pool loopbacks-pool
overload
    NAT: no portlist for proto 1 globaladdr 10.251.1.20 port 10
    NAT: deleting alias for 10.251.1.20
    NAT: remove address 10.251.1.20 from ipalias_hash[228]
    NAT: deleting alias from redundancy list for 10.251.1.20
Services(config)#
    ipnat_remove_dynamic_cfg: id 1, flag 9, range 0
    NAT: Reserved 10.251.1.20 for PAT
    ipnat_add_dynamic_cfg_common: id 1, flag 11, range 1
    id 1, flags 0, domain 0, lookup 0, aclnum A, aclname 10, mapname
idb 0x0
    poolstart 10.251.1.20   poolend 10.251.1.20
Services(config)#
```

With the "overload" keyword, our pings now succeed for all three of our loopbacks. Each is given a port number, and each has the same inside global address of 10.251.1.20. For brevity the output has been truncated:

```
Services(config)#do ping 172.16.4.1 so lo5 rep 2
Type escape sequence to abort.
Sending 2, 100-byte ICMP Echos to 172.16.4.1:
Packet sent with a source address of 10.250.15.20
!!
Success rate is 100 percent (2/2)
Services(config)#
  NAT: address not stolen for 10.250.15.20, proto 1 port 33
  NAT: Setting IP alias only flag
    mapping pointer available mapping:0
  NAT: creating portlist proto 1 globaladdr 10.251.1.20
  NAT: [0] Allocated Port for 10.250.15.20 -> 10.251.1.20: wanted 33
got 33
  NAT: i: icmp (10.250.15.20, 33) -> (172.16.4.1, 33) [127]
  NAT: s=10.250.15.20->10.251.1.20, d=172.16.4.1 [127]
  NAT: installing alias for address 10.251.1.20
  NAT*: o: icmp (172.16.4.1, 33) -> (10.251.1.20, 33) [127]
  NAT*: s=172.16.4.1, d=10.251.1.20->10.250.15.20 [127]
Services(config)#do ping 172.16.4.1 so lo6 rep 2
Type escape sequence to abort.
Sending 2, 100-byte ICMP Echos to 172.16.4.1:
Packet sent with a source address of 10.250.15.21
!!
Success rate is 100 percent (2/2)
Services(config)#
      mapping pointer available mapping:0
```

```
    NAT: [0] Allocated Port for 10.250.15.21 -> 10.251.1.20: wanted 34
got 34
    NAT: i: icmp (10.250.15.21, 34) -> (172.16.4.1, 34) [129]
    NAT: s=10.250.15.21->10.251.1.20, d=172.16.4.1 [129]
    NAT*: o: icmp (172.16.4.1, 34) -> (10.251.1.20, 34) [129]
    NAT*: s=172.16.4.1, d=10.251.1.20->10.250.15.21 [129]
Services(config)#do ping 172.16.4.1 so lo7 rep 2
Type escape sequence to abort.
Sending 2, 100-byte ICMP Echos to 172.16.4.1:
Packet sent with a source address of 10.250.15.22
!!
Success rate is 100 percent (2/2)
Services(config)#
    mapping pointer available mapping:0
    NAT: [0] Allocated Port for 10.250.15.22 -> 10.251.1.20: wanted 35
got 35
    NAT: i: icmp (10.250.15.22, 35) -> (172.16.4.1, 35) [131]
    NAT: s=10.250.15.22->10.251.1.20, d=172.16.4.1 [131]
    NAT*: o: icmp (172.16.4.1, 35) -> (10.251.1.20, 35) [131]
    NAT*: s=172.16.4.1, d=10.251.1.20->10.250.15.22 [131]
    NAT: i: icmp (10.250.15.22, 35) -> (172.16.4.1, 35) [132]
    NAT: s=10.250.15.22->10.251.1.20, d=172.16.4.1 [132]
    NAT*: o: icmp (172.16.4.1, 35) -> (10.251.1.20, 35) [132]
    NAT*: s=172.16.4.1, d=10.251.1.20->10.250.15.22 [132]
Services(config)#
Services(config)#do sh ip nat trans
Pro Inside global      Inside local       Outside local     Outside global
--- ---                ---                10.250.13.1       172.16.6.1
--- 10.251.1.141       10.250.14.1        ---               ---
icmp 10.251.1.20:33    10.250.15.20:33    172.16.4.1:33     172.16.4.1:33
icmp 10.251.1.20:34    10.250.15.21:34    172.16.4.1:34     172.16.4.1:34
icmp 10.251.1.20:35    10.250.15.22:35    172.16.4.1:35     172.16.4.1:35
--- 10.251.1.15        10.250.10.1        ---               ---
--- 10.251.1.24        10.250.11.1        ---               ---
--- 10.251.1.25        10.250.11.1        ---               ---
--- 10.251.1.142       10.250.14.1        ---               ---
--- 10.251.2.15        10.250.10.1        ---               ---
Services(config)#do un all
All possible debugging has been turned off
Services(config)#
```

7.4 Reversible NAT

So far all our translations, both static and dynamic have allowed the reverse connection, from outside to inside, without needing any intervention on our part. This changes, however, when we use route-maps and dynamic NAT, as this does not occur. There is no one-to-one mapping in the translation, therefore there is nothing to match the incoming traffic to.

Let's keep it simple and have a simple three-router set up:

```
1.1.1.1            10.1.1.0/24              20.1.1.0/24
2.2.2.2
         .1                    .2      .2               .3
         R1                    R2                       R3
```

The configurations are below:

```
R1(config)#int fa0/0
R1(config-if)#ip add 10.1.1.1 255.255.255.0
R1(config-if)#No sh
R1(config-if)#int lo0
R1(config-if)#ip addr 1.1.1.1 255.255.255.0
R1(config-if)#int lo1
R1(config-if)#ip add 2.2.2.2 255.255.255.0
R1(config-if)#router eigrp 1
R1(config-router)#net 1.1.1.1 0.0.0.0
R1(config-router)#net 2.2.2.2 0.0.0.0
R1(config-router)#net 10.1.1.0 0.0.0.255
R1(config-router)#

R2(config)#int fa0/0
R2(config-if)#ip add 10.1.1.2 255.255.255.0
R2(config-if)#no sh
R2(config-if)#int fa0/1
R2(config-if)#ip add 20.1.1.2 255.255.255.0
R2(config-if)#no sh
R2(config-if)#router eigrp 1
R2(config-router)#net 10.1.1.0 0.0.0.255
R2(config-router)#redistribute connected metric 100 1 255 1 1500
R2(config-router)#

R3(config)#int fa0/1
R3(config-if)#ip add 20.1.1.3 255.255.255.0
R3(config-if)#no sh
R3(config)#ip route 0.0.0.0 0.0.0.0 20.1.1.2
R3(config)#end
R3#ping 1.1.1.1
Type escape sequence to abort.
Sending 5, 100-byte ICMP Echos to 1.1.1.1:
!!!!!
```

```
Success rate is 100 percent (5/5)
R3#
```

We will now set up a NAT, without the reversible keyword and see what happens. We start by assigning our interfaces their relevant NAT role:

```
R2(config-router)#int fa0/0
R2(config-if)#ip nat inside
R2(config-if)#int fa0/1
R2(config-if)#ip nat outside
R2(config-if)#
```

We create a NAT pool:

```
R2(config-if)#ip nat pool NATp 172.16.1.1 172.16.1.2 prefix-length 24
R2(config)#
```

Next, we create an access-list containing both of the loopback address from R1:

```
R2(config)#ip access-list standard R1-Loops
R2(config-std-nacl)#permit host 1.1.1.1
R2(config-std-nacl)#permit host 2.2.2.2
R2(config-std-nacl)#
```

We then create a route-map to reference the access-list:

```
R2(config-std-nacl)#route-map match-R1 permit 10
R2(config-route-map)#match ip address R1-Loops
R2(config-route-map)#
```

The final step is to create the NAT statement, linking the route-map to the pool we created.

```
R2(config-route-map)#ip nat inside source route-map match-R1 pool NATp
R2(config)#
```

We can test it by pinging R3 from each of R1's loopback interfaces:

```
R1#ping 20.1.1.3 so lo0
Type escape sequence to abort.
Sending 5, 100-byte ICMP Echos to 20.1.1.3:
Packet sent with a source address of 1.1.1.1
!!!!!
Success rate is 100 percent (5/5)
R1#ping 20.1.1.3 so lo1
Type escape sequence to abort.
```

```
Sending 5, 100-byte ICMP Echos to 20.1.1.3:
Packet sent with a source address of 2.2.2.2
!!!!!
Success rate is 100 percent (5/5)
R1#

R2(config)#do sh ip nat trans
Pro Inside global      Inside local    Outside local   Outside global
icmp 172.16.1.1:10     1.1.1.1:10      20.1.1.3:10     20.1.1.3:10
icmp 172.16.1.2:11     2.2.2.2:11      20.1.1.3:11     20.1.1.3:11
R2(config)#
```

Inside-to-outside works fine and because of the extended entries that have been created, we also have a modicum of outside-to-inside traffic. It works, but is unreliable:

```
R3#ping 172.16.1.1
Type escape sequence to abort.
Sending 5, 100-byte ICMP Echos to 172.16.1.1:
!.!.!
Success rate is 60 percent (3/5)
R3#ping 172.16.1.2
Type escape sequence to abort.
Sending 5, 100-byte ICMP Echos to 172.16.1.2:
!.!.!
Success rate is 60 percent (3/5)
R3#
```

The important thing to note is that in the translation table on R2, we do not have any one-to-one mappings. This is a key factor when using route-maps with dynamic NAT. The extendable entry is created, but, unlike our previous examples, we cannot create a translation through traffic coming in from the outside.

If we let the extended entries timeout, we can try initiating a translation from R3:

```
R2(config)#do sh ip nat trans
R2(config)#

R3#ping 172.16.1.1
Type escape sequence to abort.
Sending 5, 100-byte ICMP Echos to 172.16.1.1:
U.U.U
Success rate is 0 percent (0/5)
R3#ping 172.16.1.2
Type escape sequence to abort.
Sending 5, 100-byte ICMP Echos to 172.16.1.2:
U.U.U
```

```
Success rate is 0 percent (0/5)
R3#

R2(config)#do sh ip nat trans
R2(config)#
```

It fails, as we would expect.

So, how do we let the traffic in? We can enable this by adding the keyword "reversible" to our NAT rule:

```
R2(config)#ip nat inside source route-map match-R1 pool NATp
reversible
R2(config)#
```

This does not mean however, that we will see entries in our NAT table immediately:

```
R2(config)#do sh ip nat trans
R2(config)#
```

This makes sense. How does the router know to which host to send the traffic? Does it just arbitrarily decide that address A should map to host A? This is not the router's decision to make, at least not fully. We need to first create some traffic, this will then create the mappings and in true IP address pool fashion, it is "first come, first served":

```
R1#ping 20.1.1.3 so lo0
Type escape sequence to abort.
Sending 5, 100-byte ICMP Echos to 20.1.1.3:
Packet sent with a source address of 1.1.1.1
!!!!!
Success rate is 100 percent (5/5)
R1#ping 20.1.1.3 so lo1
Type escape sequence to abort.
Sending 5, 100-byte ICMP Echos to 20.1.1.3:
Packet sent with a source address of 2.2.2.2
!!!!!
Success rate is 100 percent (5/5)
R1#
```

Now, we can see that we have one-to-one translations, as well as the extended entries:

```
R2(config)#do sh ip nat trans
Pro Inside global    Inside local   Outside local   Outside global
icmp 172.16.1.1:16   1.1.1.1:16     20.1.1.3:16     20.1.1.3:16
icmp 172.16.1.2:17   2.2.2.2:17     20.1.1.3:17     20.1.1.3:17
```

```
--- 172.16.1.1        1.1.1.1          ---              ---
--- 172.16.1.2        2.2.2.2          ---              ---
R2(config)#
```

Let us now give it a few seconds for these entries to timeout:

```
R2(config)#do sh ip nat trans
Pro Inside global    Inside local    Outside local    Outside global
--- 172.16.1.1        1.1.1.1          ---              ---
--- 172.16.1.2        2.2.2.2          ---              ---
R2(config)#
```

We still have the one-to-one entries. So let's try and put the reversible back into our reversible NAT. Without sending any traffic from R1, which we had to do previously to initiate the translation, we can send traffic from R3 to the R1 and we have a 100% success rate:

```
R3#ping 172.16.1.1
Type escape sequence to abort.
Sending 5, 100-byte ICMP Echos to 172.16.1.1:
!!!!!
Success rate is 100 percent (5/5)
R3#ping 172.16.1.2
Type escape sequence to abort.
Sending 5, 100-byte ICMP Echos to 172.16.1.2:
!!!!!
Success rate is 100 percent (5/5)
R3#

R2(config)#do sh ip nat trans
Pro Inside global      Inside local    Outside local    Outside global
icmp 172.16.1.1:22     1.1.1.1:22      20.1.1.3:22      20.1.1.3:22
icmp 172.16.1.2:23     2.2.2.2:23      20.1.1.3:23      20.1.1.3:23
--- 172.16.1.1          1.1.1.1          ---              ---
--- 172.16.1.2          2.2.2.2          ---              ---
R2(config)#
```

Once the one-to-one entries are created, they will now stay in the translation table until the table is cleared manually. They do not get timed out like the extendable entries and with them there, we are able to initiate outside-to-inside traffic.

Our last topic in this section is to look at NAT and IPv6.

7.4 NAT and IPv6

NAT-PT

NAT-PT doesn't appear on the CCIE syllabus and we'll get to why in a moment, but I have included it here as it is worth knowing about, in order to lay the framework for the technologies that we do need to know (NAT64 for example).

NAT-PT is an IPv6 transition mechanism to support an infrastructure that includes a mixture of IPv6-only hosts and IPv4-only hosts. NAT-PT (which stands for Network Address Translation/Protocol Translation) was defined in RFC 2766, back in February 2000. In 2007 it was deprecated to historic status, in RFC 4966 – meaning non-one should use it now. If you walked into a client meeting and offered up NAT-PT as a solution, they would probably question why you would want to implement something that everyone steers clear of. That said, it was around for seven years, so you may come across it in the field. Despite being declared historic back in 2007, NAT-PT is still supported in all recent versions of Cisco IOS.

Before we look at why it was deemed unsuitable as a transition mechanism, let's look at how it works – which does lead us nicely to why we shouldn't use it, and to other solutions that are applicable.

Imagine you have a router, and to the left side we have an IPv6-only network, and to the right we have an IPv4-only network.

```
         2001:1::/64              192.168.1.0/24
    :10              :1        .1              .10
  IPv6Router            NAT-PT              IPv4Router
```

The initial configurations are simple. We have an IPv6-only router (IPv6Router), connected to a dual-stack router (NAT-PT), this is then connected to an IPv4-only router (IPv4Router). We are using static routes on both sides.

```
IPv6Router(config)#int fa0/0
IPv6Router(config-if)#no sh
IPv6Router(config-if)#ipv6 add 2001:1::10/64
IPv6Router(config-if)#ipv6 unicast
IPv6Router(config)#ipv6 route ::/0 2001:1::1
IPv6Router(config)#
```

```
NAT-PT(config)#ipv6 unicast
NAT-PT(config)#int fa0/0
NAT-PT(config-if)#no sh
NAT-PT(config-if)#ipv6 add 2001:1::1/64
NAT-PT(config-if)#int fa0/1
NAT-PT(config-if)#ip add 192.168.1.1 255.255.255.0
NAT-PT(config-if)#no sh
NAT-PT(config-if)#

IPv4Router(config)#int fa0/1
IPv4Router(config-if)#ip add 192.168.1.10 255.255.255.0
IPv4Router(config-if)#no sh
IPv4Router(config-if)#ip route 0.0.0.0 0.0.0.0 192.168.1.1
IPv4Router(config)#
```

The NAT-PT configuration is below. Firstly, we enable both interfaces for IPv6 NAT. This creates a new interface (NVI0), which we will discuss later.

```
NAT-PT(config)#int fa0/0
NAT-PT(config-if)#ipv6 nat
%LINEPROTO-5-UPDOWN: Line protocol on Interface NVI0, changed state to up
NAT-PT(config-if)#int fa0/1
NAT-PT(config-if)#ipv6 nat
```

The second step is to create the mappings between the IPv4 address and the IPv6 address.

We map the address of IPv4Router's fa0/1 interface to 2001:10::10/96 and then we map IPv6Router's fa0/0 address to 192.168.10.10. The final command sets the prefix length for the IPv6 address. These are the only real requirements of NAT-PT; that we have the 2 translations, and a ::/96 prefix for the mappings.

```
NAT-PT(config-if)#ipv6 nat v4v6 source 192.168.1.10 2001:10::10
NAT-PT(config)#ipv6 nat v6v4 source 2001:1::10 192.168.10.10
NAT-PT(config)#
% Address 192.168.10.10 already in use on attached network
NAT-PT(config)#ipv6 nat prefix 2001:10::/96
NAT-PT(config)#
```

Whilst we have followed the steps to the letter, this does not work, or at best it is flaky and intermittent.

If we ping the translated address (2001:10::10) from the IPv6Router, which in turn, should be translated into 192.168.10.10, then we get a few packets (if we are lucky) and we see the translation form. This then populates the translation table on the NAT-PT router:

```
IPv6Router#ping 2001:10::10
Type escape sequence to abort.
Sending 5, 100-byte ICMP Echos to 2001:10::10:
!!.!.
Success rate is 60 percent (3/5)
IPv6Router#

NAT-PT#
%SYS-2-BADBUFFER: Attempt to use contiguous buffer as scattered src,
ptr= 67CDE1CC, pool= 67CDE038 -Process= "<interrupt level>", ipl= 1
-Traceback= 60392F00z 603A4D28z
NAT-PT#sh ipv6 nat trans
Prot    IPv4 source              IPv6 source
        IPv4 destination         IPv6 destination
---     ---                      ---
        192.168.1.10             2001:10::10

icmp    192.168.10.10,4403       2001:1::10,4403
        192.168.1.10,4403        2001:10::10,4403

---     192.168.10.10            2001:1::10
        192.168.1.10             2001:10::10

---     192.168.10.10            2001:1::10
        ---                      ---

NAT-PT#
```

We do see a lot of "badbuffer" errors on the NAT-PT router, the console will show many of these. Before we fix this, let's have a look at the other side, our IPv4-to-IPv6 translation. Does this fair any better?

```
IPv4Router#ping 192.168.10.10
Type escape sequence to abort.
Sending 5, 100-byte ICMP Echos to 192.168.10.10:
.....
Success rate is 0 percent (0/5)
IPv4Router#

NAT-PT#sh ipv6 nat trans
Prot    IPv4 source              IPv6 source
        IPv4 destination         IPv6 destination
```

```
      ---           ---                    ---
                    192.168.1.10           2001:10::10

      icmp          192.168.10.10,0        2001:1::10,0
                    192.168.1.10,0         2001:10::10,0

      ---           192.168.10.10          2001:1::10
                    192.168.1.10           2001:10::10

      ---           192.168.10.10          2001:1::10
                    ---                    ---

   NAT-PT#
   %SYS-2-BADBUFFER: Attempt to use contiguous buffer as scattered src,
   ptr= 67CDE1CC, pool= 67CDE038 -Process= "<interrupt level>", ipl= 1
   -Traceback= 60392F00z 603A4D28z
   NAT-PT#

   IPv4Router#ping 192.168.10.10 rep 2
   Type escape sequence to abort.
   Sending 2, 100-byte ICMP Echos to 192.168.10.10:
   .!
   Success rate is 50 percent (1/2)
   IPv4Router#
```

It has about the same level of success. We can see the translation building and we if enable debugging (debug ipv6 nat det), then we can see the actual order of events.

```
   NAT-PT#
      IPv6 NAT: IPv4->IPv6:
                  src (192.168.1.10 -> 2001:10::10)
                  dst (192.168.10.10 -> 2001:1::10)
                  ref_count = 1, usecount = 0, flags = 2,
                  rt_flags = 0, more_flags = 0

      IPv6 NAT: IPv6->IPv4:
                  src (2001:1::10 -> 192.168.10.10)
                  dst (2001:10::10 -> 192.168.1.10)
                  ref_count = 1, usecount = 0, flags = 2,
                  rt_flags = 0, more_flags = 0
   NAT-PT#
   %SYS-2-BADBUFFER: Attempt to use contiguous buffer as scattered src,
   ptr= 67CDE1CC, pool= 67CDE038 -Process= "<interrupt level>", ipl= 1
   -Traceback= 60392F00z 603A4D28z
   NAT-PT#
```

We still have the translations form, but our success is very hit-and-miss:

```
NAT-PT#sh ipv6 nat trans
Prot   IPv4 source             IPv6 source
       IPv4 destination        IPv6 destination
---    ---                     ---
       192.168.1.10            2001:10::10

icmp   192.168.10.10,1         2001:1::10,1
       192.168.1.10,1          2001:10::10,1

icmp   192.168.10.10,2         2001:1::10,2
       192.168.1.10,2          2001:10::10,2

---    192.168.10.10           2001:1::10
       192.168.1.10            2001:10::10

---    192.168.10.10           2001:1::10
       ---                     ---

NAT-PT#
```

If we try again we get the idea that no matter how many times we try, we will never get a 100% success rate.

```
IPv4Router#ping 192.168.10.10 rep 2
Type escape sequence to abort.
Sending 2, 100-byte ICMP Echos to 192.168.10.10:
..
Success rate is 0 percent (0/2)
IPv4Router#

IPv6Router#ping 2001:10::10
Type escape sequence to abort.
Sending 5, 100-byte ICMP Echos to 2001:10::10:
!....
Success rate is 20 percent (1/5)
IPv6Router#
```

Let's see what we can do to fix this. Firstly to clear the "badbuffer" messages that have been filling our console, we need to disable ipv6 CEF:

```
NAT-PT(config)#no ipv6 cef
NAT-PT(config)#
```

To get traffic flowing properly we also need to move to process switching on the interfaces

```
NAT-PT(config)#int fa0/0
NAT-PT(config-if)#no ip route-cache
NAT-PT(config-if)#int fa0/1
NAT-PT(config-if)#no ip route-cache
NAT-PT(config-if)#
```

We won't go into a breakdown of the differences between CEF-based switching, and process switching; we just need to know that process switching is slower. But, for our purposes, it has much improved our situation:

```
IPv6Router#ping 2001:10::10
Type escape sequence to abort.
Sending 5, 100-byte ICMP Echos to 2001:10::10:
!.!!!
Success rate is 80 percent (4/5)
IPv6Router#ping 2001:10::10
Type escape sequence to abort.
Sending 5, 100-byte ICMP Echos to 2001:10::10:
!!!!!
Success rate is 100 percent (5/5)
IPv6Router#ping 2001:10::10
Type escape sequence to abort.
Sending 5, 100-byte ICMP Echos to 2001:10::10:
!!!!!
Success rate is 100 percent (5/5)
IPv6Router#

IPv4Router#ping 192.168.10.10
Type escape sequence to abort.
Sending 5, 100-byte ICMP Echos to 192.168.10.10:
!!!!!
Success rate is 100 percent (5/5)
IPv4Router#ping 192.168.10.10
Type escape sequence to abort.
Sending 5, 100-byte ICMP Echos to 192.168.10.10:
!!!!!
Success rate is 100 percent (5/5)
IPv4Router#ping 192.168.10.10
Type escape sequence to abort.
Sending 5, 100-byte ICMP Echos to 192.168.10.10:
!!!!!
Success rate is 100 percent (5/5)
IPv4Router#
```

We can see the translations in the table:

```
NAT-PT#sh ipv6 nat trans
Prot   IPv4 source              IPv6 source
       IPv4 destination         IPv6 destination
---    ---                      ---
       192.168.1.10             2001:10::10

icmp   192.168.10.10,6          2001:1::10,6
       192.168.1.10,6           2001:10::10,6

icmp   192.168.10.10,7          2001:1::10,7
       192.168.1.10,7           2001:10::10,7

icmp   192.168.10.10,8          2001:1::10,8
       192.168.1.10,8           2001:10::10,8

icmp   192.168.10.10,1495       2001:1::10,1495
       192.168.1.10,1495        2001:10::10,1495

icmp   192.168.10.10,2018       2001:1::10,2018
       192.168.1.10,2018        2001:10::10,2018

icmp   192.168.10.10,7138       2001:1::10,7138
       192.168.1.10,7138        2001:10::10,7138

---    192.168.10.10            2001:1::10
Prot   IPv4 source              IPv6 source
       IPv4 destination         IPv6 destination
       192.168.1.10             2001:10::10

---    192.168.10.10            2001:1::10
       ---                      ---

NAT-PT#
```

So, now we have a working NAT-PT solution, but what have we broken? Many things rely on CEF – no CEF means no MPLS (on Cisco hardware, at least). NBAR and AutoQoS also rely on CEF and by using process-switching we have decreased our router's performance. NAT-PT also has constraints with DNS (well, DNS64 to be more specific), which we shall discuss shortly.

There is a solution to the issue though and that is NAT64.

NAT64

NAT64 (Network Address Translation IPv6-to-IPv4) is not available on the platform we are using and not on Cisco IOS/IOL either. It does work on a number of platforms, such as the ASR 1000, hence it being reserved for the written exam only.

With NAT64 we can have a similar setup to our last example, with one router providing the translation between the IPv4 world and the IPv6 world. It was defined in RFC 6146, in 2011, as a successor to NAT-PT.

Although we can't do a complete walkthrough, we do have enough (from looking at NAT-PT) to understand what is happening in this hypothetical example.

If we replaced our NAT-PT router with a new router, imaginatively called "NAT64", that supports NAT64, then we would not have to make many changes. The config for this new router would be as follows:

```
NAT64(config)#ipv6 unicast
NAT64(config)#int fa0/0
NAT64(config-if)#no sh
NAT64(config-if)#ipv6 add 2001:1::1/64
NAT64(config-if)#nat64 enable
NAT64(config-if)#int fa0/1
NAT64(config-if)#ip add 192.168.1.1 255.255.255.0
NAT64(config-if)#nat64 enable
NAT64(config-if)#no sh
NAT64(config-if)#nat64 prefix stateful 2001:10::/96
NAT64(config)#nat64 v6v4 static 2001:1::10 192.168.10.10
NAT64(config)#nat64 v4v6 static 192.168.1.10 2001:10::10
NAT64(config)#
```

We would then check the translations using "sh nat64 translations". As you can see there is not a huge amount of difference between NAT-PT and NAT64; both achieve the same goal.

So what are the other differences that make NAT64 the go-to transition mechanism? Well, apart from co-existing happily with CEF, it is not as reliant on DNS64, it will still need it, but it is more relaxed about where the DNS64 server is. NAT-PT introduced DNS-ALG, which also implies that the NAT-PT router has to be within the path of the DNS query. This reduces its scalability. NAT64 doesn't really mind where the DNS64 server is, just so long as it can access it.

One interesting thing to note is that instead of using "ipv6 nat inside" or "ipv6 nat outside", we used the command "ipv6 nat" on NAT-PT's interfaces, and "nat64 enable" on NAT64's interfaces. This is a newer method, called NAT virtual interface (NVI), the IPv4 equivalent is "ip nat enable" and we will discuss this shortly. Before we look at this though, we will look at how we can translate one IPv6 address into another IPv6 address.

NPTv6

We have looked at tunnelling IPv6 through IPv4 and mapping IPv6 addresses to IPv4 addresses, now we will look at mapping IPv6 addresses to IPv6 addresses. This is known as IPv6 Network Prefix Translation (or NPTv6).

Again, this is one of those syllabus topics that is reserved for the written exam.

With IPv6, we have 340 undecillion addresses (340 trillion trillion trillion). To put this in context the World population, at the time of writing, is close to 7,300,000,000. With IPv6 we now have enough addresses for each man, woman, child, dog, cat, refrigerator, car… and I am sure you get the idea.

Nevertheless, the ability to translate an IPv6 to another IPv6 address exists and was created under RFC 6296. In a nutshell, NPTv6 allows you to rewrite IPv6 prefixes, 2001:abc:def::/48 can become 2001:abc:ghi::/48. It is a one-to-one translation, the prefix lengths must be the same size and there can be no overloading.

So, why would we use this? Let's face it, it does sound less-than-fantastic. The major case is in multi-homed environments, to provide end-to-end reachability, whilst being able to translate between IPv6 prefixes. Cisco have not really embraced NPTv6, it is stateless, and breaks IPSec. Time will tell as to how much use it gets.

It is now time to leave IPv6 NAT and briefly discuss the NAT Virtual Interface (NVI), and wrap up our look at NAT.

NAT Virtual Interface (NVI)

For all our IPv4 based NATing, we used the commands "ip nat inside" and "ip nat outside". This creates two very distinct "domains"; an inside domain and an outside domain. With these domains the translations occur either before, or after the routing decisions are made, depending on the traffic flow (either inside-to-outside, or outside-to-inside).

One of the most common mistakes I have made when writing this book is to omit the "inside" keyword in the NAT statement, so instead of "ip nat inside source static 10.10.3.1

10.10.1.3", I would type "ip nat source static 10.10.3.1 10.10.1.3", for example. The IOS would take the command without complaint, but things would not work. The reason that the command is valid, is that it is used with the NVI. If my interfaces were set to use "ip nat enable" instead of "ip nat outside", or "ip nat inside" then the version entered in error, would have actually been the correct version.

This is not to say, however, that the new version would have worked anyway. To get this to work, properly, in GNS3 I had to move down a version or two.

In the end I had to downgrade to a C3600 series router, and IOS version 12.4(16).

```
R3#sh ver | i IOS
Cisco IOS Software, 3600 Software (C3640-JK903S-M), Version 12.4(16),
RELEASE SOFTWARE (fc1)
R3#
```

NVI was introduced in IOS 12.3(14)T, so try and keep to versions on or above this.

For this we will use three routers:

```
         10.1.1.0/24              10.2.2.0/24
      .1         .254          .254        .10
     R1              NVI-1                  R3
```

The basic set up for the routers is as follows:

```
R1(config)#int e0/0
R1(config-if)#ip add 10.1.1.1 255.255.255.0
R1(config-if)#no sh
R1(config-if)#exit
R1(config)#ip route 0.0.0.0 0.0.0.0 10.1.1.254
R1(config)#

NVI-1(config)#int e0/0
NVI-1(config-if)#ip add 10.1.1.254 255.255.255.0
NVI-1(config-if)#no sh
NVI-1(config-if)#int e0/1
NVI-1(config-if)#ip add 10.2.2.254 255.255.255.0
NVI-1(config-if)#no sh

R3(config)#int e0/0
R3(config-if)#ip add 10.2.2.3 255.255.255.0
```

```
R3(config-if)#no sh
R3(config-if)#
R3(config-if)#ip route 0.0.0.0 0.0.0.0 10.2.2.254
```

We then enable our interface for nat:

```
NVI-1(config-if)#int e0/0
NVI-1(config-if)#ip nat enable

%LINEPROTO-5-UPDOWN: Line protocol on Interface NVI0, changed state to
up
NVI-1(config-if)#
NVI-1(config-if)#int e0/1
NVI-1(config-if)#ip nat enable
```

Our NAT statement maps R1's e0/0 interface IP address to a new address:

```
NVI-1(config-if)#ip nat source static 10.1.1.1 10.2.2.10
NVI-1(config)#do sh ip nat nvi trans
Pro Source global   Source local  Destin local  Destin global
--- 10.2.2.10       10.1.1.1      ---           ---
NVI-1(config)#do sh ip int bri | i up
Ethernet0/0         10.1.1.254    YES manual up      up
Ethernet0/1         10.2.2.254    YES manual up      up
NVI0                unassigned    NO  unset  up      up
NVI-1(config)#
```

So, we have an entry in the NVI table, but NVI0 still does not have an IP address, and the OK? Column shows "NO". Despite this, our ping from R1 works, and we have an extended entry in the NVI NAT table:

```
R1(config)#do ping 10.2.2.3

Type escape sequence to abort.
Sending 5, 100-byte ICMP Echos to 10.2.2.3:
..!!!
Success rate is 60 percent (3/5)
R1(config)#

NVI-1(config)#do sh ip nat nvi trans
Pro Source global    Source local  Destin local  Destin global
icmp 10.2.2.10:1     10.1.1.1:1    10.2.2.3:1    10.2.2.3:1
---  10.2.2.10       10.1.1.1      ---           ---
NVI-1(config)#
```

If we enable debugging, we can see that there is no mention of an outside domain (as denoted by an (o) in previous debug outputs), we just have a source (s), and a destination (d). We do have an "i", which is inside, but not in the domain sense:

```
NVI-1#debug ip nat nvi
IP NAT NVI debugging is on
NVI-1#debug ip nat detailed
IP NAT detailed debugging is on
NVI-1#

R1(config)#do ping 10.2.2.3 rep 1

Type escape sequence to abort.
Sending 1, 100-byte ICMP Echos to 10.2.2.3:
!
Success rate is 100 percent (1/1)
R1(config)#

NVI-1#
NAT*: i: icmp (10.1.1.1, 2) -> (10.2.2.3, 2) [10]
NAT*: s=10.1.1.1->10.2.2.10, d=10.2.2.3 [10]
NAT: i: icmp (10.2.2.3, 2) -> (10.2.2.10, 2) [10]
NAT: s=10.2.2.3, d=10.2.2.10->10.1.1.1 [10]
NVI-1#sh ip nat nvi trans
Pro Source global   Source local   Destin local   Destin global
icmp 10.2.2.10:2    10.1.1.1:2     10.2.2.3:2     10.2.2.3:2
---  10.2.2.10      10.1.1.1       ---            ---
NVI-1#
```

If we enable debugging of IP routing we can see that the packet is routed via the RIB:

```
NVI-1#debug ip routing
IP routing debugging is on
NVI-1#
NAT*: i: icmp (10.1.1.1, 3) -> (10.2.2.3, 3) [11]
NAT*: s=10.1.1.1->10.2.2.10, d=10.2.2.3 [11]
IP: tableid=0, s=10.2.2.3 (Ethernet0/1), d=10.2.2.10 (Ethernet0/1),
routed via RIB
NAT: i: icmp (10.2.2.3, 3) -> (10.2.2.10, 3) [11]
NAT: s=10.2.2.3, d=10.2.2.10->10.1.1.1 [11]
IP: tableid=0, s=10.2.2.3 (Ethernet0/1), d=10.1.1.1 (Ethernet0/0),
routed via RIB
IP: s=10.2.2.3 (Ethernet0/1), d=10.1.1.1 (Ethernet0/0), g=10.1.1.1,
len 100, forward
NVI-1#
```

Our NVI interface handles the to-ing and fro-ing of the NAT traffic, but you cannot treat it as you would a physical, or loopback interface. You cannot, for example, configure the interface, and you cannot use the command "sh int NVI0". To gather the interface stats, you have to look at all your interfaces, though you can jump to the interface, not that it shows anything interesting:

```
NVI-1#sh int | b NV
NVI0 is up, line protocol is up
  Hardware is NVI
  Interface is unnumbered. Using address of NVI0 (0.0.0.0)
  MTU 1514 bytes, BW 10000000 Kbit, DLY 0 usec,
     reliability 255/255, txload 1/255, rxload 1/255
  Encapsulation UNKNOWN, loopback not set
  Last input never, output never, output hang never
  Last clearing of "show interface" counters never
  Input queue: 0/75/0/0 (size/max/drops/flushes); Total output drops:0
  5 minute input rate 0 bits/sec, 0 packets/sec
  5 minute output rate 0 bits/sec, 0 packets/sec
     0 packets input, 0 bytes, 0 no buffer
     Received 0 broadcasts, 0 runts, 0 giants, 0 throttles
     0 input errors, 0 CRC, 0 frame, 0 overrun, 0 ignored, 0 abort
     0 packets output, 0 bytes, 0 underruns
     0 output errors, 0 collisions, 0 interface resets
     0 output buffer failures, 0 output buffers swapped out
NVI-1#
```

There are a couple of useful commands, when we use NVI, though. These are the same as before, just with "nvi" added after "nat".

We can look at the statistics:

```
NVI-1#sh ip nat nvi stat
Total active translations: 1 (1 static, 0 dynamic; 0 extended)
NAT Enabled interfaces:
  Ethernet0/0, Ethernet0/1
Hits: 10  Misses: 3
CEF Translated packets: 7, CEF Punted packets: 0
Expired translations: 3
Dynamic mappings:
NVI-1#
```

We can also look at the translation table:

```
NVI-1#sh ip nat nvi trans
Pro Source global  Source local  Destin local   Destin global
```

```
    --- 10.2.2.10     10.1.1.1        ---             ---
NVI-1#
```

We have nearly reached the end now. All that's left is to cover some troubleshooting!

8. Troubleshooting

As we have gone through the book, we have seen most of the ways in which we can confirm that our tunnels, our VPNs and our DMVPN nodes have been set up correctly. This chapter is designed to be a quick refresher on the areas that we are most likely to have issues with. For many of these the same logic applies to all three technologies.

There are a few basic checks we can run through.

Are you super-connected?

In an exam environment, especially in the virtualized exam that the CCIE v5 has now become, we cannot check our physical connections, so we have to assume that everything is configured correctly there, but we can check to whom we are connected to, and that our interfaces are up.

We can check connectivity through "sh cdp neighbors" – this will tell us which of our interfaces connects to whom and to which of their interfaces. If we do not see the correct data, such as a missing neighbour, then we need to make sure that the port is up, using "sh ip int bri l e unas". If the interface is down, then bring it up.

Once we have confirmed we are connected at a physical level, then we can move on to layer 3 connectivity. We can confirm reachability through ping and traceroute, as well as confirming that we have the expected routes to enable us to connect to other routers more than one hop way (sh ip route 10.1.1.2 for example). Once we have confirmed reachability, we can move on to making sure that our tunnels (and I am using "tunnels" to cover tunnels, VPNs and DMVPN here) are up.

Troubleshooting tunnels

We need to make sure that we are talking through the right interface, the configuration command is "tunnel source <interface>". We can confirm this using "sh int tunnel 0 l i tunnel source", replacing the tunnel number as appropriate. If we are using a loopback interface as our tunnel source (or destination), then make sure that this is reachable by the other side. We should either have a static route, or it should be advertised through a routing protocol, the latter is preferred.

Do we have the correct destination IP address for the hub? Again this is an obvious one, but we should still check.

Is our encapsulation correct? We cannot mix and match encapsulation types (unless we are talking about DMVPN phase 1, where the hub can use "gre multipoint" and the spoke can be "gre point-to-point").

Let's move on to more technology specific troubleshooting

Troubleshooting DMVPN

When troubleshooting DMVPN, we need to make sure that the NHRP mappings are not the wrong way around. The mapping should be the tunnel interface to the public (NBMA) interface (ip nhrp map <tunnel> <nbma>). If the hub's NMBA address is set as the Next Hop Server, instead of the hub's tunnel IP address, then we will experience issues with our tunnel overlay, such as IGP adjacencies flapping, or not forming at all. The NHS should point to the Hub's tunnel IP address. We should also confirm that the NHRP authentication string is correct across all our devices.

Do we see flapping on our tunnels? If we do, then this can be for a number of reasons. Have we introduced recursive routing, by advertising the NBMA address into our tunnel? Configuring the NHS as the public address will also cause flapping.

We have some IGP-dependent configurational items we should check.

EIGRP - Remember the split-horizon rule (the same is true for RIP), and make sure we disable the changing of the next-hop (for phase 1 and for phase 2) "no ip next-hop-self eigrp <as>".
BGP - If we want spoke-to-spoke traffic then we need to make sure that our spokes are route-reflector clients.
OSPF – remember the OSPF network type differs depending on what phase we are using. We need to use "ip ospf network broadcast" for phase 2, and "ip ospf network point-to-multipoint" for phase 3.

If things appear to be working but we are not seeing the desired results, then we might not be getting the spoke-to-spoke traffic that we should. If this is the case, then have we broken phase 2 by summarizing any addresses? Remember that summarization works in phase 3, but not in phase 2. We will have access to the summary addresses, but our traffic will always traverse the hub. Whilst we are talking about weird behaviour, do we see large amounts of packet fragmentation? If so, then this could be because of the packet size, so we can set the MTU and MSS, comfortable values are an MTU of 1400, and an MSS of 1360.

Some quick win commands are:

```
sh ip nhrp
sh ip nhrp brief
sh ip nhrp multicast
sh dmvpn
```

Troubleshooting VPNs

Most of these are very obvious - make sure pre-shared keys match (sh crypto isakmp key) and that we are using the same transform sets (sh crypto ipsec transform-set). We need to make sure that this is configured on the correct interfaces (sh crypto ipsec sa interface), our peers are correct (sh crypto ipsec sa peer) and that our ACLs are configured correctly (the right way round for the router). Cut and paste is useful in this scenario.

Troubleshooting IPv6

Be aware of what can and cannot, run across an IPv6 transition tunnel – BGP is a good all-rounder here (because it is an application). OSPF and EIGRP can fail due to lack of link-local addresses (depending on the transition mechanism).

If we are using ISATAP, then make sure that we have turned off neighbour discovery and router advertisement suppression (no ipv6 nd ra suppress). These are enabled by default.

Make use of the general-prefix command, it is so much easier than doing hex conversion!

Troubleshooting NAT

We should make sure that our Inside and Outside interfaces are defined correctly. We should check to see if the NAT statement is missing the keywords "inside" or "outside" if we are using legacy NAT. The command will be taken, due to NVI, but the NAT will not work.

Remember that the keyword "no-alias" will prevent ARP, if we see this, then we can probably expect a route along the way to have problems communicating with us – so either change the NAT command (if we are allowed to) or add a static ARP entry to the router needing the access. We require the router(s) and any intermediate routers to perform NAT traversal. This is enabled by default, but can be disabled using the command "no crypto ipsec nat-transparency udp-encapsulation". This can be disabled if the network uses IPSec-awareness NAT, though this is not within the scope of the Routing and Switching exam.

If we have confirmed all the above and are having problems with dynamic NAT, then we should check to see if our pools are too small. Have we exhausted all our addresses? If this is the case then we need to either increase the pool size, or switch to PAT.

If our extended translations are timing out too quickly, then we can change this using "ip nat translation icmp-timeout 60" and "ip nat translation tcp-timeout 60".

Confirming end-to-end connectivity

Lastly, we should check our end-to-end connectivity. For this we will use a tcl script, and check access to Services' IP addresses from Spoke-2.

```
Services#sh ip nat trans
Pro Inside global      Inside local      Outside local    Outside global
--- ---                ---               10.250.13.1      172.16.6.1
icmp 10.251.1.15:0     10.250.10.1:0     10.10.1.3:0      10.10.1.3:0
--- 10.251.1.141       10.250.14.1       ---              ---
--- 10.251.1.15        10.250.10.1       ---              ---
--- 10.251.1.24        10.250.11.1       ---              ---
--- 10.251.1.25        10.250.11.1       ---              ---
--- 10.251.1.142       10.250.14.1       ---              ---
--- 10.251.2.15        10.250.10.1       ---              ---
Services#
```

Pinging each address by hand will become a bit arduous in an exam, especially when testing reachability between 20 – 30 different routers, so this simple script makes life much easier:

```
Spoke-2#tclsh
Spoke-2(tcl)#foreach address {
+>10.251.1.141
+>10.251.1.15
+>10.251.1.24
+>10.251.1.25
+>10.251.1.142
+>} { ping $address rep 3 si 1500
+>}
Type escape sequence to abort.
Sending 3, 1500-byte ICMP Echos to 10.251.1.141:
!!!
Success rate is 100 percent (3/3)
Type escape sequence to abort.
Sending 3, 1500-byte ICMP Echos to 10.251.1.15:
```

```
!!!
Success rate is 100 percent (3/3)
Type escape sequence to abort.
Sending 3, 1500-byte ICMP Echos to 10.251.1.24:
!!!
Success rate is 100 percent (3/3)
Type escape sequence to abort.
Sending 3, 1500-byte ICMP Echos to 10.251.1.25:
!!!
Success rate is 100 percent (3/3)
Type escape sequence to abort.
Sending 3, 1500-byte ICMP Echos to 10.251.1.142:
!!!
Success rate is 100 percent (3/3)
Spoke-2(tcl)#tclquit
Spoke-2#
```

The beauty of this script is that you can keep it in notepad and edit it, adding IP addresses, changing the packet size, adding other options such as source, then paste it into as many routers as you need. This can save you quite some time in the exam!

The actual cut-and-paste portion (for the above) would be:

```
tclsh
foreach address {
10.251.1.141
10.251.1.15
10.251.1.24
10.251.1.25
10.251.1.142
} { ping $address rep 3 si 1500
}
tclquit
```

And one last time, here is our translation table, showing the connections from Spoke-2:

```
Services#sh ip nat trans
Pro Inside global      Inside local       Outside local      Outside global
--- ---                ---                10.250.13.1        172.16.6.1
icmp 10.251.1.15:7     10.250.10.1:7      10.10.1.3:7        10.10.1.3:7
icmp 10.251.1.24:8     10.250.11.1:8      10.10.1.3:8        10.10.1.3:8
icmp 10.251.1.25:9     10.250.11.1:9      10.10.1.3:9        10.10.1.3:9
icmp 10.251.1.141:6    10.250.14.1:6      10.10.1.3:6        10.10.1.3:6
icmp 10.251.1.142:10   10.250.14.1:10     10.10.1.3:10       10.10.1.3:10
tcp 10.251.1.141:23    10.250.14.1:23     10.10.1.3:64317    10.10.1.3:64317
--- 10.251.1.141       10.250.14.1        ---                ---
```

```
---  10.251.1.15        10.250.10.1      ---           ---
---  10.251.1.24        10.250.11.1      ---           ---
---  10.251.1.25        10.250.11.1      ---           ---
---  10.251.1.142       10.250.14.1      ---           ---
---  10.251.2.15        10.250.10.1      ---           ---
Services#
```

Now its time for a little fun; a mini lab!

Troubleshooting mini lab

Load up the VPN+NAT-TS GNS3 file. It takes a few minutes for the routes to propagate, so don't dive in right away.

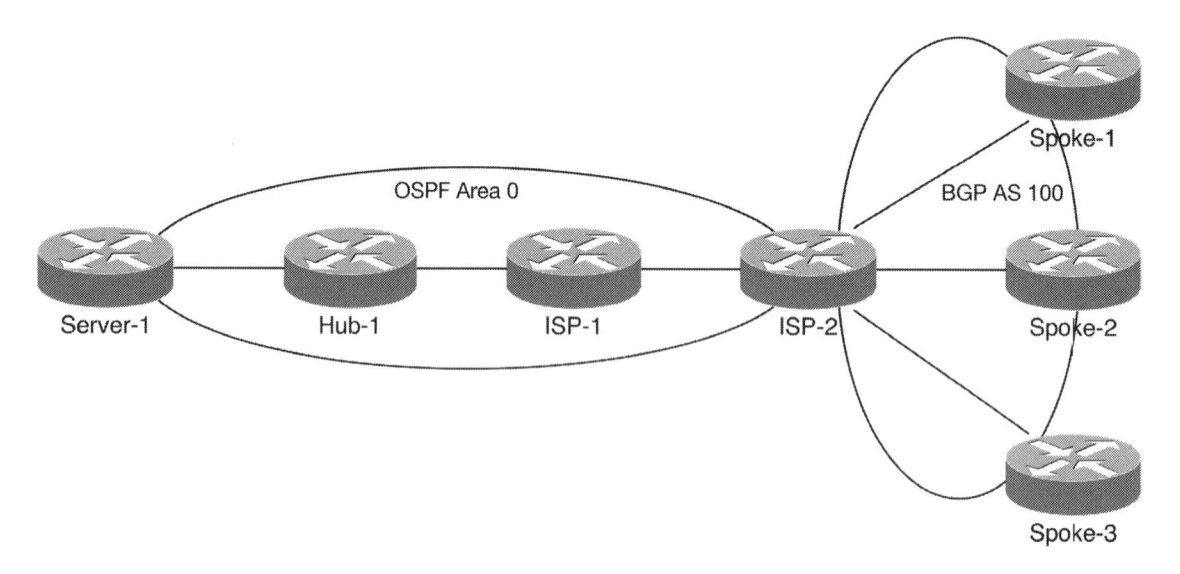

At the left-hand side we have Server-1, which will be used for a mixture of functions. It will offer a HTTP server, telnet, and more. These will be accessible through different IP addresses.

Server-1, Hub-1 and the two ISP routers will connect using OSPF and are all in area 0. The Spoke routers will connect to ISP-2 through BGP and will receive just a default route from ISP-2.

The Spoke routers will join to Hub-1 and to each other, using DMVPN.

Some faults have been introduced into the network.

Restrictions:

No commands may be removed. For example, if there is an access-list attached to an interface, you are not allowed to remove the access-list. You may edit the access-list.

You are not allowed to remove any network statements within the IGPs.

Goals:

The end goal is that we should see the following:

```
Hub-1#sh ip nhrp
192.168.1.1/32 via 192.168.1.1
   Tunnel0 created 00:00:47, expire 01:59:12
   Type: dynamic, Flags: unique registered used
   NBMA address: 10.4.1.1
192.168.1.2/32 via 192.168.1.2
   Tunnel0 created 00:00:47, expire 01:59:34
   Type: dynamic, Flags: unique registered used
   NBMA address: 55.55.55.55
     (Claimed NBMA address: 10.4.2.1)
192.168.1.3/32 via 192.168.1.3
   Tunnel0 created 00:00:44, expire 01:59:15
   Type: dynamic, Flags: unique registered used
   NBMA address: 10.4.3.1
Hub-1#

Spoke-3#sh ip route eigrp | b Gat
Gateway of last resort is 10.4.3.2 to network 0.0.0.0

      1.0.0.0/24 is subnetted, 1 subnets
D  %    1.1.1.0 [90/102400640] via 192.168.1.100, 00:43:15, Tunnel0
      2.0.0.0/24 is subnetted, 1 subnets
D  %    2.2.2.0 [90/102400640] via 192.168.1.100, 00:49:59, Tunnel0
Spoke-3#
Spoke-3#trace 2.2.2.2
Type escape sequence to abort.
Tracing the route to 2.2.2.2
VRF info: (vrf in name/id, vrf out name/id)
  1 192.168.1.2 48 msec 36 msec 28 msec
Spoke-3#

Hub-1#sh crypto ipsec sa | grep _peer | wc -l
      3
Hub-1#
```

For this one, you need to type "get" after the Open message (shown in bold):

```
Spoke-1#telnet 22.22.22.22 8432
Trying 22.22.22.22, 8432 ... Open
get
HTTP/1.1 400 Bad Request
Date: Wed, 15 Apr 2015 21:07:37 GMT
Server: cisco-IOS
Accept-Ranges: none

400 Bad Request
[Connection to 22.22.22.22 closed by foreign host]
Spoke-1#
```

For this one, use a username of "user1" and a password of "cisco".

```
Spoke-1#telnet 33.33.33.33 8423
Trying 33.33.33.33, 8423 ... Open


Congratulations!!


User Access Verification

Username: user1
Password:  Congratulations!!
Server-1>exit

[Connection to 33.33.33.33 closed by foreign host]
Spoke-1#

Spoke-1#telnet 44.44.44.44 8479
Trying 44.44.44.44, 8479 ... Open


Congratulations!!

    Line       User          Host(s)              Idle         Location
   0 con 0                   idle                 00:01:52
*  2 vty 0                   idle                 00:00:00 10.4.1.1

    Interface  User                   Mode         Idle     Peer Address

[Connection to 44.44.44.44 closed by foreign host]
Spoke-1#
```

Have a look around, do some digging and try and solve the problems before looking at the next section.

Troubleshooting process and solutions:

Look at the tasks closely. We can tell from the first output that we are using DMVPN, as the tunnels are dynamic. But from this we cannot gather if it is phase 1, phase 2 or phase 3. The second output would indicate that it is most likely phase 3. The % sign means that we are performing a next-hop override and the trace shows that we are going directly to the neighbor, rather than going through the hub. The third output shows that we have three IPSec peers. These, although not shown in the output, will most likely be the three spokes.

We cannot deduce much from the telnet commands as to what the issue may be. So we will have to dig a bit.

Looking at the console of Hub-1 we can see the following messages:

```
%CRYPTO-4-IKMP_BAD_MESSAGE: IKE message from 10.4.3.1 failed its sanity check or is malformed
Hub-1#
%DUAL-5-NBRCHANGE: EIGRP-IPv4 8211: Neighbor 192.168.1.1 (Tunnel0) is down: retry limit exceeded
Hub-1#
%DUAL-5-NBRCHANGE: EIGRP-IPv4 8211: Neighbor 192.168.1.1 (Tunnel0) is up: new adjacency
Hub-1#
```

We have two different issues. One spoke if failing the IKE phase 1, the other is flapping. Do we have any working spokes?

```
Hub-1#sh ip nhrp
192.168.1.1/32
   Tunnel0 created 00:00:55, expire 00:02:09
   Type: incomplete, Flags: negative
   Cache hits: 6
Hub-1#
```

No. We have one, but that is incomplete, and flapping as we can see above.

Let's start with confirming basic connectivity:

```
Hub-1#sh ip ospf neigh
```

```
Neighbor ID      Pri    State         Dead Time    Address       Interface
10.1.3.1          1     FULL/BDR      00:00:35     10.1.2.2      Gi2/0
10.1.1.2          1     FULL/BDR      00:00:30     10.1.1.2      Gi1/0
Hub-1#

ISP-1#sh ip ospf neigh

Neighbor ID      Pri    State         Dead Time    Address       Interface
22.22.22.22       1     FULL/DR       00:00:39     10.1.2.1      Gi2/0
10.1.3.2          1     FULL/DR       00:00:39     10.1.3.2      Gi1/0
ISP-1#

ISP-2#sh ip ospf neigh

Neighbor ID      Pri    State         Dead Time    Address       Interface
10.1.3.1          1     FULL/BDR      00:00:31     10.1.3.1      Gi1/0
ISP-2#

ISP-2#sh ip bgp summ | b Neigh
Neighbor        V   AS  MsgRcvd  MsgSent  TblVer  InQ  OutQ Up/Down    Sta/PfxRc
*10.4.1.1       4   100    173     177       2     0     0 02:35:09        0
*10.4.2.1       4   100    182     183       2     0     0 02:41:35        0
*10.4.3.1       4   100    180     183       2     0     0 02:41:26        0
* Dynamically created based on a listen range command
Dynamically created neighbors: 3, Subnet ranges: 1

BGP peergroup Customers listen range group members:
  10.4.0.0/16

Total dynamically created neighbors: 3/(100 max), Subnet ranges: 1

ISP-2#
```

Whilst we could gather from the error messages on the console of Hub-1 that basic connectivity should be pretty much ok (otherwise we wouldn't see any messages at all), troubleshooting is all about building a process and if that process is followed, there is less room for missing vital pieces.

Here we have connectivity between all our devices.

We can confirm this by pinging the outside address of each of our spokes, from Hub-1:

```
Hub-1#ping 10.4.1.1 rep 2
Type escape sequence to abort.
Sending 2, 100-byte ICMP Echos to 10.4.1.1, timeout is 2 seconds:
```

```
!!
Success rate is 100 percent (2/2)
Hub-1#ping 10.4.2.1 rep 2
Type escape sequence to abort.
Sending 2, 100-byte ICMP Echos to 10.4.2.1, timeout is 2 seconds:
!!
Success rate is 100 percent (2/2)
Hub-1#ping 10.4.3.1 rep 2
Type escape sequence to abort.
Sending 2, 100-byte ICMP Echos to 10.4.3.1, timeout is 2 seconds:
!!
Success rate is 100 percent (2/2)
Hub-1#
```

No issues here, we have eliminated any little surprises in the basic connectivity, so let's move on.

Because we can be selective with what interface supplies our tunnel source, we should also make sure that this is reachable:

```
Hub-1#sh run int tun 0 | i source
 tunnel source Loopback0
Hub-1#sh ip int bri | i Loopback0
Loopback0          11.11.11.11      YES NVRAM  up               up
Hub-1#

ISP-1#sh ip route 11.11.11.11
Routing entry for 11.11.11.11/32
  Known via "ospf 8211", distance 110, metric 2, type intra area
  Last update from 10.1.2.1 on GigabitEthernet2/0, 01:11:13 ago
  Routing Descriptor Blocks:
  * 10.1.2.1, from 22.22.22.22, 01:11:13 ago, via GigabitEthernet2/0
      Route metric is 2, traffic share count is 1
ISP-1#

ISP-2#sh ip route 11.11.11.11
Routing entry for 11.11.11.11/32
  Known via "ospf 8211", distance 110, metric 3, type intra area
  Last update from 10.1.3.1 on GigabitEthernet1/0, 01:11:23 ago
  Routing Descriptor Blocks:
  * 10.1.3.1, from 22.22.22.22, 01:11:23 ago, via GigabitEthernet1/0
      Route metric is 3, traffic share count is 1
ISP-2#

Spoke-1#sh ip route 11.11.11.11
% Network not in table
```

```
Spoke-1#ping 11.11.11.11
Type escape sequence to abort.
Sending 5, 100-byte ICMP Echos to 11.11.11.11:
!!!!!
Success rate is 100 percent (5/5)
Spoke-1#

Spoke-2#ping 11.11.11.11
Type escape sequence to abort.
Sending 5, 100-byte ICMP Echos to 11.11.11.11:
!!!!!
Success rate is 100 percent (5/5)/56/104 ms
Spoke-2#

Spoke-3#ping 11.11.11.11
Type escape sequence to abort.
Sending 5, 100-byte ICMP Echos to 11.11.11.11:
!!!!!
Success rate is 100 percent (5/5)
Spoke-3#
```

Now that we know that our spokes should not have any problem connecting to the hub, we can start to troubleshoot.

Let's have a look at the IKE issue, first.

The error we can see is:

```
Hub-1#
%CRYPTO-4-IKMP_BAD_MESSAGE: IKE message from 10.4.3.1 failed its
sanity check or is malformed
Hub-1#
```

So, let's have a look at our crypto settings on this spoke:

```
Spoke-3#sh run | s crypto
crypto isakmp policy 10
 encr 3des
 authentication pre-share
 group 2
crypto isakmp key 802-DMVPN address 0.0.0.0
crypto ipsec transform-set 802-Trans esp-3des esp-sha-hmac
 mode transport
crypto ipsec profile DMVPN-Profile
 set transform-set 802-Trans
Spoke-3#
```

We can compare this against what we have configured on the hub:

```
Hub-1#sh run | s crypto
crypto isakmp policy 10
 encr 3des
 authentication pre-share
 group 2
crypto isakmp key 8O2-DMVPN address 0.0.0.0
crypto ipsec transform-set 802-Trans esp-3des esp-sha-hmac
 mode transport
crypto ipsec profile DMVPN-Profile
 set transform-set 802-Trans
Hub-1#
```

We have the same isakmp policy number, both use 3DES for the encryption, group 2 for the Diffie-Hellman and a pre-shared key.

The key does not specify any particular peer – the "address 0.0.0.0" means anyone, but hopefully here you have spotted the difference in the key – 8**O**2-DMVPN instead of 8**0**2-DMVPN.

Before we correct this, just check the rest of the configuration. The transform sets are identical, both are set to "mode transport", we have an IPSec profile, which uses the same transform set.

Lastly, we should make sure that the tunnels are actually using this:

```
Hub-1#sh run int tun 0 | i tunnel prote
 tunnel protection ipsec profile DMVPN-Profile
Hub-1#

Spoke-3#sh run int tun 0 | i tunnel prote
 tunnel protection ipsec profile DMVPN-Profile
Spoke-3#
```

OK, so we can go ahead and change the one line here:

```
Spoke-3(config)#no crypto isakmp key 8O2-DMVPN address 0.0.0.0
Spoke-3(config)#crypto isakmp key 802-DMVPN address 0.0.0.0
Spoke-3(config)#
%DUAL-5-NBRCHANGE: EIGRP-IPv4 8211: Neighbor 192.168.1.100 (Tunnel0)
is up: new adjacency
Spoke-3(config)#
```

Our tunnel comes up straight away and we have our first working DMVPN peer:

```
Hub-1#sh ip nhrp
192.168.1.1/32
   Tunnel0 created 00:00:26, expire 00:02:38
   Type: incomplete, Flags: negative
   Cache hits: 5
192.168.1.3/32 via 192.168.1.3
   Tunnel0 created 00:00:44, expire 01:59:15
   Type: dynamic, Flags: unique registered used
   NBMA address: 10.4.3.1
Hub-1#
```

Let's look at Spoke-1.

Spoke-1 is flapping. This can either mean that the hub destination is getting advertised over the DMVPN network and therefore causing route recursion, or we have an issue with the multicast requirements for EIGRP.

We can rule out recursion, as we do not have the same kind of error messages that we would expect, which look like this:

```
%TUN-5-RECURDOWN: Tunnel0 temporarily disabled due to recursive
routing
```

Our tunnel is not actually being disabled, so we can look at EIGRP. EIGRP uses multicast, so this must be supported within our tunnel/DMVPN network. So, what do we need to have in place for multicast support in a DMVPN network? The hub must have "ip nhrp multicast dynamic" set and the spokes must have "ip nhrp map multicast" set and the command completed by specifying the address tp map this to.

We could go through each router, comparing the tunnels and the EIGRP overlay, but we can actually eliminate the Hub as the cause of the issue.

We fixed Spoke-3 a few moments ago:

```
%DUAL-5-NBRCHANGE: EIGRP-IPv4 8211: Neighbor 192.168.1.3 (Tunnel0) is
up: new adjacency
Hub-1#
%DUAL-5-NBRCHANGE: EIGRP-IPv4 8211: Neighbor 192.168.1.1 (Tunnel0) is
down: retry limit exceeded
Hub-1#
```

So, we can deduce that both spokes (and the hub) are using EIGRP, multicast must therefore be enabled correctly on the hub, otherwise Spoke-3 would be flapping the same as Spoke-1 is. Yet (and hopefully this is the same case for you), Spoke-3 is rock solid:

```
Hub-1#sh ip eigrp neigh
EIGRP-IPv4 VR(DM802101) Address-Family Neighbors for AS(8211)
H   Address         Interface  Hold Uptime  SRTT   RTO   Q   Seq
                               (sec)        (ms)         Cnt Num
0   192.168.1.1     Tu0        13 00:01:15    1   5000   1   0
1   192.168.1.3     Tu0        13 00:11:05  120   1362   0   6
Hub-1#
```

Yes, Spoke-3 is working fine. We can tell this, as the Q Cnt is 0.

Therefore, we know the cause of the issue (multicast failure within the tunnel) and where the problem exists (Spoke-1). Let's look at the configuration and compare this to Spoke-3:

```
Spoke-1#sh run int tun 0 | i multicast
 ip nhrp map multicast 11.11.11.11
Spoke-1#

Spoke-3#sh run int tun 0 | i multicast
 ip nhrp map multicast 11.11.11.11
Spoke-3
```

Both are identical. So, what else within the tunnel controls multicast? Well, we have the next-hop server as well:

```
Spoke-1#sh run int tun 0 | i nhs
 ip nhrp nhs 11.11.11.11
Spoke-1#

Spoke-3#sh run int tun 0 | i nhs
 ip nhrp nhs 192.168.1.100
Spoke-3#
```

Now we can see the issue. The next hop server (NHS) is set to the NMBA, so let's fix this:

```
Spoke-1(config)#int tun 0
Spoke-1(config-if)#no ip nhrp nhs 11.11.11.11
Spoke-1(config-if)#ip nhrp nhs 192.168.1.100
Spoke-1(config-if)#
%DUAL-5-NBRCHANGE: EIGRP-IPv4 8211: Neighbor 192.168.1.100 (Tunnel0)
is up: new adjacency
Spoke-1(config-if)#
```

Two down, one to go!

Spoke-2 has been very quiet. Too quiet. This either means that we have no tunnel configured, that the tunnel is looking to the wrong hub or its not looking in the right direction.

We know from earlier, that Hub-1 can reach the NBMA address os Spoke-2, but do we have a tunnel interface?

```
Spoke-2#sh ip int bri | e unas
Interface              IP-Address      OK? Method Status  Protocol
GigabitEthernet1/0     10.4.2.1        YES NVRAM  up      up
Loopback0              2.2.2.2         YES NVRAM  up      up
Tunnel0                192.168.1.2     YES NVRAM  up      down

Spoke-2#
```

We do, but it is down.

There are a number of requirements that a tunnel interface must have, before it will come up. These are a mode, a source, and an IP address.

```
Spoke-2#sh run int tun 0 | i mode|source|address
 ip address 192.168.1.2 255.255.255.0
 tunnel source GigabitEthernet2/0
 tunnel mode gre multipoint
Spoke-2#
```

We can see that the ip address is correct, we have a source and the mode is also correct. However, the tunnel source is pointing to the wrong interface. So, let's correct that:

```
Spoke-2(config)#int tun 0
Spoke-2(config-if)#tun so gi1/0
Spoke-2(config-if)#
%LINEPROTO-5-UPDOWN: Line protocol on Interface Tunnel0, changed state
to up
%CRYPTO-6-ISAKMP_ON_OFF: ISAKMP is OFF
%CRYPTO-6-ISAKMP_ON_OFF: ISAKMP is ON
Spoke-2(config-if)#
```

Hub-1, after a while, displays the following error:

```
Hub-1#
```

```
%CRYPTO-4-IKMP_NO_SA: IKE message from 10.4.2.1 has no SA and is not
an initialization offer
Hub-1#
```

This is not like the previous error, the sanity check one, from before. We can, therefore, rule out issues with the key. We should, for safety sake, just check this though, and compare it against a working spoke:

```
Spoke-2(config-if)#do sh run | i key
crypto isakmp key 802-DMVPN address 0.0.0.0
Spoke-2(config-if)#

Spoke-1(config-if)#do sh run | i key
crypto isakmp key 802-DMVPN address 0.0.0.0
Spoke-1(config-if)#
```

The key looks fine. So what else could it be? We know, from the error, that we are failing phase 1, so let's check that on Spoke-2:

```
Spoke-1(config-if)#do sh run | s crypto isakm
crypto isakmp policy 10
 encr 3des
 authentication pre-share
 group 2
crypto isakmp key 802-DMVPN address 0.0.0.0
Spoke-1(config-if)#
```

Again, this is identical to the other Spokes. Just for completeness, we should also check phase 2:

```
Spoke-1(config-if)#do sh run | s crypto ipsec
crypto ipsec transform-set 802-Trans esp-3des esp-sha-hmac
 mode transport
crypto ipsec profile DMVPN-Profile
 set transform-set 802-Trans
Spoke-1(config-if)#do sh run int tun 0 | i protection
 tunnel protection ipsec profile DMVPN-Profile
Spoke-1(config-if)#
```

Again, this all matches the other spokes. So, what is it that is causing the errors displayed on Hub-1? Refer back to the desired output; Spoke-2 has a "claimed" address, which means that it is behind a NAT device.

Which device is performing NAT? Let's find out!

```
Hub-1#trace 55.55.55.55
Type escape sequence to abort.
Tracing the route to 55.55.55.55
VRF info: (vrf in name/id, vrf out name/id)
  1 10.1.2.2 40 msec 28 msec 56 msec
  2 10.1.3.2 100 msec 76 msec 56 msec
Hub-1#
```

From the trace on Hub-1, it looks like the NAT address (55.55.55.55) is on ISP-2, as it is two hops away. This will never always be the case; we could have an MPLS network in between, but "hidden" from our traceroute. In this scenario, however, it is a good bet that ISP-2 is where we should be looking.

```
ISP-2#sh ip nat trans
Pro Inside global      Inside local        Outside local       Outside global
udp 55.55.55.55:450    10.4.2.1:450        ---                 ---
udp 55.55.55.55:500    10.4.2.1:500        11.11.11.11:500     11.11.11.11:500
udp 55.55.55.55:500    10.4.2.1:500        11.11.11.11:500     11.11.11.11:500
udp 55.55.55.55:500    10.4.2.1:500        11.11.11.11:500     11.11.11.11:500
udp 55.55.55.55:500    10.4.2.1:500        11.11.11.11:500     11.11.11.11:500
udp 55.55.55.55:500    10.4.2.1:500        11.11.11.11:500     11.11.11.11:500
udp 55.55.55.55:500    10.4.2.1:500        ---                 ---
ISP-2#
```

We have a number of translations for UDP port 500 (ISAKMP) and one for UDP port 450. Port 450 does not look familiar to me, but it does look a lot like 4500, which is required for IPSec NAT traversal. Let's go ahead and edit this entry:

```
ISP-2#sh run | i nat
 ip nat outside
 ip nat inside
 neighbor Customers default-originate
ip nat inside source static udp 10.4.2.1 500 interface Loopback0 500
ip nat inside source static udp 10.4.2.1 450 interface Loopback0 450
ISP-2#conf t
ISP-2(config)#no ip nat insi sou stat udp 10.4.2.1 450 int Lo0 450
ISP-2(config)#no ip nat insi sou stat udp 10.4.2.1 4500 int Lo0 4500
ISP-2(config)#
```

Once this is done, Spoke-2 shows an EIGRP adjacency forming:

```
Spoke-2(config-if)#
%DUAL-5-NBRCHANGE: EIGRP-IPv4 8211: Neighbor 192.168.1.100 (Tunnel0)
is up: new adjacency
```

Spoke-2(config-if)#

Our third tunnel is up.

And down again:

```
Spoke-2(config-if)#
%DUAL-5-NBRCHANGE: EIGRP-IPv4 8211: Neighbor 192.168.1.100 (Tunnel0)
is down: retry limit exceeded
Spoke-2(config-if)#
%DUAL-5-NBRCHANGE: EIGRP-IPv4 8211: Neighbor 192.168.1.100 (Tunnel0)
is up: new adjacency
Spoke-2(config-if)#
```

The tunnel is up, but we are not forming an EIGRP relationship to Hub-1:

```
Hub-1#sh ip eigrp neigh
EIGRP-IPv4 VR(DM802101) Address-Family Neighbors for AS(8211)
H   Address         Interface    Hold Uptime   SRTT   RTO  Q   Seq
                                 (sec)         (ms)        Cnt Num
0   192.168.1.1     Tu0            14 00:12:13   71   1398  0   5
1   192.168.1.3     Tu0            11 00:37:15  113   1398  0   6
Hub-1#sh ip nhrp
192.168.1.1/32 via 192.168.1.1
   Tunnel0 created 00:12:22, expire 01:48:25
   Type: dynamic, Flags: unique registered used
   NBMA address: 10.4.1.1
192.168.1.2/32 via 192.168.1.2
   Tunnel0 created 00:03:01, expire 01:56:58
   Type: dynamic, Flags: unique registered used
   NBMA address: 55.55.55.55
    (Claimed NBMA address: 10.4.2.1)
192.168.1.3/32 via 192.168.1.3
   Tunnel0 created 00:37:35, expire 01:35:14
   Type: dynamic, Flags: unique registered used
   NBMA address: 10.4.3.1
Hub-1#
```

Now we should dig into the tunnel a little deeper. Because the tunnel is up, nhrp is working, but it is EIGRP that is flapping, we are back to asking the same questions as we did with Spoke-1; is our multicast working correctly?

```
Spoke-2(config-if)#do sh run int tun 0 | i nhs|multicast
 ip nhrp nhs 192.168.1.100
Spoke-2(config-if)#
```

Here, we can see that our next-hop server is correct, but we have no multicast mapping. This is a quick fix:

```
Spoke-2(config-if)#ip nhrp map multicast 11.11.11.11
Spoke-2(config-if)#

Hub-1#
%DUAL-5-NBRCHANGE: EIGRP-IPv4 8211: Neighbor 192.168.1.2 (Tunnel0) is up: new adjacency
Hub-1#
Hub-1#sh ip nhrp
192.168.1.1/32 via 192.168.1.1
   Tunnel0 created 00:23:31, expire 01:37:16
   Type: dynamic, Flags: unique registered used
   NBMA address: 10.4.1.1
192.168.1.2/32 via 192.168.1.2
   Tunnel0 created 00:14:10, expire 01:45:49
   Type: dynamic, Flags: unique registered used
   NBMA address: 55.55.55.55
    (Claimed NBMA address: 10.4.2.1)
192.168.1.3/32 via 192.168.1.3
   Tunnel0 created 00:48:44, expire 01:24:04
   Type: dynamic, Flags: unique registered used
   NBMA address: 10.4.3.1
Hub-1#
Hub-1#sh ip eigrp neigh
EIGRP-IPv4 VR(DM802101) Address-Family Neighbors for AS(8211)
H   Address         Interface    Hold Uptime    SRTT   RTO   Q   Seq
                                 (sec)          (ms)         Cnt Num
1   192.168.1.2     Tu0            10 00:03:08  1027   5000  0   9
2   192.168.1.1     Tu0            12 00:39:10   191   1440  0   5
0   192.168.1.3     Tu0             9 00:39:27   185   1440  0   6
Hub-1#
```

Now, all our spokes are registered, dynamically, with our hub.

The second output is this:

```
Spoke-3#sh ip route eigrp | b Gat
Gateway of last resort is 10.4.3.2 to network 0.0.0.0

      1.0.0.0/24 is subnetted, 1 subnets
D  %     1.1.1.0 [90/102400640] via 192.168.1.100, 00:43:15, Tunnel0
      2.0.0.0/24 is subnetted, 1 subnets
D  %     2.2.2.0 [90/102400640] via 192.168.1.100, 00:49:59, Tunnel0
Spoke-3#
```

```
Spoke-3#trace 2.2.2.2
Type escape sequence to abort.
Tracing the route to 2.2.2.2
VRF info: (vrf in name/id, vrf out name/id)
  1 192.168.1.2 48 msec 36 msec 28 msec
Spoke-3#
```

Can we see this?

```
Spoke-3#sh ip route eigrp | b Gate
Gateway of last resort is 10.4.3.2 to network 0.0.0.0

Spoke-3#
```

No, Spoke-3 is not receiving any routes through Tunnel0. Neither is Spoke-1 or Spoke-2:

```
Spoke-1#sh ip route eigrp | b Gat
Gateway of last resort is 10.4.1.2 to network 0.0.0.0

Spoke-1#

Spoke-2#sh ip route eigrp | b Gat
Gateway of last resort is 10.4.2.2 to network 0.0.0.0

Spoke-2#
```

Are these routes being advertised? We can check on the hub to see:

```
Hub-1#sh ip route eigrp | b Gate
Gateway of last resort is not set

      1.0.0.0/24 is subnetted, 1 subnets
D        1.1.1.0 [90/76800640] via 192.168.1.1, 00:42:17, Tunnel0
      2.0.0.0/24 is subnetted, 1 subnets
D        2.2.2.0 [90/76800640] via 192.168.1.2, 00:26:22, Tunnel0
      3.0.0.0/24 is subnetted, 1 subnets
D        3.3.3.0 [90/76800640] via 192.168.1.3, 01:08:19, Tunnel0
Hub-1#
```

Yes they are. So Hub-1 is not readvertising the routes it receives through tunnel 0, back out of tunnel 0. Under normal circumstances this is pretty normal and is referred to as "split-horion". In this case we do want it to readvertise the routes though, therefore split-horizon should be disabled for our tunnel. There are two ways to disable split-horizon and our EIGRP version wil dictate which one we use. If we are running in "normal" mode, then we can disable it at the interface level. If we are running in 64-bit (named) mode, then we disable it within the af-interface directive in EIGRP.

```
Hub-1#sh run | sec router eigrp
router eigrp DM802101
 !
 address-family ipv4 unicast autonomous-system 8211
  !
  topology base
  exit-af-topology
  network 192.168.1.100 0.0.0.0
 exit-address-family
Hub-1#
```

Here we can see that we are running in 64-bit mode, therefore we have to disable split-horizon here:

```
Hub-1(config)#router eigrp DM802101
Hub-1(config-router)#address-family ipv4 unicast autonomous-sys 8211
Hub-1(config-router-af)#af-interface tunnel 0
Hub-1(config-router-af-interface)#no split-horizon
Hub-1(config-router-af-interface)#en
%DUAL-5-NBRCHANGE: EIGRP-IPv4 8211: Neighbor 192.168.1.2 (Tunnel0) is resync: split horizon changed
%DUAL-5-NBRCHANGE: EIGRP-IPv4 8211: Neighbor 192.168.1.1 (Tunnel0) is resync: split horizon changed
%DUAL-5-NBRCHANGE: EIGRP-IPv4 8211: Neighbor 192.168.1.3 (Tunnel0) is resync: split horizon changed
Hub-1(config-router-af-interface)#end
Hub-1#
```

This causes a resync and after that things look much better:

```
Spoke-1#sh ip route eigrp | b Gat
Gateway of last resort is 10.4.1.2 to network 0.0.0.0

      2.0.0.0/24 is subnetted, 1 subnets
D        2.2.2.0 [90/102400640] via 192.168.1.100, 00:00:58, Tunnel0
      3.0.0.0/24 is subnetted, 1 subnets
D        3.3.3.0 [90/102400640] via 192.168.1.100, 00:00:58, Tunnel0
Spoke-1#

Spoke-2#sh ip route eigrp | b Gat
Gateway of last resort is 10.4.2.2 to network 0.0.0.0

      1.0.0.0/24 is subnetted, 1 subnets
```

```
D          1.1.1.0 [90/102400640] via 192.168.1.100, 00:01:27, Tunnel0
      3.0.0.0/24 is subnetted, 1 subnets
D          3.3.3.0 [90/102400640] via 192.168.1.100, 00:01:27, Tunnel0
Spoke-2#

Spoke-3#sh ip route eigrp | b Gate
Gateway of last resort is 10.4.3.2 to network 0.0.0.0

      1.0.0.0/24 is subnetted, 1 subnets
D          1.1.1.0 [90/102400640] via 192.168.1.100, 00:01:36, Tunnel0
      2.0.0.0/24 is subnetted, 1 subnets
D          2.2.2.0 [90/102400640] via 192.168.1.100, 00:01:36, Tunnel0
Spoke-3#
```

Can we match Spoke-3 to the desired output?

```
Spoke-3#sh ip route eigrp | b Gate
Gateway of last resort is 10.4.3.2 to network 0.0.0.0

      1.0.0.0/24 is subnetted, 1 subnets
D   %    1.1.1.0 [90/102400640] via 192.168.1.100, 00:02:32, Tunnel0
      2.0.0.0/24 is subnetted, 1 subnets
D   %    2.2.2.0 [90/102400640] via 192.168.1.100, 00:02:32, Tunnel0
Spoke-3#trace 2.2.2.2
Type escape sequence to abort.
Tracing the route to 2.2.2.2
VRF info: (vrf in name/id, vrf out name/id)
  1 192.168.1.2 192 msec 80 msec 56 msec
Spoke-3#
```

Yes, we can.

The final output should be resolved if we have fixed the other tickets:

```
Hub-1#sh crypto ipsec sa | grep _peer | wc -l
      3
Hub-1#
```

The unix-style commands are available if shell processing has been enabled:

```
Hub-1(config)#shell processing full
Hub-1(config)#
```

Let's move on the the server-based items.

The first one is to initiate an HTTP call from Spoke-1 to 22.22.22.22 (port 8432). Firstly, let's find out where 22.22.22.2 actually lives:

```
Spoke-1#trace 22.22.22.22
Type escape sequence to abort.
Tracing the route to 22.22.22.22
VRF info: (vrf in name/id, vrf out name/id)
  1 10.4.1.2 36 msec 60 msec 16 msec
  2 10.1.3.1 64 msec 68 msec 28 msec
  3 10.1.2.1 116 msec 104 msec 80 msec
Spoke-1#
```

It looks like the trace stops at Hub-1. So, is Hub-1 stopping us, or is this the end of the line?

```
Hub-1#sh ip route 22.22.22.22
Routing entry for 22.22.22.22/32
  Known via "connected", distance 0, metric 0 (connected)
  Routing Descriptor Blocks:
  * directly connected, via Loopback2
      Route metric is 0, traffic share count is 1
Hub-1#
```

OK, it's the end of the line and it's up:

```
Hub-1#sh ip int bri | i 22.2
Loopback2               22.22.22.22     YES NVRAM  up                    up
Hub-1#
```

We need to connect to a non-standard port, though. This is useful, as it will show up nicely in the configuration:

```
Hub-1#sh run | i 8432
ip nat source static tcp 10.1.1.2 8443 interface Loopback2 8432
Hub-1#
```

Now we can see that the port is mapped to 10.1.1.2 port 8443. Can we get to this from Hub-1? Remember that you need to type "get" after the Open message.

```
Hub-1#telnet 10.1.1.2 8443
Trying 10.1.1.2, 8443 ... Open
get
HTTP/1.1 400 Bad Request
Date: Fri, 24 Apr 2015 14:09:40 GMT
Server: cisco-IOS
```

```
Accept-Ranges: none

400 Bad Request
[Connection to 10.1.1.2 closed by foreign host]
Hub-1#
```

Yes. So now we know that we are (most likely) to be on the router at fault. We know we are using NAT, to point this service on Server-1 at our secondary loopback interface. We know that we have connectivity (from Hub-1) and that the loopback interface on Hub-1 is also up. We can ping this form Spoke-1 just to make sure:

```
Spoke-1#ping 22.22.22.22
Type escape sequence to abort.
Sending 5, 100-byte ICMP Echos to 22.22.22.22, timeout is 2 seconds:
!!!!!
Success rate is 100 percent (5/5), round-trip min/avg/max = 52/64/80 ms
Spoke-1#
```

All signs would point to an issue wirth NAT.

The NAT statement itself looks to be all there, and will work, or not, depending on which version of NAT we have used; the "classic" approach, or the NVI method. The classic approach requires setting interfaces as either "inside" or "outside". NVI doesn't have this separation, instead each interface involved in NAT is just configured with "ip nat enable". We know that our interface connecting to Server-1 is part of this NAT translation, so we can look at that:

```
Hub-1#sh run int gi 1/0 | b interface
interface GigabitEthernet1/0
 description Connection to Server-1
 ip address 10.1.1.1 255.255.255.252
 ip nat inside
 ip virtual-reassembly in
 negotiation auto
end

Hub-1#
```

This looks like classic NAT.

Let's have a look at our other interface:

```
Hub-1#sh run int gi 2/0 | b interface
```

```
interface GigabitEthernet2/0
 description Connection to ISP-1
 ip address 10.1.2.1 255.255.255.252
 ip nat outside
 ip virtual-reassembly in
 negotiation auto
end

Hub-1#
```

So, our interfaces are set up for classic NAT, yet the statement is set up for NVI. Given that the other NAT statements are set up for classic NAT, it is most likely that our first NAT statement has been misconfigured.

Let's fix it:

```
Hub-1(config)#no ip nat source static tcp 10.1.1.2 8443 interface Loopback2 8432
Hub-1(config)#ip nat inside source static tcp 10.1.1.2 8443 interface Loopback2 8432
Hub-1(config)#
```

Now do we have access form Spoke-1? (Remember that you need to type "get", as shown below)

```
Spoke-1#telnet 22.22.22.22 8432
Trying 22.22.22.22, 8432 ... Open
get
HTTP/1.1 400 Bad Request
Date: Fri, 24 Apr 2015 14:24:24 GMT
Server: cisco-IOS
Accept-Ranges: none

400 Bad Request
[Connection to 22.22.22.22 closed by foreign host]
Spoke-1#
```

Excellent, let's move on.

Now we need to telnet to 33.33.33.33 on port 8423. Again this is a non-standard port, so will be easily spotted in the configuration. But let's test the basics first:

```
Spoke-1#ping 33.33.33.33
Type escape sequence to abort.
Sending 5, 100-byte ICMP Echos to 33.33.33.33, timeout is 2 seconds:
```

UUUUU
Success rate is 0 percent (0/5)
Spoke-1#
```

We don't have basic reachability.

The trace stops at ISP-2

```
Spoke-1#trace 33.33.33.33
Type escape sequence to abort.
Tracing the route to 33.33.33.33
VRF info: (vrf in name/id, vrf out name/id)
  1 10.4.1.2 12 msec 176 msec 4 msec
  2 10.4.1.2 !H  !H  !H
Spoke-1#
```

Because 22.22.22.22 is on Hub-1 it would be a fairly reasonable assumption to think that 33.33.33.33 is also on that router. If we look for that port number in the configs of Hub-1, then this assumption is proved to be correct:

```
Hub-1#sh run | i 8423
 ip nat inside source static tcp 10.1.1.2 23 interface Loopback3 8423
Hub-1#
```

Now we need to look at the loopback interface:

```
Hub-1#sh ip int | i back3
Loopback3 is administratively down, line protocol is down
Hub-1#
```

It's down, so let's bring it up:

```
Hub-1(config)#int lo3
Hub-1(config-if)#no shut
Hub-1(config-if)#end
Hub-1#
```

Giving our IGPs a few moments to pick up the change, we can then test from Spoke-1, using the username of "user1" and when prompted, a password of "cisco":

```
Spoke-1#trace 33.33.33.33
Type escape sequence to abort.
Tracing the route to 33.33.33.33
VRF info: (vrf in name/id, vrf out name/id)
```
```

```
    1 10.4.1.2 16 msec 128 msec 20 msec
    2 10.1.3.1 80 msec 44 msec 32 msec
    3 10.1.2.1 72 msec 48 msec 44 msec
Spoke-1#telnet 33.33.33.33 8423
Trying 33.33.33.33, 8423 ... Open


Congratulations!!

User Access Verification

Username: user1
Password:  Congratulations!!
Server-1>exit

[Connection to 33.33.33.33 closed by foreign host]
Spoke-1#
```

It just goes to show; always check the obvious!

Our last, and final, little test; telnetting to 44.44.44.44, port 8479.

Again, we have a non-standard port. So let's check Hub-1 straight away:

```
Hub-1#sh run | i 8479
 ip nat inside source static udp 10.1.1.2 79 interface Loopback4 8479
Hub-1#
```

Again, we can see that Hub-1 is performing NAT, to and address on Server-1. This time, Spoke-1 does have reachability to the desired address:

```
Spoke-1#ping 44.44.44.44
Type escape sequence to abort.
Sending 5, 100-byte ICMP Echos to 44.44.44.44, timeout is 2 seconds:
!!!!!
Success rate is 100 percent (5/5), round-trip min/avg/max = 40/61/120 ms
Spoke-1#
```

So, let's look at Hub-1, again. Does it have access to this service on Server-1?

```
Hub-1#telnet 10.1.1.2 79
Trying 10.1.1.2, 79 ... Open
```

```
Congratulations!!
    Line         User         Host(s)              Idle         Location
   0 con 0                    idle                 03:36:58
*  2 vty 0                    idle                 00:00:00  10.1.1.1

   Interface    User                     Mode     Idle         Peer Address

[Connection to 10.1.1.2 closed by foreign host]
Hub-1#
```

Yes, it does.

So, we have reachability, but only partial accessibility. Hub-1 can reach the desired destination, but Spoke-1 cannot. Our NAT rule has the "inside" keyword, so that is fine.

Let's see if we can find some help on this one (unless you have already spotted the issue).

We know the service is hosted by Server-1, therefore we can look to see what has been enabled on Server-1, that might occupy port 79. As the enabling of services starts with the command "ip" we can narrow our search down to that:

```
Server-1#sh run | i ip
no ip icmp rate-limit unreachable
no ip domain lookup
ip cef
no ipv6 cef
ip finger
ip tcp synwait-time 5
ip ssh version 1
 no ip address
 ip address 10.1.1.2 255.255.255.252
 no ip address
ip forward-protocol nd
ip http server
ip http port 8443
no ip http secure-server
Server-1#
```

So we have a few that we know about, cef, http, but here was also have "finger", which if we look at the other routers, is not enabled:

```
Hub-1#sh run | i finger
Hub-1#
```

```
Spoke-1#sh run | i finger
Spoke-1#
```

So, we can deduce that port 79 matches up to the finger service. Looking at the NAT statement again we can see that we are trying to NAT finger, using UDP.

```
Hub-1#sh run | i 79
ip nat inside source static udp 10.1.1.2 79 interface Loopback4 8479
Hub-1#
```

Do we have enough information to ascertain whether finger uses UDP, or TCP? Not really, not from what we are limited to in the exam. The documentation CD may be available, but is not searchable. So how long do you spend trying to find information on this service?

In this instance it would be easier to edit the NAT to TCP, and see of that works:

```
Hub-1(config)#no ip nat inside source static udp 10.1.1.2 79 interface Loopback4 8479
Hub-1(config)#ip nat inside source static tcp 10.1.1.2 79 interface Loopback4 8479
Hub-1(config)#
```

Now, let's give it a try:

```
Spoke-1#telnet 44.44.44.44 8479
Trying 44.44.44.44, 8479 ... Open


Congratulations!!

    Line       User       Host(s)            Idle       Location
   0 con 0                idle               00:04:53
*  2 vty 0                idle               00:00:00 10.4.1.1

  Interface    User              Mode         Idle       Peer Address

[Connection to 44.44.44.44 closed by foreign host]
Spoke-1#
```

Bingo! We have completed all of the tickets.

The last few pages cover relevant items in the syllabus, as well as some further reading and the Cloudshark capture links.

All that is left, is for me to say that I hope you enjoyed this book and I wish you the very best of luck in your studies, your work and your life.

9. This book and the CCIE

This section is just to give you a quick reference to the CCIE syllabus requirements (pertinent to this volume).

LAB	Written	Section
3.1.c		**Implement and troubleshoot encapsulation**
3.1.c (i)		GRE
3.1.c (ii)		Dynamic GRE
3.1.d	4.1.d	**Implement and troubleshoot DMVPN (single hub)**
3.1.d (i)	4.1.d [i]	NHRP
3.1.d (ii)	4.1.d [ii]	DMVPN with IPsec using preshared key
3.1.d(iii)	4.1.d [iii]	QoS profile
3.1.d(iv)	4.1.d [iv]	Pre-classify
	4.1.e	**Describe IPv6 tunneling techniques**
	4.1.e [i]	6in4, 6to4
	4.1.e [ii]	ISATAP
	4.1.e [iii]	6RD
3.2	4.2	**Encryption**
3.2.a	4.2.a	Implement and troubleshoot IPsec with preshared key
3.2.a (i)	4.2.a [i]	IPv4 site to IPv4 site
3.2.a (ii)	4.2.a [ii]	IPv6 in IPv4 tunnels
	4.2.a [iii]	**Virtual Tunneling Interface [VTI]**
	4.2.b	Describe GET VPN
3.3		**Troubleshooting VPN technologies**
3.3.a		Use IOS troubleshooting tools
3.3.a (i)		debug, conditional debug
3.3.a (ii)		ping, traceroute with extended options
3.3.a (iii)		**Embedded packet capture**

5.3.d	6.3.d	**Implement and troubleshoot IPv4 network address translation**
5.3.d (i)	6.3.d [i]	Static NAT, dynamic NAT, policy-based NAT, PAT
5.3.d [ii]	6.3.d [ii]	NAT ALG
	6.3.e	**Describe IPv6 network address translation**
	6.3.e [i]	NAT64
	6.3.e [ii]	NPTv6

10. Further reading

Here is a few other resources you might find useful. I have included the original RFCs throughout the book, so won't include them here, but these are also worth reading.

Other books in this series:

BGP for Cisco Networks
MPLS for Cisco Networks

A cool GETVPN "on-a-budget" solution:

http://blog.ine.com/2009/11/21/minimalistic-get-vpn-example

Cisco GETVPN design guide:

http://www.cisco.com/c/dam/en/us/products/collateral/security/group-encrypted-transport-vpn/GETVPN_DIG_version_1_0_External.pdf

How to decrypt ESP packets in Wireshark:

http://packetpushers.net/ipv6-ospfv3-esp-packets-and-decrypting-with-wireshark/

Cisco DMVPN design guide:

http://www.cisco.com/c/en/us/td/docs/solutions/Enterprise/WAN_and_MAN/DMVPDG.html

11. Cloudshark capture links

If you are not already aware, Cloudshark is a website that you can upload Wireshark captures to. It is really useful, and so, instead of increasing the download file size, I have uploaded all of the Wireshark captures here.

Capture 1:   http://l.802101.com/802101vpnscap1
Capture 2:   http://l.802101.com/802101vpnscap2
Capture 3:   http://l.802101.com/802101vpnscap3
Capture 4:   http://l.802101.com/802101vpnscap4
Capture 5:   http://l.802101.com/802101vpnscap5
Capture 6:   http://l.802101.com/802101vpnscap6rd
Capture 7:   http://l.802101.com/802101vpnscap7
Capture 8:   http://l.802101.com/802101vpnscapNHRP
Capture 9:   http://l.802101.com/802101vpnscap9
Capture 10: http://l.802101.com/802101vpnscap10

Printed in Poland
by Amazon Fulfillment
Poland Sp. z o.o., Wrocław